ADVANTAGE

ADVANTAGE

How American Innovation
Can Overcome the Asian Challenge

ADAM SEGAL

W. W. NORTON & COMPANY
NEW YORK · LONDON

Copyright © 2011 by Adam Segal

For information about permission to reproduce selections from this book,
write to Permissions, W. W. Norton & Company, Inc.,
500 Fifth Avenue, New York, NY 10110

For information about special discounts for bulk purchases, please contact
W. W. Norton Special Sales at specialsales@wwnorton.com or 800-233-4830

Manufacturing by RR Donnelley Harrisonburg
Book design by Kristen Bearse
Production manager: Julia Druskin

Library of Congress Cataloging-in-Publication Data

Segal, Adam, 1968–
Advantage : how American innovation can overcome the Asian challenge /
Adam Segal. — 1st ed.
p. cm.
Includes bibliographical references and index.
ISBN 978-0-393-06878-8 (hardcover)
1. Technological innovations—Economic aspects—United States.
2. Technological innovations—Economic aspects—Asia. 3. Diffusion of
innovations—United States. 4. Diffusion of innovations—Asia.
5. Entrepreneurship—United States. 6. Entrepreneurship—Asia.
7. United States—Economic policy—21st century.
8. Asia—Economic policy—21st century. I. Title.
HC110.T4S38 2011
338'.0640973—dc22

2010041867

W. W. Norton & Company, Inc.
500 Fifth Avenue, New York, N.Y. 10110
www.wwnorton.com

W. W. Norton & Company Ltd.
Castle House, 75/76 Wells Street, London W1T 3QT

1 2 3 4 5 6 7 8 9 0

FOR MY PARENTS,
FREYA AND TONY SEGAL

Contents

ADVANTAGE

Chapter One

GOING NANO

Recessions tend to lead people toward reordering their priorities and concentrating on what works. Thus, the fiscal and economic crisis of 2008–2010 has raised serious questions about the very purpose and direction of American capitalism from the early 1990s to the present. Consumption, once thought of as the engine of endless growth and revival, is now viewed as one of the sources of the crisis. Decades of liquidity and easy leverage have left companies, households, and even the federal government mired in debt. While, in late 2006, President George W. Bush asked the American people to "go shopping more" to beef up the slowing economy, it is now clear that the country cannot buy its way into renewed affluence.[1] Achieving growth by sending the average American out to purchase more stuff has proved untenable.

The United States does have, however, a powerful alternative to debt-fueled consumption—namely, technological innovation and entrepreneurship. The resolution of some of the country's biggest challenges—fiscal crisis, energy dependence, and affordable health care—lies in *innovation*. As President Obama stated before an audience of America's most prominent scientists and technologists at the National Academy of Sciences in April 2009, the current crisis demands a national movement that would inspire young people "to be makers, not just consumers of things."[2] To achieve this end, Americans will have to break from their recent past and mastermind innovations that will not only spur the growth of industries and jobs but also address the consequences of climate change and reduce America's dependence on foreign oil.

The burning question is, after several decades of frenetic spending, can the United States find salvation through innovation? At first glance, the outlook is not good. Since 2004, observers in Washington and Silicon Valley have warned of the erosion of the United States' technological lead.[3] They attribute this downhill slide to the rise of Asia and to a series of self-inflicted wounds to the American innovation ecosystem: flat spending on basic research, declining enrollment in science and engineering courses, irrational immigration policies, cheap debt, irresponsible spending, and a lack of focus and seriousness. "Every one of the early warning signals is trending downward," former Intel chairman Craig Barrett told *U.S. News & World Report* in 2006. "We're all fat, dumb, and happy, which is one reason why this is so insidious."[4]

Furthering the ring of alarm, America is by no means alone in the quest for advanced technology. In Asia, new players such as China and India have entered the arena. Take the field of nanotechnology— that is, the manipulation of molecules and individual atoms—and the case of Cui Fuzhai, a professor at Tsinghua University in Beijing, the MIT of China. In 2003, Cui announced a breakthrough that one day could transform how doctors treat broken arms and legs. Using nanotechnology, he had created "nanobones" to replace the metal pins traditionally used to hold fractured bones together. The nanobones were designed to be placed in a person's arm or leg and then to slowly degrade as the real bones healed. This technology would save patients from the multiple surgeries they usually need when doctors first put metal plates in place and then, several months later when the fractures are healed, remove them. For fractures so severe that the bones would always need some support, Cui had engineered the nanobones to last but to cause less shock to the body and thus reduce the risk of infection.

Cui, who had been working on the bones for almost six years, was especially eager to complete the final clinical tests in late 2002. Unfortunately his work was soon swept up in the confusion and panic created by the outbreak of severe acute respiratory syndrome, or SARS. The pandemic first emerged in Guangdong and then spread to other parts of China as well as the rest of the world, resulting in more than seven hundred deaths in 2002 and 2003. While high-level officials kept on insisting that there was no SARS in Beijing, and that the outbreak was under control in the south, hospitals in the capital were closed to the outside world as they filled with infected patients, cutting off Cui from access to his test subjects. In April 2003, the Chinese government was embarrassed by a surprising whistle-blower as the website of *Time* magazine published a letter from Jiang Yanyong, a prominent surgeon in the Chinese military and a Communist Party member, exposing the cover-up. The government was forced to admit not only that it had closed some hospitals, but also that it had rushed to build an emergency quarantine center on the outskirts of town to house the growing number of patients. When the epidemic passed and the controls on the hospitals were finally lifted, Cui rushed to discover that the artificial bones had done what they were designed to do—slowly dissolve as the patient's own bones hardened.[5]

While some of the claims made for the future of nanotechnology—supercomputers so small as to be invisible to the naked eye, or swarms of "nanobots" that break down the metal in enemy tanks—are rooted more in science fiction than reality, this emerging technology still has the potential to radically change how medicines are developed and delivered, the scale and speed of computing, and the portability and efficiency of power cells. Already nanotechnology is used in over eight hundred products, from air purifiers and stain-resistant fabrics to camera sensors and organic light-emitting diodes. The U.S. National Science Foundation predicts that within a decade nanotechnology could have a $1 trillion impact on the economy.[6]

Beijing has made it clear that it has no intention of missing what could be the catalyst for a new industrial revolution. In fact, Cui's work is part of a determined push for China to situate itself at the forefront of nanotechnology. The entire budget for nanotech research in China may be in the range of $300 to $400 million, and the National Science Foundation of China funds over 650 projects with *nanotechnology* in the title, according to the Center for Nanotechnology in Society at the University of California, Santa Barbara.[7] The huge Taiwanese electronics manufacturer Foxconn has invested more than $40 million in a nanotechnology center at Tsinghua University, directed by Fan Shoushan, one of the top experts on carbon nanotubes. Housed in a modern steel and glass building near the campus gate, the center employs more than sixty researchers and is equipped with lab equipment so advanced that one visiting Japanese scientist described it as "the best equipped research center I have ever visited in China."[8]

As a result, China leads the world in some specialized areas of nanoscience and ranks second in the world in the publication of nanotech research papers. Although U.S. spending on nanotechnology totals more than $3 billion, with half of the funding coming from the federal government, the founder of the U.S. government's National Nanotechnology Initiative, Dr. Mihail C. Roco, has cautioned, "The U.S. does not have the overwhelming advantage we have in other technologies. We have to compete harder."[9]

Thus, the efforts of Cui and tens of thousands of other scientists and high-technology entrepreneurs in India, China, Korea, Japan, Taiwan, and Singapore are clear signs that fundamental change is coming. No longer will workers in Asia be content to provide low-cost manufacturing labor while someone in a garage outside of San Jose or a lab in Cambridge sparks the next generation of high-paying jobs with a "next big thing" idea. Already China is the world's largest exporter of high-technology products, followed by the United States and Japan. And the established science and technology powers of Japan and South Korea are retooling themselves for the future. BYD, a battery firm at the forefront of developing an electric car, is only one of the most prominent Chinese companies pushing to transform China from the world's factory to a more creative innovation-based economy. In the face of the global economic crisis, South Korea in December 2008 introduced the 577 Initiative: an ambitious plan to, by 2012, raise the share of its GDP dedicated to research and development to 5 percent (the 5 in the 577 Initiative), make South Korea the world's seventh science and technology power (yes, the first 7 in 577), and funnel money to seven major technology areas, including consumer electronics, automobiles, robotics, and nanotechnology.

While the Asian powers clearly have their eyes on the prize, the United States has appeared distracted, neglecting science and underfunding basic research. While Americans built McMansions, Asia spent on science, technology, and infrastructure. After World War II, the United States accounted for 50 percent of the world's research and development; today it is responsible for close to one-third. While the United States was a clear leader in most scientific fields for most of the last century, that position has slipped, according to the National Science Foundation, especially in new areas such as national cyberinfrastructure networking.[10] America's innovation system is on even shakier ground today as a result of the economic crisis. Capital for high-risk technology development has evaporated. In October 2008, the venture capital firm Sequoia Capital captured the spirit of the moment in the title of a presentation delivered to portfolio companies: "R.I.P. Good Times." With little potential to sell themselves to larger companies or list on the stock market, many early-stage technology companies closed shop; many that survived delayed expansion, cut costs, and laid off staff.

Also complicating technological development in the United

States is an inescapable reality deeply embedded within national power and political influence. Two powerful groups have conflicting ideas about the role of technological innovation: the chief executive officers of global companies and many economists versus officials in the Pentagon and members of Congress. The former tend to see the globalization of innovation as a "win-win" for all parties involved. In their view, the movement of technology across borders is the natural outcome of ever-expanding R&D networks and international business collaborations, and thus it is already beyond the control of states. Besides, the CEOs believe their companies are particularly well placed to enter into cooperative agreements that leverage new innovations, no matter where they occur. "During the Cold War," according to IBM CEO Samuel Palmisano, "innovation pitted nation against nation." Now, the United States is not the only source of innovation; it must collaborate where and whenever it can. "We're much better off," Palmisano says, "if we focus on enlarging the pie rather than on divvying it up . . . American leadership can take the world to a better place."[11]

This sanguine corporate view sits uncomfortably with the hawkish stance taken by many in the Pentagon and at the U.S. Capitol. Military and government policy makers still tend to see the international economy as a competition between nation-states for economic and technological resources, and no state brings out their wariness like China. In the 2006 *Quadrennial Defense Review*, the Pentagon concluded, "Of the major and emerging powers, China has the greatest potential to compete militarily with the United States and field disruptive military technologies that could over time offset traditional U.S. military advantages."[12] These concerns have not disappeared under the Obama administration. In 2009, General Michael Maples, the director of the Defense Intelligence Agency, testified to the Senate Armed Services Committee about the Chinese developing "systems and technologies" that could disable U.S. communication and intelligence satellites.[13] Put simply: for most of Washington, innovation is a zero-sum game where, for example, the decision of Intel to locate a semiconductor factory in Dalian is a gain for China and a loss to the United States. As they see it, pies are for cutting, not for enlarging.

The spread of technology creates two negative outcomes for American security: diffusion of new technologies to potential competitors, and unreliable suppliers. Through diffusion, new technologies and "know-how" strengthen the Chinese military. Shifting research centers to China and developing collaborative relations with Chinese companies inadvertently involves American technology companies in the diffusion process, speeding Beijing's military modernization. Second, as more technology development occurs in places like Shenzhen, Washington fears that Chinese intelligence agencies will find it hard to pass up the opportunity to slip malware into programs or to compromise hardware that eventually ends up being used by the U.S. military or government. Already a fake microchip has been found in the flight computer of an F-15 fighter jet.[14]

The more hawkish worldview is certainly correct in its diagnosis of the problem. Technology diffusion has and will continue to improve Chinese military capabilities. But the policy responses— tighter export controls and greater scrutiny of foreign students and scientists in the United States—ignore a central paradox: globalization ensures American security at the same time that it creates new security threats for the United States. Private companies, not federal labs, provide much of the technology required by the U.S. military to keep its qualitative lead over potential challengers. Those same private companies need access to markets in developing economies, especially China, to remain competitive. In parallel, tens of thousands of Chinese students, scientists, and business people now regularly study and work in the United States. They manage America's most prominent technology companies and are graduate students in labs in American research universities. In this globalized world, nearly everything is intertwined.

DEFINING INNOVATION

Before I delve into innovation in Asia and the United States—a huge topic both conceptually and geographically—let me define some terms. While there is much public discussion of innovation, there is not a great deal of agreement about what the term actually means or how it should be applied. Students of innovation have tried to distinguish among *invention*, the discovery of a new idea; *innovation*, the first commercialization of that idea; and *diffusion*, the widespread profitable adoption of the resulting product. In some rare cases, the three occur in sequence fairly rapidly; in others, it can take several decades before the original idea reaches a commercial application. In most instances, however, invention, innovation, and diffusion occur as part of a continuous, overlapping process. The car, airplane, computer, and cell phone we know today bear little resemblance to their original designs; the original idea for each was subsequently transformed by a long series of alterations, some groundbreaking, others minor. The path an idea takes usually involves a series of starts and stops: detours that may be failures, and wrong turns that eventually lead to new breakthroughs.

There is also a distinction between *process innovation*, or "new to the market," and *product innovation*, or "new to the world." Process innovation often involves adapting existing technologies to create new business models to deliver cheaper goods or services to consumers. While FedEx now invests heavily in tracking software, wireless technology, artificial intelligence, and geospatial analysis, its original innovation was the creation of a more efficient distribution system that delivered packages in one or two days. Home Depot and Wal-Mart possess innovative business models, but they are not companies known for their R&D departments.

Product innovation more closely fits the popular conception of the radically new invention, the revolutionary change that creates new industries. It is the innovation of the microchip or the development of Microsoft Windows. While these categories are analytically useful, in reality they often blur, with changes in process feeding the discovery of new products and vice versa.

In this book, when I refer to *innovation* I mean the creation, commercialization, and spread of novel ideas. I am using the term expansively—innovation with little bits of invention and diffusion and a primary focus on science-based product innovation.

Of course, some countries can do very well without product innovation. Both China and India have had jaw-dropping runs of growth—China's average rate of growth has been more than 9 percent for close to thirty years, India's closer to 6 percent since 1991—that have been grounded not in the development of their own technologies, but rather in the large-scale mobilization of labor and capital and the importation and diffusion of foreign technology.

In addition, according to Georgia Tech political scientist Dan Breznitz and management consultants John Hagel III and John Seely Brown, China and India's future (and present) is process, not product, innovation. The danger, Hagel and Brown warn, is that Western companies value product innovation too highly, and that by ignoring the disruptive process innovations emerging in China and India, they set themselves up for "innovation blowback."[15] What some Indian commentators have called "jugaad-innovation" is a good example of how this works. A *jugaad* is a low-cost, locally built, often jury-rigged truck or car used in the countryside. In the same way that the makers of these trucks have to improvise in the face of scarcity and shortage, Indian companies develop ingenious responses to the underdeveloped capital markets, inadequate infrastructure, and opaque government regulations they face in their home markets. These skills not only give them a competitive advantage over the Western companies trying to do business in India, but also allow them to be the dominant players in other developing economies.[16]

I have been observing technology development, politics, and security in Asia for about twenty years, visiting Taiwan and China for the first time in 1990 and India, Japan, and Korea since 2000. Writing about Chinese technology policy and military modernization, I have witnessed the importance of process innovation firsthand. In 2007, for example, I gave a talk at Oracle, the enterprise software giant, to a small group of the company's partners and venture capital firms investing or thinking of investing in China. After I finished laying out what I thought were some of the significant barriers to new technological development in China, Kevin Walsh, who at the time managed Oracle's China development centers, told me he did not disagree with the basic thrust of my argument. He thought it unlikely that a Chinese company would emerge any time soon to compete with Oracle in any of its core technologies. But a couple of smaller companies were adapting existing software to the needs of Chinese users, and they were building a service and support network that let them reach customers spread throughout several provinces. At the end of the day, they did not need product innovation if they had process innovation; small tweaks in the software and better service created a potential market of several hundred million dollars.

Whereas process innovation is clearly very important to Asia, I focus on the creation of new technologies for two reasons. First, many political leaders in Asia are extremely dissatisfied with the role of process innovator while leaving product innovation to the West. There is real concern, especially in Beijing, that process innovation will not be enough. Asian firms will be stuck making low-cost products in markets with low margins. Or as one Chinese analyst put it, "They eat the meat and we have the bone; they eat the rice and we have the husk."[17] Fearing that reliance on process innovation is not a tenable long-term development strategy, these countries are struggling determinedly to move from "Made in" to "Innovated in." As governments dedicate serious resources to this goal, they also siphon off people, ideas, and money from the United States.

Second, product innovation continues to matter for the economic health, the political influence, and the military power of the United States. There is a long debate over the economic impact of different types of innovation; in fact, according to *The Oxford Handbook of Innovation*, the "bulk of economic benefits comes from incremental innovations and improvements."[18] Amar Bhidé, a Columbia Business School professor, argues that the emphasis on the production of technological breakthroughs is misplaced; the widespread use of technologies by "venturesome" companies and customers is the true heart of America's advantage. "Wal-Mart and its followers are as much a part of the technological success of America as Silicon Valley," says Bhidé.[19]

Still, incremental change, diffusion, and use cannot be severed from invention and discovery. Basic scientific research remains a central component to technological advance and is essential to other American priorities, including military power as well as the development of new clean energy sources and the reduction of the country's dependence on foreign oil. Assuming a choice between discovery at the front end and diffusion at the back is unrealistic and artificial. The focus needs to be on systems that ensure that the front and the back continue working together.

LOOKING TO THE FUTURE

The focus here is on Asia, with a spotlight on India and China, and on how the United States can meet the challenges they present. The scale and scope of India and China put them in a different category than South Korea, Japan, and Taiwan. While the three Asian tigers experienced rapid growth in the 1970s and 1980s and now make up approximately 10 percent of the world's GDP, if they were to become true science-driven innovators it would be a change in degree. The rise of China and India as technological powers, however, would be a change in kind, a remaking of the world's economic and political structure. Two centuries ago, China and India accounted for more than 40 percent of the world's wealth, and they could soon regain that status. By 2030, the top-four world economies could be China followed by the United States, Japan, and India.

In addition, while Japan and South Korea have traditionally represented an alternative to the American model of innovation, China and India seem intent on beating the United States at its own game. South Korea and Japan were the archetypal "developmental states," where central government bureaucracies defined national economic objectives and actively intervened in markets. The Chinese and Indians have experimented with many different models, but today they are pushing small start-ups, university-industry collaboration, and venture capital. This is an archetypal American model, tied specifically to Silicon Valley, Austin in Texas, Route 128 in Boston, San Diego, and the Research Triangle Park in North Carolina, and to the success of American companies in the information technology and biotechnology sectors. It also reflects the way East Asians have carried the expertise they picked up during their education in the United States back to their own countries.

Still, the United States cannot sit idly by and merely observe the rise of new technology powers. Instead Washington must help shape the institutions and networks that promote and support science and technology in a globalized world. In foreign policy circles, it has become a widely noted observation—almost a cliché—that the "unipolar moment" is over; the United States is no longer "the center of world power, the unchallenged superpower," in journalist Charles Krauthammer's words.[20] The United States might remain the world's predominant military power, but it cannot impose its political and economic will on the rest of the world. The rise of Iran in the Middle East, North Korea's nuclear program, the collapse of the Doha round of trade negotiations in July 2008, and the Russian invasion of Georgia are all signs of the limits of American influence.

Limits does not mean, however, the end of U.S. power or the ascendance of the "rest" over the "West." Rather, it reflects the restrictions placed on American power by the growing capabilities of new actors—states with new influence, such as Brazil, China, and India, as well as large foundations, multinational companies, terrorist groups, and other less traditional players in foreign affairs. As the Indian foreign policy analyst Brahma Chellaney wrote, "In 2050, the United States is likely to still be influential enough to do almost anything, but not powerful enough to do everything by itself."[21]

Unable to act alone, the United States will have to work with a shifting set of partners on a range of different issues. Washington and Delhi, for example, have similar views on combating terrorism and building regional stability, but have not been able to find common ground on farm subsidies or on India's close economic relationship with Iran. Washington has praised China's sponsorship of six-party talks and the efforts to contain North Korea's nuclear program, but has criticized Beijing's relationship with Iran, Sudan, and Burma.

Unipolarity was an anomaly bound to end, and if managed properly, its demise should not lead to a crippling contraction of the United States' role in international affairs. The strength and influence of the United States since the Second World War were not simply the outcomes of having a larger military and more vibrant economy; they derived in part from the way in which America helped create a liberal international order—open markets, international organizations, and security alliances spanning Europe and Asia—with itself at the center. This open and rule-based system allowed the United States to turn "power into order and domination into legitimate authority," in the words of Princeton political scientist G. John Ikenberry.[22] Similarly, in science and technology, size is not everything. Influence, growth, and innovation can be found in the open, inclusive institutions and networks that connect the United States to the rest of the world.

The current economic crisis is also not an insurmountable challenge. America has rebounded from severe downturns through technological innovation before. As economist Alexander Field observed, the "most technologically progressive" period in U.S. economic history was not the 1990s, but the years from 1929 to 1941.[23] During the Great Depression, for example, DuPont made the breakthroughs in chemical engineering that led to nylon, Lucite, and Teflon. In 1935, Douglas Aircraft rolled out the DC-3, a plane whose speed and range revolutionized air travel. These discoveries helped propel the United States out of economic freefall.

More recently, Microsoft and Genzyme emerged during recessions in the 1970s and 1980s, and a decade from now we may be able to look back and see this period as critical to the founding of a revolutionary alternative energy company. There are some early signs of the innovation system stirring. In 2008, venture capital invested about $4 billion into solar power, coal gasification technology, biofuels, green building materials, and batteries, although this amount declined significantly in 2009 to $1.9 billion.

Big companies such as Microsoft, Freescale Semiconductor, and Intel are either protecting R&D spending against cuts or actually increasing it. Jeffrey Immelt, CEO of GE, sees opportunity in the crisis, claiming, "Companies and countries that really play offense vis-à-vis technology and innovation are going to come out ahead."[24] The government has stepped in with new funding for science. The

American Recovery and Reinvestment Act, the 2009 stimulus package of $787 billion, provided more than $21 billion for research and scientific infrastructure, including $10 billion for the National Institutes of Health, $3 billion for the National Science Foundation, and $1.6 billion for the Department of Energy. In April 2009, President Obama set spending 3 percent of GDP on research and development as a goal, up from around 2.7 percent. "We will not just meet but we will exceed the level achieved at the height of the space race," said the president. "This represents the largest commitment to scientific research and innovation in American history."[25]

This crisis could be cathartic, ending the reliance on debt and leverage. Inventing things other than complex financial instruments could become cool again, ushering in an era of "geek chic." In May 2009, Intel started running a TV commercial with the tagline "Our rock stars aren't like your rock stars." In the ad, an actor portraying Ajay Bhatt, the inventor of USB, saunters through the break room, dressed in tie and sweater vest, winking at and signing autographs for swooning groupies. After years of registering for finance classes, students might rediscover careers in the sciences and engineering or start their own companies. According to the *Harvard Crimson*, the number of students in the 2009 graduating class seeking jobs in finance and consulting fell by more than half compared to 2007.[26] Rawi Abdelal, a professor at Harvard Business School, tells me that his students, driven overachievers who just recently thought they could not afford *not* to take a job on Wall Street, are now leaning toward entrepreneurship.

Two outcomes for the United States are possible in the wake of the economic meltdown: an innovation system, already neglected, slowly crumbling and shunted aside by rising technology centers in Asia; or one renewed and revitalized, tightly linked to new ideas and talent around the globe. The challenge? To recover a culture of innovation that was driven underground, overshadowed by sexy credit default swaps and easy spending. The drive to invent and make is deeply American, and the economy has corrected itself in the past, but this time the United States cannot count on the innovation system to right itself. The economic crisis is too big, and challengers like China are pressing too hard. Action is critical. But to act usefully and make appropriate policy decisions, business leaders and policy makers need a realistic view of the emerging world of globalized innovation, and I hope to offer one here.

Chapter Two

STAKES AND FORCES

Those who point to Asia as the source of the next wave of innovation can back their claims with impressive raw numbers. Asia is spending heavily on science and technology. In China, expenditures on research and development rose from 0.6 percent of GDP in 1995 to 1.49 percent ($102 billion) in 2007; the goal for 2020 is 2.5 percent of GDP. India jumped from 0.84 percent in 1997 to 1 percent ($24 billion) in 2004, fell to 0.8 percent in 2007, and has set a goal of reaching 2 percent in 2012.

Korean expenditures moved from 2.25 percent of GDP in 1999 to approximately 3.5 percent (about $10 billion) in 2007 and are expected to reach 5 percent in 2012. In absolute numbers, the United States still remains the world's largest spender by far—bigger than the next seven countries combined—with funding for federal and private research and development totaling $397 billion in 2010. Growth in the budget was flat until President Obama's April 2009 announcement of dramatic new funding goals. Before then, as a percentage of GDP, U.S. spending fluctuated from a high of 2.74 percent in 2001 to a low of 2.54 in 2004 and to 2.67 percent in 2007.

Governments throughout Asia are not the only ones investing in science plans; foreign investors are jumping into the game as well. Major venture capital players—Sequoia Capital, Kleiner Perkins Caufield & Byers, Draper Fisher Jurvetson, and the Mayfield Fund—are involved in China, either directly or through partnerships. In 2006, foreign venture capital firms invested $1.89 billion in 214 deals in China, and investments almost doubled to $3.2 billion in 2007. Foreign venture capital was almost as bullish on India: $928 million in eighty deals during 2007, up from $349 million invested in thirty-six deals in 2006. The money flow is not likely to stop: a 2006 survey of 505 investors conducted by the National Venture Capital Association identified China and India as the top-two countries of interest over the next five years because of their low costs and, for India, an emerging culture of entrepreneurship.[1]

New spending on labs results in demand for new workers to staff them, so countries throughout Asia are expanding their talent pipelines. Educational systems are being revamped and universities built in order to produce bumper crops of graduates with degrees in science and engineering. In the 1960s, the United States became the world's largest producer of doctorates in the sciences, and while no nation has overtaken the lead, the American share is steadily shrinking. Today there are more students in Asia graduating with doctorates than in America, and America's overall share of doctorates in the world will shrink to about 15 percent in 2010, according to Harvard economist Richard Freeman.[2] South Korean universities awarded more than 3,779 doctoral degrees in science and engineering in 2006, up from 945 in 1990. In 1987, there were only a few hundred people with doctorates in China; in 2006, China graduated 36,247 doctoral students, approximately 63 percent with degrees in science and engineering.[3] China's long-range plan is to raise higher-education enrollment among the college-age population from a current 20 percent to 50 percent by 2050.

More people working in science and engineering plus increased spending on research are beginning to produce results. The percentage of patents issued to scientists in Asia is rising: Taiwan, Japan, and South Korea now account for more than 25 percent of industrial patents granted in the United States, and China now follows Japan and the United States in the total number of patents filed globally. In 1993, China was barely a presence in the research world, ranking seventeenth in its percentage of the world's scientific articles. By 2007, it had climbed to second. According to *BusinessWeek*'s Info-Tech 100 index, American firms made up 43 of the world's 100 most competitive high-tech companies in 2009, down from 75 in 1998; Asia is home to 30.[4] "The bottom line," according to Craig Barrett, former chairman of the board of Intel, "is that the United States no longer has a lock on the ideas and innovations of the future."[5]

The stakes couldn't be higher. Technological innovation is widely believed to be a decisive source of national wealth and prosperity, the most important competitive edge in the twenty-first century, and Asia's leaders are thoroughly wedded to this view. Questioned by foreign journalists about the wisdom of spending approximately $1 billion annually on space exploration when more than 200 million citizens still live below the poverty line, Prime Minister Manmohan Singh of India defended the space program: "In the increasingly globalized world we live in, a base of scientific and technical knowledge has emerged as a critical determinant of the wealth and status of nations and it is that which drives us to programs of this type."[6]

In China, innovation is becoming a dominant political priority. In October 2007, at the seventeenth National Congress of the Communist Party of China, a normally staid affair with the real decisions usually made behind the scenes, interest ran feverish since two leaders, Xi Jinping and Li Keqiang, were being elevated to the Politburo Standing Committee and thus marked as potential successors to President Hu Jintao. With hundreds of millions of people inside and outside of China glued to televisions and two thousand delegates watching in the imposing Great Hall of the People, Hu, in a speech lasting over two hours, dictated China's directions for the next five years. Technology was a clear centerpiece: "Innovation is the core of our national development strategy and a crucial link in enhancing the overall national strength."[7]

To meet Asia as a viable competitor, we must dissect the forces that shape it. Three pairings are critically important: hardware and software; high and low politics; and the local and global sides of innovation. If we focus on only one side or the other, we get a flat representation of the world, when we really require an atlas with rich topographical detail that can depict the barriers and fissures in the landscape of technological development.

Even experts can easily focus on one side of these couplets but miss the other. For hardware, clear metrics such as the number of scientists and patents are easy to measure and report, while the software—the abstract web of institutions, relationships, and understandings that move ideas from lab to market—is more complex. For high and low politics, the argument that openness is critical to U.S. national security is difficult to make and counterintuitive. The cost of being wrong—explaining to the enraged public why some important piece of technology ended up in the wrong hands—is concrete. And if there is any consensus about globalization, it is that the local will suffer. Distance is dead. Everything that can move, will.

We may ignore a side of these pairings for worthwhile reasons, but our blinkered perspective does us no good. Business leaders, policy makers, and university administrators must truly understand the strengths and weaknesses Asia and the United States bring to the playing field if they are going to make the correct decisions.

THE HARDWARE AND SOFTWARE OF INNOVATION

Chen Jin, the dean of the School of Microelectronics at Shanghai Jiaotong University, became a national hero in 2004 for his work on the Hanxin chip, China's first digital signalprocessing computer chip. The chip, which can be used in modems, cellular phones, high-capacity hard disks, digital cameras, and digital TVs, is critical to China's drive to become the preeminent player in information technology markets. Through numerous interviews and background pieces, the Chinese press praised Chen as a patriot, particularly since he had left a good job at Motorola to return to China. And Chen, who had a master's degree and a doctorate from the University of Texas, had made sacrifices; he had a bright future at Motorola, working his way through the company as a senior engineer and a manager for chip design. He led development on several system-on-a-chip projects, with the goal of creating integrated circuits that contain all the components of a computer on one chip, at Motorola's semiconductor research center. In 1999 and again in 2000, he won internal Motorola awards for excellence.

In 2000, Chen gave it all up for China, returning first to the garden town of Suzhou, which aspired to become the chip capital of the country, and then moving to Shanghai with a position at Shanghai Jiaotong University, one of China's most prestigious universities. In March 2001, he set up the lab within Jiaotong's department of computer science that would eventually develop the digital signal chip. Soon, Chen attracted the attention of and received support from the Shanghai municipal government. The press promoted the lab's accomplishments, and ever-more powerful government officials from provincial and central government offices visited Chen. By the end, government support for research on the chip totaled more than 100 million yuan, or approximately $13 million (yuan is also known as renminbi, RMB), and the Ministry of Education made Chen a "Yangtze River Scholar," the highest academic award given by the government of China.

The chip was a fake. When he left Motorola, Chen had taken a chip with him: after scratching the letters *MOTO* off, he stamped on

No. 1 Hanxin. When he needed to upgrade, he did so by stamping *No. 2, 3, 4,* and *5* on other chips he had brought back from the United States. Until an assistant exposed him, Chen used connections at various universities and bribed government officials to receive fake certifications of design and testing. After the fraud was revealed, the university removed Chen, and he was required to return the investment funds.

It is not easy to be a scientific star in China. Lured home with promises of cutting-edge equipment and brand-new labs staffed by eager graduate students, showered with attention by the media, feted by a government that desperately wants its own technology to compete with Western standards, celebrity professors like Chen face extraordinary pressure to produce tangible outcomes, usually within a bureaucrat's time frame of three to five years. A scientist who is unable to come up with the goods might be tempted to plagiarize or falsify research results. But the pressure to perform is only part of the problem. In the wake of the Chen scandal, Fang Shi-min, who runs a website tracking scientific misconduct, wrote, "The higher the position a cheater occupies the easier for him to avoid investigation and punishment."[8] Fraud and plagiarism are prevalent because of a lack of accountability and effective oversight in Chinese society.

Regardless of how fervently China races to build the *hardware* of innovation, on this side of the Pacific we should not mistake the inputs to the innovation process for actual innovation. As Cheng Jing, CEO of Beijing biotech company Capital Biochip, says, "To construct a research building takes a year. To fill it with something really meaningful easily takes ten to twenty years."[9] Labs can be built, money invested, students enrolled, and prominent professors recruited, but without respect for the rule of law and intellectual property rights, as well as a culture of individual initiative and openness, these steps will not produce the intended results.

Asia is underdeveloped in the *software* of innovation, which includes both the specific organizations and relationships that structure innovation and the underlying cultural framework, the "source code." Historically, any country looking to develop new technologies has had to make certain decisions: What is the appropriate relationship among government, academia, and the private sector? Should universities be centers of research and development, focus on education and training, or somehow combine the two? How much research should occur in government labs, and should it focus on basic or applied research? Where should investment for new technologies come from? And who should benefit from new inventions—the individual scientist, or the university or government lab where the work was done?

The American answer to most of these questions has historically diverged from the responses of the rest of the world. While the federal government funds most basic research, the private sector is the main engine of technological growth, funding more than two-thirds of research and development. Universities not only train the next generation but are themselves a significant source of discovery and invention. Although certainly not immune to stove-piping (the failure to share information and ideas across organizational boundaries) and turf battles, for the most part academia, industry, and government work relatively closely together. They develop a wide range of collaborative research projects, such as Bio-X, a massive multidisciplinary research program at Stanford University working at the intersection of medicine, science, and engineering. People and ideas circulate freely, through informal gatherings and the planned meetings that Bio-X hosts—cocktail and coffee hours where bright graduate students can make pitches to the venture capital firms clustered on Sand Hill Road in Menlo Park.

It is not enough that ideas are free to flow. The U.S. system also creates strong incentives to move inventions from the lab to the market. In America, your ideas can make you rich. Intellectual property is protected, and individual scientists are able to exploit their breakthroughs for commercial gain. Financial markets (at least until recently) are flexible and transparent. Entrepreneurs looking for capital can turn to venture capitalists interested in high-risk, high-return opportunities, and there can be (again, until recently) distinct, and often lucrative, avenues of exit: selling the company to an established, bigger company, or listing it on NASDAQ. The young entrepreneur has many role models to emulate: the Sergey Brins, Steve Jobs, and others who demonstrate the massive rewards that come to those who execute good ideas well.

In addition to concrete incentives and brick-and-mortar institutions encouraging innovation, something more intangible is in the air. Bio-X and the Sand Hill Road firms operate within a larger social and political environment where scientists and entrepreneurs embrace risk, and while not courting failure, they accept it as part of the process. For some, failure is a badge of honor, an entrepreneurial rite of passage. Furthermore, invention and innovation are locally driven. Yes, the federal government was the driving force for large-scale projects such as ARPANET (Advanced Research Projects Agency Network), the predecessor to the Internet, but the tradition of the individual tinker and the culture of making things in the backyard with a group of like-minded friends remain strong. Not to deny rivalries and jockeying for position, but in America competition is able to occur in parallel with collaboration. Scientists and technology entrepreneurs know that today's rivals may be tomorrow's partners. In addition, entry is based on the strength of ideas, not on background or pedigree. Max Weber, the German sociologist, observed that science is an aristocracy of merit, not a democracy.[10] The American innovation system operates in a similar way, and it can continue to thrive only if the best people, from inside and outside the United States, develop their talents here. Finally, marketing and distribution skills have developed here in tandem with invention and discovery. All eyes remain firmly on the prize of new markets and customers.

Even in this highly idealized vision of how the American system works, some important components need to be replaced or repaired, as I will discuss in later chapters. Nonetheless, these cultural strengths still match up extremely well with Asia's transformation. Besides, simply trying to win a hardware-driven arms race with Asia is a losing proposition. In the future, China is likely to invest more in research and development than the United States; almost inevitably China and India will one day produce more engineers than the United States; and, with a growing middle class, Indian and Chinese consumers will eventually become more important final consumers. It is time to realize that software in its most expansive sense offers the most opportunities for the United States to ensure its competitive place in the world.

THE HIGH AND LOW POLITICS OF INNOVATION

Prior to Chen Jin, the most notorious perpetrator of scientific misconduct in Asia was Hwang Woo-Suk, the South Korean scientist who published papers in *Science* in 2004 and 2005 with faked data claiming to have been the first to clone eleven patient-specific stem cell lines. Hwang's purported accomplishment created a near frenzy in South Korea, and he became an even larger national hero than Chen Jin in China. Honored as the country's first "supreme scientist," he was given free first-class tickets on Korean Air for ten years; sixteen biographies of Hwang lined the shelves of Seoul bookstores, including a comic book meant to instruct children on how to be more like the great scientist; and Hwang's image was put on a postage stamp. Government subsidies for his research totaled $65 million.[11]

Soon after the article on human stem cells was published, a website run by young South Korean scientists alleged that Hwang's results were faked. In November 2005, a South Korean television show called *PD Notebook* broadcast critical stories, claiming that some of the eggs used to create the stem cell line had been donated by women in his lab, perhaps under pressure from Hwang. The government and the general public, however, rallied around Hwang, questioning the patriotism of his attackers. But doubts about the authenticity of Hwang's experiments eventually drowned out the defense, and in December 2005, Korea University determined that all eleven of the stem cell lines were fabricated.

While the Chen and Hwang stories clearly reveal the difficult process of building the institutions and culture of effective innovation, they are also side effects of the political drive behind much of the technology development in Asia. Corruption, inefficiency, and waste are more likely to occur in a system without transparency or checks and balances, and they divert resources and attention away from real innovation. Furthermore, Chen Jin's and Hwang Woo-Suk's rise and fall were the result, in part, of a political process attempting to foster technological autonomy. Beijing supported Chen's efforts to develop China's first digital signal processor as part of a larger government-led effort to reduce Chinese dependence on foreign, primarily American and Japanese, technology through what the government called "indigenous innovation." Or as former Chinese minister of science Xu Guanhua put it in January 2006, when he unveiled a new plan designed to make the country one of the world's leading science powers by 2020, "China still lacks capability in innovation, particularly in those strategically important areas. We would never buy or borrow the key technologies from the global leading economies."[12]

Hwang's story is also tied in with the nationalist agenda in science and technology. "We became crazy for our work and were blind to everything else," Hwang told the press soon after his fabrication was revealed. "The only thing that I could see was the hope South Korea could stand high at the top of the world." Hwang was passionately embraced as a symbol of South Korean pride, and many nationalists attacked the whistle-blowers and journalists who had humiliated him. "You're America's dog," criticized one posting on an online bulletin board. "Those who buried the greatest scientist in the history of the Korean people will incur the wrath of the heavens."[13]

If these references to national pride sound anachronistic and out of place, it is because we tend to misperceive the globalization of science and technology as primarily a technological and economic process, not a social and political one. We see technology as a force of its own, free from any real constraints. When we notice the flow of technology across borders, it is usually in terms of a company like General Electric locating an R&D center in Bangalore or a Chinese-born Yale biochemist returning home to a new lab at Fudan University after thirty years in the United States.

While the multinational companies and individual scientists are important engines, technological development in Asia is still in large part driven by political goals. Politics precede and shape globalization. America's emerging competitors are not interested in globalization simply for globalization's sake—that is, for the economic benefits alone. They are reinterpreting and filtering the rules that govern the flow of technology in accordance with their culture, their drive for autonomy, and their demands of national power. All of the countries in East Asia think of civilian technology as a national security issue. Since the Meiji period (the era of Japan's modernization from 1868 to 1912), Japan has pursued, as MIT scholar Richard Samuels observed, the goal of "Rich Nation, Strong Army" through a strategy that closely linked technology and security, pairing the defense industrial base with civilian industry.[14] China is currently trying to create its own "dual-use" industrial base, one that is equally adept at turning out the flash drives used in MP3 players as the microchips used in the radar systems of advanced fighter jets.

None of this should be surprising. Americans did the same thing. More than two hundred years ago, Secretary of the Treasury Alexander Hamilton called on Congress to protect and subsidize domestic manufacturers in order to "render the United States independent on foreign nations for military and other essential supplies."[15] The problem is that today Hamilton's strategy is neither possible nor in the country's best interests. The changing structure of world trade and the nature of technology mean that the United States must exploit the relationship between high and low politics to thrive.

For most of the Cold War, the *high politics* of foreign policy rarely overlapped with the *low politics* of trade and economic relations. The Soviet Union was a security and political competitor, but it never really presented a meaningful economic challenge. Trade with the Eastern Bloc was minimal, and Khrushchev's threat to bury the West seemed less ominous as the failures of central planning became obvious. Japan, an ally, was an economic rival during the 1980s, but it never posed a security risk. Although negotiations with Tokyo over the valuation of the yen and car imports caused friction, Japan did not present a strategic threat—except to some, like the late novelist Michael Crichton.

Today, the high and the low, the strategic and the economic, merge in China. The United States trades heavily with China, and technology relations with China are, paradoxically, both central to American security and a threat to it. It works this way: Federally funded research currently plays a much smaller role than it used to in maintaining the United States' security capabilities. Instead of looking to government-funded defense labs, the Pentagon now depends on private companies to push the technological envelope and help keep it ahead of its rivals. Many of the leading technologies that determine success on the battlefield are developed in the labs of commercial companies. These same companies must be in the China market—for access to customers and talent—to remain competitive. Yet by building manufacturing and R&D centers in China, American companies cannot help but raise the technological capabilities of Chinese companies, which could, in turn, transfer technology and know-how to the Chinese military.

In the face of this spillover of know-how, it makes sense, especially after the terrorist attacks of September 11, 2001, to take a "zero-risk" approach to technology trade, to build high walls around as many technologies as possible. And this is what has happened: government agencies have fought to keep an expanding array of commercial technologies out of the hands of the Chinese military through new export control laws and visa restrictions, which make it more difficult for foreign students and scientists to come to the United States.

Unfortunately, the export control policies are futile, and the visa restriction policies are completely divorced from the realities of how science and technology work today, and impose perilous costs on America's own innovative capabilities. As Edward Teller, the theoretical physicist known as the father of the hydrogen bomb, wrote in 1999, "Our continuing security is acquired by new knowledge rather than by conserving old knowledge."[16] Yes, technology must be protected, but the range of technologies the United States can effectively keep secure is small. Openness is risky, but the United States must embrace it as a driver of innovation, the ultimate safeguard of American security.

THE LOCAL AND THE GLOBAL

Maine's economy conjures clichés—lobstermen, L.L. Bean, and sailboats. Currently Maine is trying to update this list to add biotechnology, software, and wood composites. During the 1990s, Dr. Habib J. Dagher, director of the University of Maine's Advanced Engineered Wood Composites Center, tried—initially without much luck—to interest the U.S. Navy in building a small speed boat out of composite wood. Compared with aluminum, wood composites produce much less vibration in a boat moving rapidly on the water, reducing the chances of injury. At the time, however, the navy was primarily focused on open-ocean missions far from the coastline and wanted specialty metals for large ships. After the terrorist attacks of September 11, the Pentagon began to think about how to land small teams of Navy SEALs in hostile areas quickly and safely. In 2005, the lab received a Defense Department grant to develop a prototype special-operations boat in cooperation with Hodgdon Yachts in East Boothbay.

Launched in 2006, the North Star Alliance Initiative—a partnership involving small companies, the University of Maine, community colleges, and the state government—is attempting to build a new regional economy. The plan is to leverage the research on composites to spur the development of a wide range of other industries, including marine and waterfront infrastructure and ballistic armor. But the scientific breakthrough involved in developing the wood composites is only the first, and perhaps the smallest, step toward developing a local innovation ecosystem. To succeed, communities have to work together to create specialized workforce training programs, identify marketing opportunities, and grow infrastructure.

During a visit in May 2007, Karen Gordon Mills—who worked in private equity and venture capital for twenty years and was chair of Maine's Council on Competitiveness and the Economy for two years before she became head of the Small Business Administration in 2009—described to me the challenges the state faced. For years, in its effort to create new jobs by luring large companies to the state, Maine had been frustrated by high energy costs and an unfriendly business environment. Employment was flat; many young people were leaving the state for opportunities elsewhere; and the impending closing of Brunswick Naval Air Station, scheduled for 2011, could mean the loss of nearly 5,000 jobs (out of almost 500,000 non-farm jobs) and $135 million in annual earnings. The pressure to act was growing.

The state needed a fresh strategy: not simply to attract companies to Maine but to create brand new industries by exploiting cooperative relationships, especially in areas like boatbuilding where the state already boasted a competitive advantage. Maine's small size and the fact that everyone—academics, boatbuilders, and state officials—knew everyone else meant few social or political barriers stood in the way of cooperation. "The increased globalization of the world economy is making things tough for companies across the United States," writes Mills, "but maybe it will play to our state's strengths."[17] In effect, Maine made the decision to turn social and personal ties, a sense of community, and a willingness to build public-private partnerships into the building blocks of competitiveness.

While public money plays an important role in the process, the investments are not huge. Rather, money is being used to reinforce collaborative networks and build capacity. The North Star Alliance Initiative received one of the first WIRED (Workforce Innovation in Regional Economic Development) grants from the Department of Labor. The grant was not large, $15 million over three years, but it allowed the Initiative to function as a matchmaker, consultant, and clearinghouse for industry. Money from the state—in particular a $55 million R&D bond passed by voters in 2006—funds technological entrepreneurship through matching grants. Since grantees must partner with local companies, technology development is grounded within Maine.

Maine is exploiting one of the fundamental truths obscured by the hype around globalization. Location still matters. Globalization has changed the competitive environment. American companies monitor and actively engage market opportunities abroad. New competitors are emerging throughout the Pacific. Cheap telecommunications and broadband, in conjunction with low-cost, highly skilled labor, allows companies to move not only manufacturing but also high-value research and development out of the United States. According to Craig Barrett, these circumstances mean that Intel "can never hire another worker in America again and still be a great company." (He also admits that this worries him as an American.)

Even though they can go just about anywhere, there is good reason for companies to orient themselves in clusters. Proximity—to new start-up firms, established companies, research universities, venture capital, and new graduates—is important. As innovation has become increasingly collaborative, companies are drawn to technology hubs that provide the concentration of ideas, talent, and capital needed for future competitiveness. These technology hubs in turn gain a competitive advantage over their neighbors as companies arrive and set up shop. Richard Lester, director of MIT's Industrial Performance Center, put it very clearly: "As the competition between firms globalizes, the competition between places intensifies."[18]

Creating the right environment for collaborative innovation is no easy task, though many governors, mayors, and business associations across the United States are now trying. These efforts have been heavily influenced by the idea of clusters. Popularized by Harvard Business School professor Michael Porter, clusters are geographic concentrations of firms, suppliers, and supporting businesses and institutions—bankers, lawyers, professional associations, research universities—all from the same industry.[19] While economists and geographers speak of "agglomeration effects" and "positive externalities," the basic idea is that individual firms benefit from being located next to each other.

Clusters do not serve as an instant panacea. As Charles Cogan, a professor of public policy at the University of Southern Maine, told me, "The world is spiky. I do not worry about Southern California or Boston. It is the small and rural states that are scrambling." Some fear that Maine has gotten into the game too late; Pennsylvania, California, and other states have initiatives that began a decade or two ago. One Maine official told me that she worried that the governor and his supporters are "raising expectations that the government can simply build a cluster. Creating networks is frustrating work that takes time and cannot be measured."

Helping new start-up companies should be at the center of any regional development strategy. The dynamism of the American economy is rooted in the constant interaction between large and small firms, and the very real possibility that they may soon swap places, the small start-up dethroning the established player. One-third of the Fortune 500 companies in 1970, for example, had disappeared by 1985, and the median life span for an information technology company is less than five years. Of the twenty largest software companies, only one occupied the same position in 1993.[20]

Most Asian countries have either big firms or new start-ups, but not both. Asian governments often subsidize and protect their large firms so they cannot fail, while their inhibitory regulatory environment and tight restrictions make it difficult to found and grow new companies. Around 50 percent of bank lending in China, for example, goes to large state-owned enterprises. In Korea, Samsung, LG, and the other large family-owned business conglomerates known as *chaebol* conduct the vast majority of research and development. Even after the government introduced a raft of new policies designed to support small start-ups, the large companies, universities, and government research institutes all watch to see what markets the chaebol enter, and then organize their own research, training, and development to follow suit. In the United States, the rapid rise and fall of technology companies weeds out low performers and encourages experimentation. Failure can be painful, but it has the salubrious effect of releasing people, ideas, and capital to pursue more promising projects.

Small companies are increasingly likely to deliver the benefits of innovation to the American economy. Cisco, Microsoft, and other large companies must operate globally, and while they might prefer to conduct research, develop new markets, and build capacity at home, they will do so wherever it is most cost-effective. Moving research and development abroad may be good for shareholders, but its impact, at least in the short term, on American workers and the American economy is not beneficial. As a board member of a large electronics company told me, "When we look at the world, we do it as a global company. Our strategic plans involve the European Union, the United States, and Asia. As people go global, the national is less important. Still, in the back of my mind we are an American company, but I don't know for how long." By contrast, small companies anchor innovation to a place, assembling scientists and engineers, well-trained workers, venture capital, and all the other components of success locally.

An understanding of the dynamic interaction between the local and global, economic and political, and software and hardware is missing from both the well-worn descriptions of a rising Asia and the debates on how the United States can best respond. In almost all areas, policy makers have tended to see only one side of each of these couplets, and either ignore or underestimate the importance of the other. As a result, they have overblown the threat of Asia and suggested similarly one-dimensional policy responses focused on hardware—more money for federal research budgets and expanding the pipeline of talent in math, engineering, and the sciences through scholarships and fellowships. There is nothing wrong with more money. Indeed, the country should be spending more money on research.

Such responses, however, are fundamentally backward looking, harkening back to the shock of Sputnik and the National Defense Education Act, the 1958 legislation that increased federal funding for science and mathematics education. They are also unlikely to be effective. Eventually, China will outspend America. Today, the United States needs to focus on building the platforms, especially at the local and regional level, that allow it to exploit its cultural and social strengths. As David Tennenhouse, a former director of the Information Technology Office at the Defense Advanced Research Projects Agency, told me, "What the U.S. is really good at is sifting through all these wacky ideas and turning them into something bigger." The United States needs to lead the world in championing risk taking, technological entrepreneurship, and a start-up culture; educating scientists and engineers in multiple linked technical fields and connecting them to like-minded thinkers and doers; and integrating a range of disparate ideas from various disciplines and localities and matching them to emerging markets around the world.

Chapter Three

KNOW THY COUPLETS

In May 2006, I was in a cab in Beijing riding past the new National Stadium being constructed for the 2008 Olympics. I was on my way to interview the managers of a new research center built in the Wangjing Science and Technology Park by one of the United States' most advanced telecommunications companies. Modern office buildings housing Motorola, Nortel, Ericsson, Agilent, Samsung, and Lucent now sat on what had been, six years before, farmland. The labs were stocked with the most advanced equipment and were staffed by young, motivated, and talented Chinese. I was about to get a glimpse of China, the technological superpower.

Over our lunch of *he fan*, vegetables and fish over rice in a Styrofoam box, and numerous cups of green tea, the two senior managers of the lab, both foreigners with several decades of experience in the telecom industry in the United States and Europe, listed the rationale behind their company's choice to open an R&D center in China. They particularly wanted entrée to a growing and increasingly sophisticated technology market. In 1999, approximately 108 million Chinese had access to a fixed line phone and 49 million to mobile phones; by 2009, those numbers had ballooned to 314.7 million and 747.4 million, respectively.[1]

Not only do more Chinese have more phones, they are increasingly sophisticated and demanding consumers. According to the marketing firm Grey Global Group, it is now fashionable to upgrade cell phones every three months in Shanghai, Beijing, and other large Chinese cities.[2] In a January 2007 issue entitled "The Mobile Phone Man (Shoujiren)," *New Weekly*, a Chinese news magazine, profiled nine cell phone fanatics, including a man who has changed his mobile phone every month since 2002, lovers who send as many as three thousand text messages a month, and a freelance photographer who owns twenty mobile phones and gives different mobile phone numbers to the different women he meets.[3]

The research center managers also expected to reduce manufacturing costs by working in China. Labor costs in the chip industry, for example, can be as much as 90 percent lower in China than in the United States, and Semiconductor Industry Association president George Scalise claims that Chinese government incentives—tax breaks or building subsidies over ten years—can make it $1 billion cheaper to build and operate a semiconductor manufacturing facility in China than in the United States.[4]

There is also an unspoken but palpable pressure from the Chinese government to move a company's advanced R&D unit to Beijing if the company wants entrée to the Chinese market. Under the terms of China's acceptance into the World Trade Organization, the government agreed to stop requiring technology transfers to Chinese companies in return for allowing foreign firms access to the domestic market. Demands may no longer be made openly, but multinational companies know that officials are more likely to reward those who actively contribute to China's technology development. "Friends of China" get first dibs on land to build new factories, find the electric and water companies more responsive and helpful, and are unlikely to be bothered by overly zealous safety and tax inspectors. Eager to be a good friend of the Chinese government, foreign firms move R&D centers and higher-level design to China.

The advanced telecommunications company had also established the R&D center to keep an eye on competitors, both those from its home market and up-and-coming Chinese companies. Most companies now believe that to be a truly global player they need to have a strategic presence that encompasses sourcing, manufacturing, and research and development in China.

Finally, and perhaps most important among all the reasons listed, the company had come to Wangjing tech park in search of young, talented engineers and software programmers. Engineers are not only in high supply but also of high quality. Bill Gates has said that some of Microsoft's best computer science researchers are in China, and Microsoft Research Asia competes with the company's R&D centers in other parts of the world in number of patents received and publications produced. In an interview in 2004, Craig Barrett of Intel stated that the Chinese are "capable of doing any engineering, any software job, any managerial job that people in the United States are capable of doing."[5]

Even with all of these reasons to move research to Beijing, details emerged, as the managers and I talked, that made China sound less like a brave new world of technological development and more like a work in process. The quality of the engineers graduating from Tsinghua or other local schools was good, but new employees often lacked language, management, and project skills. Government policy was opaque and often capricious. The managers of the center had real concerns that the company's main Chinese competitor was stealing their technology.

Strangely, the office in which the interview was taking place looked like the hothouse at a botanical garden. Each desk was covered with at least three rather large, leafy green plants. In fact, almost every newly constructed R&D facility I went into in Beijing seemed to have its own greenhouse. This was not the result of a liberal office decoration policy. Sometime after lunch, the fourth or fifth cup of tea caught up with me and I had to excuse myself and ask for directions to the restroom. Standing at the urinal, I noticed a large banner in Chinese telling me, "Do not worry. All the toxins have been removed." Of course, this exhortation had the opposite effect on me. Returning to the office, I asked what the story was with the poison and the poster.

A little sheepishly, the managers explained. The buildings were new, and the staff believed that the paints and other materials used in their construction were giving off toxic fumes. Several weeks earlier, they had threatened not to show up for work. This was not an outlandish idea with regards to the quality of building materials in China. Many of the young engineers who worked in the labs had renovated their own apartments and knew that, in order to cut costs, contractors frequently substituted substandard and often deadly materials. During an inspection of buildings across the city in 2005, for example, the Beijing Municipal Government discovered at least thirty-two products that did not meet the standards for their content of dangerous materials. Even though the foreign management called in several government agencies to confirm the building's safety, Chinese employees understandably believed that their workplace could be as dangerous as their homes.

Finally, after several weeks of negotiation, a compromise was reached. Since the workers believed that green leaves filter out the most dangerous chemicals, the company agreed to put several plants on every desk. The scientists and engineers could go back to their labs, and management could announce the toxin-free workplace through restroom banners.

The innovation process has four steps: producing new ideas, training new talent, launching new companies, and fostering policies that encourage the preceding three steps. The desk plants in Wangjing are symbolic of the glitches that exist throughout this process in Asia—the physical infrastructure is changing rapidly while the politics and psychology of innovation lag. Policymakers, scientists, and entrepreneurs in India, China, Japan, and Korea are not blind to these software glitches, and they are laboring hard to build a culture of technological entrepreneurship. The globalization of science and technology gives them a reason for optimism that the work will go quickly since they can leverage the unprecedented circulation of people, money, and ideas around the world to boost their own scientific and technological capacities.

To be sure, there are always unforeseen contingencies—political crisis or the emergence of new technologies and business models—that can radically shorten timelines and shift technological trajectories. What might look like a weakness in the current climate could be an advantage under a different model of economic growth. New leaders can push countries down different development paths, and the next generation of scientists and students could be willing to adopt radically different ways of doing things. Still, despite all of the ideas, resources, and talent available to Asia's leaders, building an effective innovation system is a political process and thus, progress will be slow and uneven.

NEW IDEAS

In India, at the end of 2006, a growing sense of crisis gripped many scientists and analysts. They feared that the nation was falling behind, if not outright failing, in generating new scientific ideas. Despite all the talk in India and the West about India's rise as a science superpower, C. N. R. Rao, the scientific adviser to Prime Minister Manmohan Singh, declared, "Science in India is dying." Newspapers complained that government labs lagged significantly behind their Chinese counterparts in the production of scientific papers and that Chinese scientists had more resources at their disposal. Funding for research in China was almost fivefold that in India. "Unless India changes the scientific policies and practices that it has been following for the last five decades, its science could be dead in the next five years," continued Rao.[6]

Indian government research institutes are the crown jewels of the national innovation system, the legacy of the first Indian prime minister Jawaharlal Nehru's commitment to science and technology, and at the same time subject to poor management, chronic underfunding, and bureaucratic interference. Historically, money has been in short supply. Government spending on science and technology was flat for most of the 1980s and 1990s, and declined in the first half of this decade. The government, however, announced in 2008 its intention to double spending on research and development from about 1 percent to 2 percent of GDP.[7]

In 2006, when asked what it would take to make India a scientific power, Ashok Parthasarathi, the scientific adviser to former prime minister Indira Gandhi, answered, "The problem is not one of increased funding alone, but bringing about a cultural transformation."[8] Ajit Balakrishnan, founder and CEO of Rediff.com, echoed this sentiment, telling me that science is mismanaged. Although nominally independent, research labs in India are hampered by long decision cycles, inappropriate research areas, and an emphasis on procedures over results. "Diversity of research or personality is often frowned upon," said Anita Mehta, a physicist at the S. N. Bose National Centre for Basic Sciences. "Those who don't match stereotypes or work on subjects that have been hammered to death are labeled 'too independent.'"[9] Perhaps most important, scientists in government labs are civil servants, rewarded and promoted for seniority more often than for creativity.

The Council of Scientific and Industrial Research (CSIR), under the leadership of the extremely able R. A. Mashelkar from 1995 to 2006, became a notable exception. When I visited India in 2005, almost everyone I spoke with praised how he had made the labs more business oriented and productive. Mashelkar's personal story is inspiring: As a schoolboy he studied by the light of the street lamps, and he almost dropped out of school when his widowed mother could no longer afford the fees. He eventually became one of the country's most prominent chemical engineers, the winner of numerous awards and honors, and a fellow of the Royal Society in London and the U.S. National Academy of Engineering. But despite all of his successes, the shifts Mashelkar inspired in the government labs were relatively narrow. Almost 70 percent of American patents earned by CSIR were granted to only three laboratories, and the mindset in the other thirty-five labs remained unchanged. When I returned to India for a follow-up trip in 2008, Mashelkar had moved on, the scientists working in the CSIR labs were still government employees, and their work was relatively untouched by market pressures.

Indian scientists can only envy the funding and government attention their counterparts in Beijing and Shanghai receive. That said, more money and state involvement create their own set of concerns. Many Chinese scientists fear that too many resources are being wasted on high-prestige, politically important "big science" projects.

The ambition of China's plans, many of which were announced in January 2006, is breathtaking: thirteen engineering "megaprojects" in areas such as high-end generic chips, extra-large-scale integrated circuit manufacturing, and manned aerospace and moon exploration, along with four science "megaprojects" in developmental biology, nanotechnology, protein science, and quantum research. The review process for these projects remains opaque, and administrators and politicians, not experts, make promotion and funding decisions. No one can guarantee that down the line these areas of focus will be worthwhile. Committing to specifically designed areas, especially in a national plan, will make it more difficult for labs to change course and hone in on the most fruitful research paths. "The most innovative ideas come from very few creative scientists at rare moments," according to Yi Rao, a neurobiologist at Northwestern University in Evanston, Illinois, and deputy director for academic affairs of China's National Institute of Biological Sciences, "whereas planning of large-scale projects requires the consensus of many scientists."[10]

NEW TALENT

Despite all the talk in the United States about hundreds of thousands of engineers and scientists as well as the rapid expansion of university education in China and India, it is uncertain whether these countries will be able to keep pace in the second of the four steps—new talent development. In a widely reported 2005 study, McKinsey consulting company found that only 10 percent of graduates in China and 25 percent of those in India had the practical, analytical, and teamwork skills that foreign companies required. Cong Cao of the Levin Institute in New York and Denis Fred Simon of Penn State, in their 2009 book, *China's Emerging Technological Edge: Assessing the Role of High-End Talent*, found huge gaps in the skills students acquire in college and those they need to be successful in the market. They predict over the next few years (2009–2012) a shortfall of fifty thousand scientists and engineers in China, with the most extreme shortages at the top of the skill ladder. By 2017, the number of workers in the age range of fifty-five to sixty-five will be greater than the number in the age range of eighteen to twenty-two. As a result, experienced managers and engineers will be leaving the workforce through retirement faster than they can be replaced.[11]

The Chinese leadership is aware of these challenges and has ambitious plans for higher education. Enrollment rates at universities are exploding. Chinese universities now have greater autonomy from the Ministry of Education than in the past, though they remain tightly regulated. Students have more opportunities for interdisciplinary study and research than they did previously, but higher education remains mainly theoretical, tied to outdated textbooks and syllabi. Instruction is top-down and rewards memorization and rote learning. Technical knowledge is divorced from creative thinking, and students are not encouraged to challenge authority or pose critical questions.

The experience of Wang Yin, a twenty-eight-year-old student in the doctoral program in computer science at Tsinghua, is emblematic. Wang created a stir in 2005 by appearing on national television and in the mainstream press after posting a letter on his blog telling of his decision to drop out of one of China's most prestigious universities. In "The Smashing of the Tsinghua Dream," Wang complained that he had learned little in his Ph.D. program. Since university administrators and professors were more concerned with the production of meaningless research papers than with practical training or creative thinking, he decided he would be happier doing something else.[12]

Freedom of expression and inquiry is limited within China's restrictive political and cultural context. Liu Daoyu, the former president of Wuhan University, criticized China for thinking that growth serves the same role as reform: "China boasts the biggest college population, the largest campuses and is the second biggest academic paper generator in the world, but it can barely foster a world-class scholar or a school of thought." The solution, according to Liu, is that China "must lift the screws on people's minds and tap into their initiative and enthusiasm."[13] Mu-Ming Poo, head of neurobiology at the University of California, Berkeley and director of the Institute of Neuroscience, Chinese Academy of Sciences, in Shanghai, made a similar argument in the journal *Nature* about the difficulties of developing a creativity-based research tradition when there is "strong bureaucratic control of research agendas and scientific careers, a profound bias towards short-term commercial results and applications, and an environment that reflects a cultural predisposition of deference towards authority."[14] When the China supplement of *Nature* tried to reprint Poo's critique as part of a general discussion of Chinese science and technology, the General Administration of Press and Publication, the media overseer, pressured the journal to cancel the issue.[15]

There are also widespread concerns about plagiarism and academic dishonesty in China. In a survey quoted in *China Daily* of 180 graduates with doctorates, 60 percent admitted to paying for their work to be published in academic journals, and another 60 percent said that they had copied someone else's work. In 2010, the BBC reported that underemployed masters and doctoral students were hard at work writing papers for other people, creating a $100 million market in ghost-written papers and bloating publication lists. A member of the Chinese Academy of Sciences, a president of a university, and a member of the Chinese Academy of Engineering were involved in prominent plagiarism cases, and all kept their jobs.[16]

This academic malfeasance is fueled by the methodology behind evaluation and promotion. Graduate students need to publish papers in a few core journals in order to graduate, and academics need to publish in the same journals in order to get promoted, but the number of journals has increased only slightly while enrollments have exploded. *China Newsweek* estimates that Chinese journals can publish only 300,000 articles annually, while the country's academics are expected to produce some 530,000 papers.[17] The result is bribery and intense pressure on editors, and those who cannot get their papers accepted are sometimes tempted to create fake journals and articles. Liu Hui, assistant dean of Tsinghua's medical school, was removed after his qualifications were found to be faked; Yang Jie, dean of the School of Life Science and Technology at Tongji University in Shanghai, met the same fate.

While incidences of plagiarism, falsification of data, and scientific misconduct are also rising in India, the most dramatic problem the country faces is a severe shortfall of talent. By 2020, if the economy continues growing at 6 to 7 percent annually, the shortfall in engineers could be more than two million.[18]

The Indian Institutes of Technology (IITs) and Indian Institutes of Management, though richly praised in the business press, are a minuscule part of the Indian educational system, reaching less than 1 percent of the student population. The vast majority of India's eleven million college students attend the other eighteen thousand colleges and universities, which rarely make the pages of Western newspapers. A 2007 government study rated two-thirds of these universities and found that 90 percent of the degree-granting colleges were of poor or middling quality. Colleges stress rote memorization, fail to develop marketable skills, use old and outdated curricula, and often fail to provide any instruction in English, which cuts graduates off from jobs in the outsourcing, business process, and information technology sectors.[19]

Moreover, democracy does not insulate India's universities from political interference and corruption. In fact, no area of activity in India may be more politicized than education. Sixteen different agencies supervise higher education, few of which are independent. Universities have little or no autonomy; permission is required to set admission standards, start new courses, and revise syllabi. Bureaucratic regulation stifles reform and innovation. Recruitment of faculty and administration staff is often treated as another spoil to be doled out by political parties, and there is a strong market for fake degrees, leaked exams, and sham credentials.

All is not right at the top of the education hierarchy either. Individual "IITians" have gone on to great things—almost 30 percent of NASA scientists, as well as numerous CEOs in Silicon Valley, come from IITs. But the Indian Institutes of Technology are not producing nearly enough, in terms of students or research, to meet the demands of the growing Indian economy. The IITs are really focused on teaching, not research. At a December 2006 gathering of IIT alumni, former president A. P. J. Abdul Kalam, who is an aerospace engineer, criticized the complacency of the institutes. The direct benefit of the IITs to the nation in terms of knowledge products and intellectual property, Kalam told the four thousand alumni, "is rather minimal."[20] The schools are too exclusive and distant from the needs of India.

The government of India has plans to raise enrollments by creating new universities and colleges. In July 2008, the cabinet approved eight new Indian Institutes of Technology (bringing the total to fifteen), and the Planning Commission has proposed spending $760 million over seven years on seven new Indian Institutes of Management (total of fourteen), two additional Indian Institutes of Science and Engineering Research (total of five), twenty more Institutes of Information Technology, and thirty additional universities.

While this is a necessary and farsighted plan, who is going to teach in all of these new institutes? India graduates fewer than seven thousand doctoral candidates in science, engineering, and technology each year. The majority of Indians with a Ph.D. are in the United States, not India. Only thirty-five to fifty doctorates in computer science are earned each year in India, compared with close to a thousand in the United States.[21] And despite the rapid growth of the Indian economy, salaries for professors—$15,000 a year for those at IIT Bombay—are paltry compared to what the software and service firms offer. Thus, recruiting and retaining graduates with doctoral degrees is becoming increasingly difficult for universities and research institutes, leaving many institutes, even the elite IITs, unable to fill up to a third of their positions.[22]

NEW COMPANIES AND NETWORKS

It would not be much of an exaggeration to say that the average mid-level bureaucrat at one of the science and technology agencies in China, Japan, Korea, or India knows as much as, if not more than, most Northern Californians about the history and workings of Silicon Valley. In the late 1990s, I often gave AnnaLee Saxenian's classic study of Silicon Valley, *Regional Advantage*, as a gift to the Chinese officials whom I met and who had befriended me. Less than two years after its publication in English, they often waved the book off—they already had it and were adopting its ideas. Planning documents for the Zhongguancun Science and Technology District in Beijing trumpeted the development of *chuangxin wangluo* (innovation networks)—the flexible, informal connections that circulate people, ideas, and money, connections Saxenian described as one of Silicon Valley's central competitive strengths.

When policy makers in Asia talk about the founding, funding, and support of new technology companies—the third step in the innovation process—they have in mind a specific image: the story of Silicon Valley. The recipe appears simple and easy to replicate: concentrate universities, research institutes, and factories in the same area; build good schools, parks, and nice housing; offer preferential tax rates and financing to attract smart people and new companies; and eventually, so the theory goes, new clusters of regional innovation will flourish. Perhaps more so than any nation, China has pursued recreating the trappings of Silicon Valley locally: there are now hundreds of high-technology zones all over the country, although many have little to do with actually encouraging high technology.

Indian policy makers are also interested in cloning the success of Silicon Valley, especially collaboration between universities and industry. One of the major weaknesses of the Indian national science and technology system has been the lack of participation of universities in the innovation chain. Part of the problem is funding. The central government provides the lion's share of R&D funds (almost 80 percent of all the money spent), but since most of that money (60 percent) is funneled through strategic programs—Department of Atomic Energy, Indian Space Research Organisation, Council of Scientific and Industrial Research, Defence Research & Development Organisation—it has little immediate commercial use. Higher-education institutions account for 3 to 4 percent of national R&D expenditures, significantly less than the approximately 10 percent spent on research and development at universities in South Korea and China.

Traditionally, Indian universities have shown little concern for what industry needs or wants. Academia rewards professors for publishing, not for patenting or consulting. Academics can be snobby about outside projects, believing that industry projects offer little intellectual challenge or pay. When they do work with industry, Indian professors are more likely to engage in joint development with foreign companies than with local ones. The bad feelings flow both ways. From industry's perspective, professors are out of touch and difficult to work with. If an Indian company needs help from an academic partner, it looks abroad.

There has been a push in India to close this gap. The National Research Development Corporation, a department under the Department of Science and Technology, licenses technologies developed in university- and government-run labs and invests in new ventures. The National Science and Technology Entrepreneurship Development Board, whose mission is to generate entrepreneurship among scientists and engineers, establishes industry-university cells, science and technology entrepreneur parks, and technology business incubators. The Society for Innovation and Entrepreneurship at IIT Bombay, which receives financial support from the government, provides office space to engineers and professors in return for a share of ventures. By 2005, there were some seventy parks and incubators, with the government adding another five a year, although government officials estimated that perhaps only forty of them were effective.

These are not the problems of developing economies alone; similar roadblocks slowed collaborative work between academia and industry in Japan. As in India, Japanese universities historically played a minor role in innovation; the most important players were always the R&D departments of large companies like Toyota, Sony, and Hitachi. Programs supporting university-industry collaboration are part of a larger push for technological entrepreneurship, which includes a new venture capital law, the establishment of regional incubators, and the encouragement of university spin-offs. On a research trip I made to Japan in 2005, every government official I met proudly trumpeted these projects, especially the one thousand new start-ups created by university collaboration.

I nearly left Japan impressed with the success of the projects, but on my last day there, *Nikkei Business* coincidentally published a cover story on the topic.[23] My breakfast interviewee, a Japanese engineer who had spent years at MIT, kindly translated the title for me: "The Delusion of University-Oriented Ventures." Government bureaucrats had fixated on a nice round number for the new start-ups, but few firms had survived for long, and even fewer were actually working at the technological edge. Most were happy to receive government support because they would have gone under without it.

Robert Kneller, an American who teaches at the University of Tokyo, explained why successful entrepreneurial start-ups are rare, contrary to the government hype.[24] The largest companies still dominate the technological landscape and pursue their own research agendas in-house; since they also have preferential access to people and ideas at Japanese universities, they crowd out smaller firms. Labor mobility is severely limited. Even during the "lost decade," the economic downturn that stretched through the 1990s, Sony, Hitachi, and the other big firms managed to keep their R&D units together, and unlike Silicon Valley or Beijing, Japanese engineers generally do not leave jobs at the big companies for new opportunities at start-ups.

Young Japanese entrepreneurs who risk starting their own companies face a distrust of youth and entrepreneurialism. Ito Masahiro, the CEO of the YAPPA Corporation, founded his first company soon after he graduated from high school, the International School in Osaka. Clearly an outlier, Ito was so independent that he rented an apartment by himself rather than commute four hours to school every day. As graduation approached, his parents gave him a choice: he could attend college in the United States or start a business. While buying some food at the local 7-Eleven in Japan, he noticed that the cashiers were always entering data about customers and their purchases. He soon wrote a horoscope program for cell phones that would collect personal data for mobile phone companies.

The company that Ito founded to develop this program and other software for cell phones failed after he was unable to get anyone from the leading mobile telecommunications company, DOCOMO, to hear about his project. No one would meet with a seventeen-year-old, no matter how good his idea. For the next eleven months, Ito searched the Internet for a new business idea. He decided on three-dimensional imaging software and came across an Israeli company that seemed to have excellent technology but had failed commercially. He brought the Israeli founders over to Japan for a meeting. "The fact that they came even after they knew I was a recent high school graduate shows how desperate they were," Ito told me.

The Israelis were impressed with Ito's understanding of their technology and his knowledge of the Japanese market. After much pleading and begging, Ito raised seed money from NEC and Mitsubishi and founded YAPPA in 2000. By 2008 YAPPA had over two hundred clients, seventy employees, sales of about $13 million, and branch offices in Paris, New York, and Israel. But things, according to Ito, are still very difficult, and no step in the process is easy. Even after it began to grow, YAPPA's application for grants from the government innovation fund was turned down several times. Recruitment was challenging. In the minds of most Japanese, according to Ito, start-ups are neither glamorous nor highly regarded. Besides, "being young is bad here," Ito says. "People expect you to be humble and understated. Anything else is seen as too aggressive."

As Ito's experience demonstrates, whatever courage it may take to start a new company, starting is only the first step. The company has to find capital to grow—an especially difficult task when the state still plays a large role in shaping the financial markets. Bank lending in China, for example, is still a social and political policy instrument; over 50 percent of loans are made to state-owned enterprises, often under the direction of city officials who want to avoid high rates of urban unemployment. Big state-owned enterprises employ people, even if they lose money. Small start-ups employ few and can easily fail. As a result, small technology companies cannot just approach a bank with a business plan and hope to get a loan; instead they must provide collateral, often real estate.

The obvious place to turn for capital in China is one of the funds set up by the Chinese government to support the development of specific technologies—a measure that, while bringing financial support, also creates incentives that push against riskier innovation. Entrepreneurs are likely to spend more time trying to cultivate good relations with government bureaucrats than developing strong ties to research institutes, partners, suppliers, and customers. Since these personal ties to bureaucrats can be tenuous—who knows when the official you have spent months wooing with expensive dinners and nights of karaoke will be transferred?—it makes sense to pursue short-term gains over longer-term investments.[25] In addition, the money is often tied to specific technologies the government wants to pursue. While such funding may help a new firm survive, it also makes it less likely that young entrepreneurs will pursue their original idea, the one they were passionate about. Few, when forced to choose between pursuing a technology that might ultimately fail, leaving them with nothing, and a guaranteed payout from the government, choose the former.

The explosion of venture capital firms, both domestic and foreign, could break the dependence of technology enterprises on the Chinese government for money. They could also be carriers of the culture of innovation, since venture capitalists often advise entrepreneurs about how to develop and market products in addition to introducing them to potential funders, managers, and clients. Successful companies in India such as Sasken Communication Technologies and Ittiam have received venture funding, and Baidu, the Chinese search engine company, received funding from Integrity Partners, Peninsula Capital Partners, Draper Fisher Jurvetson, and IDGVC Partners. But the venture capital industry, and more broadly the relationship between investor and entrepreneur, is still developing.

People I interviewed in China, India, South Korea, and Japan were almost universally dismissive of local venture capital firms, describing them as no different from bankers, as risk averse, and as lacking the necessary expertise in selecting, monitoring, and supporting new ventures. Their description is apt: state officials manage the majority of domestic venture capital firms in Asia. Over 80 percent of the venture capital funds in China, for example, are actually state funds. In 2008, close to 40 percent of South Korean venture capital came from the government and national pension funds. Ito of YAPPA described Japanese venture capital firms as a bad influence.

"All they do," he told me, "is come in and observe. They are interested in reporting, not growing the company. They are not thinking about a future public offering but current cash flow, and they are too worried about themselves getting sacked."

Foreign firms are more likely to accept real risk, but they are less interested in science-based innovation. There is simply too much money to be made in lower-risk, high-profit areas such as services, telecom, or retail. As K. P. Balaraj of Sequoia Capital explained to me in his office in Bangalore, "It is a pretty clear choice for most. Do you go after immediate opportunity in a very large market, or one-off exceptions in a very uncertain market?" In addition, many of the ideas being brought to venture capitalists are neither new nor innovative, and some, especially in China, are based on the theft of intellectual property. In 2005 and 2006, China saw an explosion of MySpace, eBay, and YouTube rip-offs, what the Chinese call "C2C," or copy to China. Such companies and their investors seek to get in and sell out quickly; few are committed to the time and risks necessary to develop new technologies.

This discussion of venture capital leads to one of the more fundamental challenges for innovation in China: the development of robust capital markets able to provide start-up capital as well as longer-term incentives to entrepreneurs. Since opportunities for exit—that is, selling a company to a larger one or going public—are limited within China, technology companies list themselves on foreign markets. When Baidu went public on August 5, 2005, Li Yanhong, the company's thirty-seven-year-old founder, became a billionaire, and over a hundred of its employees became millionaires. Baidu went public on NASDAQ.

For at least a decade, the Chinese government continually announced and then postponed the creation of a NASDAQ-like board to provide exits for venture capital–backed technology companies. A market for small enterprises in Shenzhen opened in 2004, but this board has been plagued by poor accounting, insider trading, and corporate theft. And, like much of business in China, the board has been dominated by state-owned enterprises.

In April 2009, plans for a second board were announced, but public comments within China were highly skeptical about what the final board would look like. Some worried about the wisdom of opening a new market in the midst of a global recession. Others feared that the Chinese government lacked the regulatory power to protect investors' interests, punish insider trading, and prevent market manipulations. "After a few scandals," said Jin Chen, a partner at Chinese private equity fund CMHJ Partners, "investors will lose faith in the growth market."[26]

History is on the side of the doubters. Effective capital markets are not easy to set up: they require clear standards, laws, and transparency, as well as independent regulatory bodies, courts, and penal systems—all of which China lacks. Professors William Goetzmann at the Yale School of Management and Philippe Jorion at the University of California, Irvine estimate that of approximately forty stock markets founded in the nineteenth century, only a half dozen are active today.[27] Without reliable institutions, stock markets in Latin America, Africa, and the Middle East have emerged, closed, and then returned in new forms. This is the likely pattern for China as well.

THE HAND OF GOVERNMENT

The market, of course, is never actually free. In Asia, the state's role in technology markets has been especially prominent. Governments throughout the region fund research and development, pick and support individual firms to commercialize technologies, and define technology standards. Thus, the larger political and social context of each of the countries in question shapes the culture of innovation, though it does not set it in stone. South Korea's historical disregard and current enthusiasm for small technology ventures, for example, has its roots in political concerns.

Indeed, South Korea is the poster child for the new model of technological development. From almost nothing—at the beginning of the 1960s, it had only two public research institutes and fewer than five thousand scientists and engineers—South Korea became a major force in global technology markets. Essentially the state and the chaebol, the large business conglomerates, were involved in a two-step partnership. The government first identified a promising technology and made massive investments in research and development. At the same time, the government encouraged the largest firms to compete internationally. Companies that did well were given access to better business and investment opportunities, and grew even larger. This scale and size meant that the big firms had the resources necessary to undertake risky research and development on their own, and over time the private sector took over the responsibility for investment in research. In 1981, the government funded over 50 percent of total R&D investment; by 1994, that funding had declined to 16 percent.[28]

There is, however, a growing skepticism about the effectiveness of top-down directives in an age of globalized innovation. When I visited Seoul in 2006, Dr. Chung Sung Chul explained to me that South Korean bureaucrats now believe that traditional tools have to be complemented with more bottom-up, multifaceted efforts to create business environments supportive of innovation and entrepreneurship. Chung, a science and technology adviser to former South Korean president Roh Moo-hyun, pointed out that the government had realized that the real effect of policy on innovation was very much reduced. "The private sector will dominate," according to Chung, "with government's role best described as facilitator or promoter." And officially, this is the direction of policy. Vision 2025, South Korea's long-range plan for science and technology, calls for the transformation of the national innovation system from "government-initiated and development focused to privately-led and distribution-oriented."[29]

Less clear, however, is how comfortable policy makers are with letting go in Korea. The IT839 strategy, for example, looks like a reversion to the past. As part of the strategy, the government identified eight services, three infrastructures, and nine devices it thinks critical to the future—things like radio-frequency identification technology, or RFID, and digital mobile television—and funneled over $1 billion into research. With the government taking care of the R&D side—the government's share rose to 27 percent by 2009—Samsung, LG, and other firms are concentrating on commercializing these new technologies, introducing state-of-the-art cell phones, digital televisions, and networked robots.

While the government cannot seem to cut the apron strings with the big companies, efforts to support small start-ups have created a mixed set of incentives, not all of them leading to innovation. Over the past four decades, the South Korean government has shied away from, if not actively handicapped, small companies. South Korea believed it needed the large conglomerates to succeed in international markets and to compete with Japan in particular. A large body of regulations prevented small and medium-sized companies from directly competing with the chaebol.

The situation changed after the 1987 democratic transition. The social, labor, and religious groups that had opposed military rule split their votes between two candidates in the first national election in 1987, allowing Roh Tae Woo, a former general and the ruling Democratic Justice Party's chosen successor, to win. But when the civilian Kim Young Sam finally won the presidency in 1993, he brought to office a deep distrust of the large companies. The CEOs of the chaebols were personally close to and financially supported the military regime. Kim and the opposition believed that promoting small firms could serve as a counterbalance to the political influence of the large companies. Kim's efforts, however, soon stalled in the face of an undeniable reality: the dependence of the South Korean economy on the chaebol for economic growth. In particular, the chaebol were and continue to be the primary sources of technology; today the twenty biggest companies conduct more than half of South Korea's industrial research and development.

Policy initiatives directed at small and medium-sized enterprises took off again after the 1997 Asian financial crisis created widespread unemployment and, in part, discredited the large companies. The 1997 Venture Business Promotion Special Act, for example, created a new category of "venture businesses" and offered tax benefits, credit loans, and public venture capital funding to these technology companies. The government lifted the military service requirement for entrepreneurs and engineers, lowered the financial requirements for initial public offerings, and deregulated the Korean stock market, the KOSDAQ.

Today, the scope of financial support for small companies in South Korea is huge. All this money, however, has not easily translated into great technological capability. A survey by the Korean Small and Medium Business Administration revealed that only 10 to 30 percent of government-funded projects resulted in commercialization, owing to poor project selection and lack of resources for market entry. Small companies easily game the system, claiming to undertake research in order to receive government funds, and then fail to engage in any real development work.

If the Korean government can be too heavy-handed, others can have too light a touch in creating environments supportive of private enterprise. The World Bank, for example, ranks India near the bottom among the nations—133 out of 183—in terms of ease of doing business. In the United States, starting a new business takes an average of six procedures and six days. Indian entrepreneurs have to go through an average of thirteen procedures and wait thirty days. Dealing with government agencies in India remains a huge headache; it takes an average of 195 days to obtain all the licenses, complete the inspections, and obtain utility connections needed to build a warehouse. Firing workers is difficult and almost impossible for companies employing one hundred or more workers. And if a company sues a business partner, it takes an average of 1,420 days—nearly four years—for the issue to be resolved.

On the World Bank charts, China, at number 89, ranks better than India in ease of doing business, but it is still lower than Rwanda, Pakistan, and Kazakhstan. Recent research by Yasheng Huang of MIT's Sloan School of Management shows that despite the impression that China is becoming more market-oriented, in fact it is becoming harder for private enterprises in China to operate. "The growth of onerous regulatory burdens and weakening of property rights," according to Huang, "have affected politically weak but economically nimble small entrepreneurs."[30] The vast majority of China's $586 billion stimulus package in 2008 flowed to government infrastructure projects and state-owned enterprises. Bao Yujun, chairman of the China Private Economy Research Center, found that private companies were sidelined, cut off not only from the original contracts, but also from the downstream business for supplies and subcontracting jobs.[31] Chinese policy makers are increasingly willing to intervene in markets. Seeing the fiscal crisis and recession in the United States as the outcome of the failure to regulate the economy, they are confident that intervention is the right course of action.

The most pressing regulatory challenge for technology companies is the protection of intellectual property rights (discussed in more detail in chapter 7); the failure to protect them undermines Chinese businesses as much as, if not more than, it does Western businesses. A recent study conducted for the European Commission concluded that "lax intellectual property rights in many ways keep Chinese companies lazy in terms of their own research and development."[32] With quick profits available to companies that successfully reverse engineer already proven technologies, it makes little sense to risk failure by putting money and effort into further technological innovation.

In addition, smaller companies have a difficult time rebounding from piracy, especially when it is pervasive. In the 1990s, China Star competed aggressively with Microsoft through an operating system that was bilingual, stable, and, perhaps most important, sold at 30 percent of the official price of Windows. But pirated copies of Windows were widely available on Chinese streets for $1.20—a price with which China Star could not compete—and eventually the company disappeared. Microsoft, grousing the whole time about the theft of its intellectual property, could afford to ride out the losses. Although Microsoft is still complaining about piracy, its operating system is now the standard of choice, installed (illegally) on the majority of home, business, and government computers in China.

Given the difficulties involved in generating new ideas, training new talent, starting new companies, and building a regulatory environment supportive of entrepreneurship, Asia's rise as a technological power will be gradual, stretched out over the next several decades. Building a system of trust, transparency, flexibility, and creativity—one where there is no need for green plants to reassure people that their workspace is safe—will be protracted and political. Innovation will happen, but it will be on islands of excellence within larger national economies that will still lag behind the United States in technological capability.

POSSIBLE CONTINGENCIES

Still, the history of predictions about the future of economic development is strewn with faulty assumptions and misguided conclusions. At the beginning of the 1950s, development experts, had they been asked which Asian country they thought would develop the fastest, would likely have guessed Burma, with its relatively stable government, educated population, and vast natural resources. South Korea was thought of as a basket case, ravaged by the war, plagued by corrupt rulers, and holding to a hierarchical Confucian culture widely considered incompatible with rapid development. In 2009, Korea's GDP was $800.3 billion; Burma's, $56.5 billion.

Similarly, for much of the 1960s, 1970s, and early 1980s, many observers argued that the Japanese would never do anything but copy American technology. "The Japanese," according to *Time*, "often feel it is better to mimic or borrow than originate."[33] The success over the last two decades of companies like Sony and Nintendo and the growing popularity of anime (animation) and manga (comics) are sharp rebuttals to any critiques of Japanese creativity and innovativeness.

In light of such developments, my views about the development of innovative technology may not take account of several possible contingencies. For one thing, given Japan's and Korea's remarkable track records over the last fifty years, they may continue to succeed despite some of the barriers outlined in this chapter. Since the late 1990s, they have invested huge amounts in research and development, and the number of patents being filed has grown. In both countries, a generation of entrepreneurs in their twenties and thirties, like Masahiro Ito of YAPPA, are slowly working their way through the system. As George Packard, the president of the United

States–Japan Foundation told me, "The Japanese have never missed a wave of technology since the Meiji period and this one is not going to be different."

Also, the next wave of innovation may center on technologies that mesh better with the Japanese and South Korean models. The majority of research and development in both of these countries occurs in the big companies, which have large budgets, huge staffs, and well-developed patent portfolios, as well as strong links to customers. Unlike small start-ups, the big companies can make something first and then slowly over time improve its quality and cost, inventing new uses as they go along. Their deeper pockets allow them to hold on to their research staffs during economic downturns. These assets have meant success in the automobile industry as Toyota and Hyundai developed capabilities over decades, and they could translate to technology industries that produce solar cells or batteries, where Japanese companies are trying to bring the price down even though others think the technology will never be cost-effective. Japanese investment in battery technology has trumped that of the United States by tenfold over the last decade, according to Charles Gassenheimer, CEO of the U.S. green-car firm Ener1.[34]

Another contingency is that emerging institutions and cultures of innovation in India and China will not be easily identified and understood. Such institutions will hardly look like those in the United States: there will be no Silicon Valley in the state of Karnataka or Jiangsu Province. Rather, China and India will combine top-down and bottom-up initiatives with bits and pieces borrowed from the United States and, in smaller measure, from Europe. In fact, these hybrid models are already appearing.

In India, the main action is found not in the central government–dominated Delhi, but—as with so many spheres of activity—in the states driven by public-private partnerships. Indian companies, for example, are now in the education business, taking up the slack where the central government consistently fails. Many of the for-profit training companies are little more than diploma mills (founded by corrupt politicians), but the information service giants are playing a much more productive role. Tata Consultancy Services trains over 1,500 computer science graduates annually, and Infosys works with local colleges in developing courses on how engineers should be trained.

Technology entrepreneurs and returnees are especially important in building a culture of innovation. Between 2001 and 2007, according to the National Association of Software and Service Companies, thirty-five thousand information technology professionals returned to India; the recession in the United States has accelerated the process. A survey of Indian executives living in America found that 68 percent were actively looking for an opportunity to return home, and 12 percent had already decided to do so. "If you want to be in the latest trends," Dutt Kalluri, who returned to India after six years in Maryland, told the *Washington Post*, "you have to be in India."[35]

The Berkeley scholar AnnaLee Saxenian has called the flow of returnees from Silicon Valley to China and India "brain circulation."[36] These individuals no longer represent "brain drain" and a loss to their home countries, but neither are they a clear-cut "brain gain" since they often retain business and personal connections to the United States. Rosen Sharma, with degrees from IIT Delhi and Cornell University, lives in California and travels to New Delhi and Pune to oversee local employees of Solidcore, a developer of security software. Rajiv Mody, who founded Sasken Communication Technologies in Silicon Valley and moved the company to Bangalore, now travels back to the United States and pays U.S. taxes.

Many of these "new argonauts," as Saxenian calls those traveling between two worlds, have taken on technological entrepreneurship as their mission. Consider the story of the Wadhwani Foundation, a nonprofit that has launched the National Entrepreneurship Network (NEN) in partnership with five academic institutions. The NEN develops coursework on entrepreneurship for universities, fosters networking activities, and provides assistance to new, high-growth start-ups. The foundation is the brainchild of Romesh Wadhwani, a serial entrepreneur whose first start-up was a student-run cafeteria at IIT Bombay. Wadhwani raised initial capital by selling shares to his classmates, and soon the cafeteria was popular and profitable. Jealous students eventually derailed the project, questioning why a private enterprise was operating on the campus of a public university. The cafeteria was "nationalized," and the new managers soon ran the cafeteria into the ground.

After graduation, Wadhwani went to Carnegie Mellon University to study for a Ph.D. in electrical engineering, and then he founded three software companies in Silicon Valley. In 1999, i2 Technologies acquired Wadhwani's third company, Aspect, for $9.3 billion, the largest merger in software industry history at the time. With the sale completed, Wadhwani wanted to do more. Having seen the power of entrepreneurship in the United States, he wanted to harness the force for the good of India. Wadhwani told an Indian newspaper, "I'm a first generation entrepreneur. To succeed as an entrepreneur, I had to come to the United States. The purpose of a national entrepreneurship network is to make it possible for millions of Indians like me to start and build large and successful businesses in India, businesses that create jobs for tens of millions of professional workers."[37] In five years, the foundation went from having approximately five hundred students in entrepreneurship clubs around the country to having fifty-five thousand. Wadhwani is not alone. While there are still strong middle-class biases to starting a company—it is safer to work for a multinational—every CFO, CTO, or CEO I met in India was an evangelist for entrepreneurship, often involved in activities like coaching new graduates in business plan competitions, providing early-stage investment for new start-ups, and creating support groups for young entrepreneurs.

Likewise in China, change and creativity come from either the outside or the bottom. The returnees, called *hai gui*, or sea turtles (the Chinese characters used for sea turtles, which return from the sea to lay their eggs, are a homonym for "return from overseas"), and the multinational companies have already dramatically changed how business is done in China. Over one million Chinese have studied abroad since the 1980s, though more than two-thirds have not yet returned. It is hard to read migration patterns over the short term, but a wave of returnees could be beginning, accelerated by a prolonged recession in the United States. Taiwanese and Korean students began to return in the late 1980s as economic conditions improved at home, and approximately thirty thousand Chinese graduates returned in 2008 seeing brighter prospects in their homeland than they could hope for in the United States.

Over coffee at the Starbucks at the Lido Holiday Inn in Beijing, Jie Liang explained to me how returnees were raising the bar for all. Jie, who had previously worked in Austin and Boston, started a company in Beijing during the first Chinese Internet boom in the late 1990s. In 1998 and 1999, it was enough simply to open a company to attract people to work for you. This time, in 2006, working on a MySpace-like website for performing artists, he competed for talent with many other start-ups founded by returnees from Silicon Valley. He had to demonstrate to potential employees that a human resource system was in place and that his management was transparent and flexible.

The R&D centers like the one I visited in Wangjing could have a similar effect on the innovation ecosystem. In a decade, the number of foreign R&D centers in China rose from zero to over a thousand. The majority of these centers develop and modify technology for the local market rather than pursue cutting-edge research—in one survey, over 80 percent were involved in efforts to make foreign technology suitable for local markets, though this could gradually change.[38] Microsoft now conducts research on voice recognition and wireless multimedia in Beijing, and Nokia recently expanded its Chengdu R&D center, aiming to make it one of the most important sites for research on products intended for global markets.

China may benefit more from the people who pass through these foreign research centers than from the work that is actually done within them. Employees of Nokia, Intel, and Vodaphone learn to manage complex research projects, often across disciplines. They develop collaborative agreements with other companies. They connect with local universities and recruit new graduates. And some day these employees will leave, possibly to start their own firms or to work for a Chinese multinational company. In September 2009, Lee Kai-fu, formerly head of Google's operations in China and before that vice president of Microsoft's operations in China, left the search engine company to start his own venture capital firm to fund Chinese start-ups, especially in the areas of mobile computing and the Internet. Chinese engineers, according to Lee, were ready to become an entrepreneurial force, but they needed help. "If a smart engineer trusts me, he should come join me," said Lee in an interview. "We'll do an idea and if it fails, we'll do the next idea."[39]

Bottom-up, outside-in, and top-down forces are combining to change the culture of science in China as well. Fang Shi-min, a molecular biologist with a Ph.D. from Michigan State, is the person mentioned earlier who runs the website that attacks scientific "fakeness." The site, New Threads, has exposed academic corruption, criticized the medicinal claims of DNA nutritional supplements, and raised questions about the qualifications of some prominent returned Chinese scholars. New Threads raised the first questions about Liu Hui, the assistant dean of the medical school at Tsinghua who was later removed from his job for using fake credentials.

Returnees like Mu-Ming Poo, the scientist who wrote the piece in *Nature* about the cultural barriers to innovation, also play an important role by introducing international standards to their new institutes. At the Center for Bioscience, Poo instituted a regular review system of its scientific staff. In an email purportedly from Poo and posted on a Chekiang (Zhejiang) University discussion board, he informed the director of a lab, who was refusing to submit to an internal academic review, that he would have to remove him. In his email response, the director claimed that his election to the Chinese Academy of Sciences was proof enough of his leadership in the scientific community to make him not subject to review. Moreover, the scientist believed that his exalted position as an academician guaranteed his right to continue his research activity indefinitely. Unmoved, Poo offered two choices: show up for the review, or accept an honorary position with the same level of salary, a move that would effectively terminate his position as lab head.[40]

The government has responded to these grassroots public forums on scientific and academic wrongdoing. In September 2005, on its website, the National Natural Science Foundation of China (NSFC) published for the first time the names of three scientists punished for misconduct and banned them from applying for NSFC funding for three years.[41] NSFC claims that it has recorded 542 cases of alleged misconduct since 1998, but most were resolved without being made public. In July 2006, the Ministry of Science and Technology announced it would set up a center to track R&D funding as well as create a "credibility evaluation system" to assess institutions that apply for funding.[42] And in July 2007, in order to encourage risk taking and reduce the pressure to cheat, the ministry introduced a policy that would allow scientists to report failure without fear of risking their chances for future funding.

Finally, China's ability to tackle its innovation challenges should not be underestimated. Over the past twenty years, there have been several instances when outside commentators believed that Chinese economic growth would hit a wall or, more drastically, go off the rails. In the early 1990s, as regional identities reasserted themselves and tax remittances from the provinces to the central government declined, pundits began writing articles with titles like "Will China Collapse?" At one point, the taxes the central government was able to collect were lower than those the government in Belgrade collected before the demise of Yugoslavia; but the crisis passed as the Chinese leadership introduced a new tax system and maintained tight control over personal appointments in the provinces.

Later in the decade, many predicted that the banking system would crumble under the weight of bad loans to state-owned enterprises. Estimates of nonperforming loans—that is, loans in default—reached 38 percent of the total for loan portfolios, or RMB 2.5 trillion, approximately 34 percent of China's GDP in 1998. Again, China dodged the bullet: it saw the problem clearly, got the best advice, mobilized the people and the money needed, recapitalized the banks, and took foreign banks on as new partners. Thus, facing seemingly insurmountable challenges is nothing new for China.

Nonetheless, what worked for China in the past may not be enough to overcome the innovation challenge. The current government has made little progress on the issues a culture of innovation requires: greater transparency, individual initiative, willingness to question authority, and freedom of expression, which in turn demand some form of political reform and liberalization.

While the New Threads website, for example, signals a new, bottom-up approach, it also demonstrates that such efforts remain limited in China. Fang and New Threads have been positively portrayed in the *People's Daily* and on China Central Television, but the site itself is intermittently blocked to viewers in China. New Threads, like any nongovernmental, web-based initiative, must contend with the Great Firewall of China, the system of Internet filtering and censorship that controls the internal flow of information. The big question remains: Can China become innovative without becoming more free?

China's leaders think it can. In January 2010, Google announced that its systems had been hacked into and that the company would either stop censoring search results in China or withdraw from the market. The Chinese wished them well. "Foreign companies in China should respect the laws and regulations," said Foreign Ministry spokesman Ma Zhaoxu. "There is no exception for Google."[43] But history suggests that it will be difficult to build a truly innovative economy while tightly controlling information. At best, blocked or repressed information, be it on the web or elsewhere, slows the development of a culture of innovation. Of the 784 scientists who responded to a survey conducted by *Nature*, 84 percent said that Google's departure would "somewhat or significantly" hamper their research; 78 percent said it would "somewhat or significantly" affect international collaboration.[44] At worst, the overly restrictive control of information can lead to economic stagnation. The Soviet Union looked like a technological superpower at the height of the Cold War, but everyone now knows that it could produce quantity, but not quality.

Creativity, individual initiative, and critical thinking cannot be mandated from above. Singapore, for example, attempted to promote unconventional thinking through government diktat and failed. While a move to a multiparty democracy isn't required for China to foster innovation, the Communist Party needs to give more space to civil society. This development would require a degree of political reform unlikely in the near term.

In China, politics can stand in the way of innovation, but India is a democracy with a boisterous free press and a vibrant civil society. India's greatest potential stumbling block will be scale—or lack thereof. India could be held back by a different type of politics: failure of Indian institutions to take discrete breakthroughs, build on them, and reproduce them on a national level. What is happening in India is primarily individual ingenuity, which, according to Rishikesha T. Krishnan, a professor of strategy at the Indian Institute of Management Bangalore, "does not have an organizational base or support, but rather tends to be a one-time activity with few subsequent improvements."[45] There are innovative companies, and there are universities and research institutes full of smart and enterprising scientists. But India right now lacks the system to reproduce individual success more widely.

Diffusing success widely requires improved infrastructure, and—as everyone who has ever heard the stories of the sorry state of India's roads, airports, and power systems knows—expanding on the hardware has been a slow and frustrating process. After many years of delays, Bangalore finally completed a brand new airport north of the city, but unfortunately it did not build a highway that would allow people to get there. In 2008, the Economist Intelligence Unit downgraded India by two positions, to number 48 in a global information technology industry competitiveness ranking, placing the blame on deteriorating human resources and technology infrastructure.[46] Projects are hamstrung by an antiquated eminent domain law, widespread corruption, a glacial judicial process, and competing lines of authority. Democracy makes some things more difficult. Unlike China, India cannot relocate whole populations to make room for new development.

The challenge for South Korea and Japan is neither politics nor scale, but how to develop a new model of adaptation. Both of these societies have histories of rapid, often dislocating, change. They have adapted and widely diffused foreign technologies and institutions and, over the course of time, made them their own. But the shift from "catch-up" to innovation will require a more flexible, international model. As Dr. Arinobu Mutsuhiro, director of research and development at Toshiba, told me, competing was easier in the past because everyone knew who the challengers were: big American companies such as IBM. The mission then, he continued, was to provide what people wanted cheaper, faster, and smaller. Today, in advanced economies, most basic goods are provided for and demands are changing. To be a follower is no longer sufficient.

If they want to compete at a higher level, South Korean and Japanese firms have to become more innovative and thus become more open to the rest of the world. It has not been easy. The old models worked well; the big companies—Samsung, LG, Sony, Panasonic, Canon, Fujitsu, and Hitachi—have deep technological capabilities; and neither South Korea nor Japan has fully embraced the reality of a flat world without any borders.

While LG and Samsung have been successful in China, India, and other global markets, South Korea has had a hard time opening itself to the world. South Korea is one of the world's most ethnically homogeneous countries, with attitudes toward the outside world often bordering on suspicious, if not downright xenophobic. In a 2002 poll conducted by the Pew Survey on Global Attitudes, five out of six Koreans thought their culture should be protected from foreign influences. In another Pew survey, only 54 percent of Koreans saw foreign companies as having a positive impact on their country.[47] For most of the last three decades, the government has erected barriers to foreign investment. The Koreans, wanting to reduce their dependence on foreign technology, developed much on their own. Any multinational companies that did invest in the country were restricted to a minority share in a joint venture with a Korean partner. The public remains wary of foreign investors buying and selling Korean companies for profit.

Until recently, the strength of Korean identity and the state's ability to mobilize people based on a shared sense of "Korean-ness" were seen as essential components to the country's success and survival. South Korea accomplished in twenty years what it took Japan fifty years to achieve, in part because the former's citizens were eager to work hard and sacrifice for the nation. Today's cultural attitudes need to change for South Korea to remain competitive in the global economy. "We have to get out of this uni-country, uni-cultural mindset; otherwise we will not survive," Dr. Chung, the former science and technology adviser and now president of the Science and Technology Policy Institute in Seoul, told me.

The question of how South Korea will best be able to exploit and interact with globalized innovation looms large in Seoul. Culture is an obstacle, but geography is also a major barrier: if a company is going to relocate research to Asia, why would it choose South Korea over China? In fact, foreign investment declined in South Korea by almost 30 percent a year at the beginning of the decade, and hovered around $11 billion per year by the end of the decade. The ratio of the amount of funds from foreign sources to the total spent on research and development (0.2 percent) is low compared with that for the United Kingdom (17.7 percent).

In 2003, only a handful of companies were doing real research in South Korea; the vast majority of research centers were adjusting for the local market products that had been developed elsewhere. By 2009, the government had succeeded in luring only twenty-seven new R&D centers to Korea. During the presidency of Roh Moo-hyun (2003–2008), South Korea actively promoted itself as the R&D hub of Northeast Asia. Touting South Korea's location between China and Japan, government agencies offered cash grants, subsidies for land and labor, and tax breaks to multinational companies willing to locate R&D facilities in South Korea. Over the next several years, Microsoft, Sun, Hewlett Packard, and others opened small research centers, and the South Korean government provided a subsidy of more than $130 million to Institut Pasteur, the private French biological research foundation, to set up a lab in Seoul.

These policies, however, have not been able to overcome the pull of China, where cheap labor is more plentiful, the pool of scientific talent wider and deeper, and the domestic market several times larger. Most of the few companies that relocated R&D units to Korea employ fewer than twenty researchers, and they supply components to Korean firms, not conduct basic research. Those that do engage in more basic research are specialized producers of LCD screens or wireless equipment, areas where Korea leads the world. More common is the trajectory of Alcatel-Lucent, which briefly considered locating in Korea but ultimately chose China; or of Intel, which expanded the size of its lab after President Roh asked it to do more in Korea, and then virtually closed the lab two years later.

While Sony, Toyota, Honda, Hitachi, and other Japanese companies are global brands, Japan has historically struggled with how open it wants to be to the rest of the world. Even today, only 20 percent of the Japanese economy is exposed to global competition. Information and communication technology firms have been caught in a pattern of what the political scientist Kenji E. Kushida calls "leading without followers."[48] Although Japanese communication companies invest heavily in research and development, build infrastructure rapidly, and often develop technologies that are more sophisticated than those found anywhere else in the world, they soon find that the rest of the world has gone in a different technology direction. This pattern is clear with Japanese cell phones, where Japanese producers were the first to introduce email, music downloads, camera phones, and digital TV, but insisted on technology standards used only in Japan. In short, Japanese companies get trapped in domestic markets.

This is more than a question of markets, though. It is also cultural. One of the world's great cities, Tokyo is not particularly hospitable to foreigners. In November 2008, the *Asahi Shimbun*, Japan's second largest newspaper, published "Opening the Nation: Time to Make

Choices," a long article about cultural and political discrimination against foreigners, as well as regulations and practices that make even long-term residents feel unwelcome. And Japanese students do not have the English language skills their counterparts in China and South Korea do. All attend years of mandatory instruction, but Japanese students still rank among the lowest in Asia on the Test of English as a Foreign Language, usually right below Burma and right above North Korea.

The rise of China (and to a lesser extent India) raises uncomfortable questions within Japan about how prepared the country is for the globalization of science and technology. In 2005, as South Korean newspapers and government officials were warning that China would soon close the technological gap with the nation, one senior official at the Japanese Ministry of Economics, Trade, and Industry told me that he did not see Chinese companies as potential competitors, and neither did Japanese business. The Chinese competed at the lower end, on price. Chinese companies were followers. The real competition, he insisted, would continue to be American companies and a few South Korean firms, such as Samsung and Hyundai.

This situation may change, according to this official and to many others I spoke with in Tokyo, because of the question of talent. China is huge, and Japan's population is aging and slowly declining. While the best Chinese and Indian students go to the United States, restrictive visa and employment policies, as well as a culture seen as unwelcoming to outsiders, combine to make it extremely difficult for Japan to attract talent of the highest quality.

Japan is taking steps to attract Chinese, South Korean, and Indian students. The president of one of Tokyo's most prestigious technological universities told me that they were working to become more hospitable to Chinese students, but that he would be able to attract better-quality students only if Japanese companies offered Chinese graduates the same contract terms they offered their classmates, not the short-term contracts offered to foreigners. Although this president holds, in the context of Japan, rather liberal views about immigration, the best he thought Japan would be able to offer was a five- to seven-year stay in the country for Chinese students. By comparison, in the United States, in March 2009, Congress introduced a bill that, if passed, would give foreign graduates permanent residency. (As of April 2010, the bill was still in subcommittee.) The outer limit in Japan is five years; in the United States, it is indefinite.

Firms like Sony and Fuji Xerox have sought to impart greater knowledge about the rest of Asia, particularly China, to young Japanese. Internships send Japanese students on homestays with Chinese families, and Chinese students with Japanese families. Still, as with all efforts to globalize, history (and history lessons) still intrudes. Sony was considering lowering the age of the homestay participants from college to high school and possibly to middle school after finding that students who had already sat in several years of history classes inflexibly held nationalistic attitudes toward their Chinese or Japanese counterparts. Once they reached college, the educational system had already imprinted them, and by then it was too late.

Despite all the hype about the rise of China and India as technological superpowers, the reality is that while some science and technological capacity is shifting to Asia, the spread is incremental. The pace of innovation is slowed by the persistence of green leafy plants, the gap between the huge buildup of the hardware of innovation and the grind of creating software. The gap will take at least several decades to close.

The drive for innovation is composed of many layers, like a Russian *matryoshka* nesting doll—individual within company within region within country. A wide range of motivations drive the individual scientist or technology entrepreneur: the desire to push the boundaries of knowledge, to receive public acclaim or the regard of colleagues, to get rich, to create new markets, to help the "motherland," to change the world. At the corporate level, companies seek profit and competitive advantage. Local communities have their own development and social goals, often new jobs and the creation of a regional identity. Finally, the scientist, the entrepreneur, the company, and the innovative region all exist within a country—and the country pursues technology to bolster its economy, as well as its power, autonomy, and prestige.

American policy makers not only need to see the gap between hardware and software but also need to understand how the interplay of economics and security, high and low politics—the second critical couplet—shapes technology. Since it will take time for Asia to become a technology power, we have the time to prepare our own science and technology policy responses. On the other hand, each Asian country's drive for power and prestige will pose immediate and direct political challenges to our country: we will have to meet them as we go along, constantly shifting our response in order to preserve the openness vital to the American innovation system without sacrificing security.

Chapter Four

THE OPEN DOOR

China and India—and in a broader sense, Asia as a whole—have liberalized and matured with astonishing speed. The rapidity of their transformation has made it easy to forget that their policy makers welcome money, ideas, and people so long as such outside forces aid in the pursuit of economic and political goals. GE, Intel, Cisco, Siemens, and other foreign high-technology companies were given the green light to set up shop in China and India not because of any abstract commitment to the ideals of free trade, but because they were expected to help improve the technological capability of domestic companies, which in turn would increase national power and influence. "Today, an economic superpower, an information technology giant and a custodian of nuclear capability, it has been such a long journey," declared an editorial in the *Hindustan Times* on India's Republic Day in 2008, the national holiday marking the anniversary of the adoption of the Indian constitution.[1] This prosperity and power were possible in part owing to globalization. Strategic purpose is designed in conjunction with economic objectives, thus high politics is an inevitable part of low politics.

At the same time, leaders throughout Asia realize that even if openness fits with their long-term goals, it can bring unwanted short-term outcomes. The technological capabilities of Chinese firms, for example, undeniably improved as the country opened to the world. But while China may now be the world's largest exporter of high-technology products, few of the exported technologies are "Chinese." In 2009, foreign-invested firms—local firms employing Chinese laborers but using foreign investment and technology—accounted for 83 percent of China's high-tech exports. Chinese companies have proven that they can follow technological trends, but not that they can develop new technology.

To many Chinese leaders, this setup appears a trap. Foreign firms reap high profits from the control of intellectual property, and Chinese companies survive on the thin margins made in manufacturing. Manufacturing is a dirty business, with a heavy price to pay in natural resources, energy, and environmental damages. Further, it is insulting to a country that has a glorious past as the inventor of paper, printing, the compass, and gunpowder. Reflecting this aggrieved nationalistic feeling, articles in the Chinese press complain that foreign companies own the technology used to enter Chinese characters—"the embodiment of five thousand years of Chinese civilization," in the description of one Chinese commentator—on a cell phone keypad.[2] So with each of the tens of millions of cell phones sold in China, a payment is made to a foreign company for the use of character input technology.

The Chinese have a plan to break their technological dependence on the West: the "Guidelines on National Medium- and Long-Term Program for Science and Technology Development," released in January 2006. The guidelines clearly define China's goals until 2020: "markedly enhance our overall ability to conduct basic science research and cutting-edge technology research" and to "join the ranks of innovative countries." At the center of the guidelines is a call for "indigenous innovation" (*zizhu chuangxin*). By 2020, China must reduce its "degree of dependence on technology from other countries to 30 percent or less." Reliance on other countries, and on the United States and Japan in particular, is a threat to Chinese economic and national security. "Facts tell us that we cannot buy true core technologies in key fields that affect the lifeblood of the national economy and national security," state the guidelines. "To gain leverage in fierce international competition," the document continues, "China must improve its independent innovative capabilities and master a number of core technologies, own a number of proprietary intellectual property rights, and groom a number of internationally competitive enterprises in certain important fields."[3]

One of the most controversial tools deployed in China's hunt for autonomy has been a set of Chinese technology standards, developed despite the preexisting technical standards already widely used in the United States, Japan, and Europe. A standard establishes uniform engineering and technological codes and thus allows a wide range of hardware and software to work together. The company that defines a particular standard captures much of the economic value in a specific technology market—think Microsoft and the Windows operating system, Intel and the Pentium chip, Qualcomm and CDMA (code division multiple access) in cell phones. Those locked out see their market share shrink. Or as a phrase popular in technology circles in China puts it, third-class companies make products, second-class companies develop technology, first-class companies set standards.

In December 2003, the government announced that WLAN Authentication and Privacy Infrastructure, or WAPI, would be the mandatory standard for any wireless product sold in China. Foreign companies such as Intel reacted with a mixture of shock and frustration. The Chinese standard essentially came out of nowhere, mandated by a government agency without consultation with private companies. In addition, Beijing's decision—due to "national security concerns"—not to share an algorithm included in WAPI would have forced Intel and other foreign companies to cooperate with one of twenty-four Chinese vendors licensed to develop the competing standard.

What the Chinese called cooperation, the Western companies saw as stiff-arming—an attempt to force the transfer of proprietary knowledge to rivals, since all twenty-four officially sanctioned companies were competitors. Intel's Craig Barrett described his concern: "The Chinese were suggesting we needed to bring our intellectual property to the table to play in the marketplace."[4] Intel and Broadcom announced that they would not comply with the regulations and would stop selling their wireless chips in the Chinese market.

Along with the threatened boycott, American firms enrolled the support of the U.S. government to roll back the standard. In March 2004, the Bush administration sent a letter about WAPI, signed by Secretary of State Colin Powell, Commerce Secretary Don Evans, and U.S. Trade Representative Robert Zoellick. "We are particularly concerned," said the letter, "that the new rules would require foreign suppliers to enter into joint ventures with Chinese companies and transfer technology to them." Arguing that regulations compelling technology transfer were incompatible with China's trade commitments, the letter implicitly threatened to pursue the case at the World Trade Organization.[5]

The Chinese government backed down. A month after receiving the letter, Vice Premier Wu Yi announced the indefinite suspension of the implementation of the Chinese standard as a wireless encryption standard. Beijing agreed that it would revise the standard after soliciting comments from Chinese and foreign firms.

Although this ended the battle over enforced technology transfer, it was not the end of the WAPI story. After Wu Yi's announcement, the Chinese submitted the standard for consideration at several meetings of the International Organization for Standardization, the body responsible for recognizing and managing technology standards. These meetings did not go well. When several Chinese delegates were denied entry visas to a meeting in Orlando, the Chinese press saw an underhanded effort by the U.S. government to secure the Wi-Fi standard, the wireless standard used by many American companies, including Cisco, 3Com, and Intel. When Chinese delegates later walked out of a meeting in Frankfurt, claiming that procedures were stacked against them, Chinese reporters were outraged: "It is not as accurate to say that the foreign monopolistic forces trampled on international regulations as to say that they barbarically trampled on human civilization."[6] The two competing standards were eventually placed on the ballot for a voting period that extended from October 2005 to March 2006. After the 19-to-3 decision was announced in favor of Wi-Fi, the Chinese accused Wi-Fi's backers of mounting a campaign of dirty tricks, deception, and misinformation.

Officially, the Chinese were adopting the WAPI standard because of security concerns—not a ridiculous claim since at the time Wi-Fi had widely noted vulnerabilities. But by refusing to make their own standard more transparent, Chinese officials never let outside observers validate assertions that it was more secure. Since 85 percent of the chips used in wireless technology in China are imported from abroad, the most likely rationale behind WAPI was to reduce licensing and royalty payments to foreign firms. The market for wireless networking in China promises to be particularly lucrative: The number of Internet users topped 380 million in 2009, and more than 90 percent of those users were on broadband. Increasingly, consumers in Shanghai, Guangzhou, and other large cities are going on the web through cell phones, netbooks, or handheld devices. The supporters of WAPI wanted to lock in the standard early in the market's development and see future royalties go to Chinese companies.

WAPI may eventually fade into history, but not without a fight. By December 2009, the Chinese resubmitted the standard to the International Organization for Standardization two more times, and when Apple finally introduced the iPhone in China, it included WAPI. Still, Scott Kennedy, a political scientist at Indiana University, argued that we should not read too much into the case since efforts to develop other standards in China, like those used in home networking, have been much less nationalistic, much more transparent and open.[7] While the Chinese organizations promoting the WAPI wireless standard are linked to the military and the internal security ministries, the groups working on the home network standard are from private industry and have little contact with the government. These Chinese firms have not cut themselves off from the global market and are cooperating with companies in Japan, Korea, and Taiwan. Lenovo, a Chinese computer manufacturer, and TCL, an electronics company, are now members of both the Chinese and the international alliances for home networking standards, making it possible that the two groups will cooperate, not compete.

But, as Professor Kennedy noted, standards policy may recede into the background only to be replaced by other protectionist initiatives. Chinese commentators argue that the Anti-Monopoly Law should be used as a weapon against foreign commercial interests, U.S. technology companies in particular. In October 2009 Beijing released a new policy blocking foreign companies from selling to the Chinese government unless their products included "indigenous innovation." This was not an empty threat since the government is a massive customer for high technology. Whatever shape new policies take, the political objective of technological autonomy will persist and likely spur new initiatives.

This fixation is not a singularly Chinese one. Throughout the region, reform programs, energized by an analogous set of political demands, have taken a very similar form. Of course, China's reform and opening to the world have their genesis in Chinese economic structures and political institutions, just as India's dismantling of its growth-choking regulations and curtailment of bureaucratic interference are rooted in the Indian context. Still, technology development strategies that encourage small start-ups, welcome foreign investment, and reduce the influence of government bureaucracies are common not only in China and India but throughout the region. For leaders in China, India, Japan, Taiwan, and South Korea, concerns about autonomy, security, and rising inequality have led to similar strategic solutions. Policy makers can intervene in domestic and international markets whenever the free flow of technology works at cross-purposes to these larger political concerns. Their intervention may take the form of support of national champions, protection of domestic industrial sectors, and purchase of strategic assets abroad by sovereign wealth funds.

Some policies—an openness to foreign investment, an expanded role for American and other foreign multinational companies in Asian domestic technology policy, the promotion of technological entrepreneurship—are congruent with Washington's larger political and economic goals. Other more interventionist policies can run counter to American interests. The challenge for American businesses and policy makers, then, is to understand a shifting spectrum of policies in Asia, some motivated by economic objectives, others by political goals, and still others by some combination of the two.

REFORM, OPENING, AND INNOVATION IN CHINA

Since the late 1970s, the innovation systems in Asia, especially in China and India, have changed dramatically. Before liberalization, they were isolated and relatively backward. Today, every step of the process, from basic science to the marketing of new products, has been revitalized through the movement of people, ideas, and money.

Before "Gaige Kaifang," the reform and open door policies associated with the rise of Deng Xiaoping in 1978, China's science and technology institutions were afflicted with all the weaknesses characteristic of central planning. Copied almost completely from the Soviet Union, the system was highly hierarchical and stratified, with a great deal of institutional redundancy. The steel, light manufacturing, and machine tool industries, for example, had their own labs, and these research institutes had few ties to each other or to the final users. Technology was treated as a public good and provided to state-owned enterprises at little or no cost. During the Cultural Revolution, science and education were attacked as elitist. The ideologically fervent and politically trusted "Reds" were promoted over technical and scientific "experts." With the exception of nuclear weapons and intercontinental ballistic missiles, the Chinese system failed to develop advanced technologies.

Since 1978, the science and technology system has been drastically remade. The state slashed budgets, forcing research institutes to make up financial shortfalls by cooperating with industry. Scientists and engineers were given both the right to develop their own ideas and a direct financial stake in their inventions. Universities and research institutes "spun off" start-up technology companies like Lenovo and the software developer Founder. It is, however, the importation of foreign technology that had the most dramatic impact on Chinese capabilities.

In the first two decades of the reforms, the strategy was simple: trade access to the domestic market in return for technology. Beijing brokered joint venture agreements with the explicit understanding that the Western partner would transfer 'know-how to its Chinese counterpart. ITT Belgium, for example (subsequently acquired by Alcatel-Lucent), made substantial technology commitments to its Shanghai Bell joint venture manufacturing facility and, in return, received not only market access guarantees but also the ability to sell imported telecommunications switches to Chinese clients.

The partnering strategy was not a huge success, and delays and disputes plagued many of the biggest projects. American Motors' joint venture to build the Jeep became the most famous symbol of all the things that could go wrong with a joint venture: walkouts over pay and staffing, disputes over the control of foreign exchange, cultural and professional divisions between Chinese and American managers, and frustration in finding qualified local suppliers. Similar problems afflicted joint ventures in the high-technology sector, compounded by a tendency among Chinese government officials to chase after technologies they thought were the "most advanced" with little understanding of the technologies themselves and how they might be applied in the Chinese market. Visitors to China at the time often returned with stories of unopened crates of expensive equipment sitting on factory floors, or of IBM computers going unused because no one knew how to operate them or there was no steady supply of electricity.

In the mid-1990s, Beijing shifted course, opening wide the door to foreign investment. Foreign investment was welcomed everywhere, not just Shenzhen, Zhuhai, and the other special economic zones, and it flooded into electronics assembly and other technology sectors. The scale has been huge—$90.3 billion in 2009—and foreign investment almost certainly emerged as the predominant source of technology transfer. By contrast, foreign investment has only recently increased in India. For much of the last two decades, it was almost ten times larger in China than in India.

The massive inflow of foreign money pushed Chinese firms up the technology ladder. Take the semiconductor sector: In the mid-1990s, after ten years of partnering, China was still about a decade behind the technological frontier, perhaps even farther behind than when it first entered the market.[8] After the shift to the foreign investment–intensive strategy, the Chinese rapidly caught up. Advanced semiconductor manufacturers flocked to Shanghai, and by 2002, according to a study conducted by the U.S. Government

Accountability Office, China had closed the gap, producing chips less than one generation behind the commercial state of the art.[9]

China, as used in this report, however, does not necessarily equate with Chinese origin. Rather, most technology in China traces back to Taiwan, Japan, and Europe. The management of the most prominent semiconductor company in China, SMIC (Semiconductor Manufacturing International Corporation), is Taiwanese. Five of China's eight newest major integrated circuit manufacturing facilities are joint ventures. The other three are wholly Chinese-owned entities funded with foreign capital.

The benefits China has reaped from foreign investment extend far beyond the inflow of money. With investments came networks, contracts, and alliances that link Chinese firms to foreign customers, investors, and suppliers. Close contact with Western companies has had a dramatic impact on corporate culture and human resource management. Lenovo, for example, slowly evolved from a patriarchic, top-down company to one with a more participatory management style through its joint ventures with companies from the United States and Europe. Liu Chuanzhi, founder of Lenovo, has called Hewlett Packard "our earliest and best teacher."[10]

END OF THE LICENSE RAJ, AND INNOVATION IN INDIA

Owing to my background as a China expert, my meetings and conversations in India invariably end with people asking me to compare the two countries. Pausing to come up with some new insight gives the person I am speaking with an opening to tell me how he or she thinks the two countries differ. I have heard many comparisons, and over the years I have assembled a large list of the pairings that people use to capture the often-stark differences between the two (with characteristics of China presented first): communist versus democratic; top-down versus bottom-up; hardware versus software; manufacturing versus services; stable surface, chaotic underneath versus chaotic surface, stable underneath; linear versus Brownian motion; public goods versus individual rights; and system of success versus pockets of excellence.

These simplifications capture some of the massive differences between the two societies. Nonetheless, both stifled technological entrepreneurship in similar manners, at least before India opened to the world in 1991. Central planning, high barriers to foreign investment, and the complex and convoluted system of licenses and regulations required to set up a business, known as the "license Raj," all conspired to choke innovation in India. Private entrepreneurs had to submit applications to bureaucrats in Delhi for approval to invest in specific sectors, grow their companies to a certain size, and import particular types of technology. Gurcharan Das, the author and former CEO of Procter & Gamble India, described an "untrained army of underpaid, third rate engineers . . . operating on the basis of inadequate and ill-organized information and without clear-cut criteria, who vetted thousands of applications on an ad hoc basis."

Eighteen industries, including telecomminications, were reserved for the public sector, and over eight hundred products were listed as reserved for small-scale industries, where investment in plant and machinery was not allowed to exceed $250,000. In the 1980s, with China surging as a manufacturing power, only small-scale industries were allowed in sectors with high export potential such as garments, shoes, and toys. The inability to increase investment and scale in companies in these sectors severely hampered India's export competitiveness, as compared to China's. At the same time, the license Raj created a parallel, profligate bureaucracy, as large businesses camped out in Delhi to follow up on their files, organize bribes, and win licenses. "Licensing," according to Das, "was an unmitigated disaster. It raised costs, brought delays, arbitrariness, and corruption, and achieved nothing. We killed at birth any hope for an industrial revolution."[11]

Both India's communist left and the nationalist right viewed trade, foreign investment, and multinational activity as a threat to economic independence. The first Industrial Policy (1947) declared that "as a rule, the major interest in ownership and effective control of an undertaking should be in Indian hands"; and India adopted a strategy of import substitution and domestic ownership.[12] High tariffs and import barriers were implemented in the hope that Indian companies would begin producing the manufactured goods it was importing. This strategy also involved handicapping foreign firms when necessary. Multinational companies faced tight restrictions on what sectors they could invest in and at what levels. IBM, for example, withdrew from India in 1977 rather than comply with a government order to sell 60 percent of its operations to Indian nationals.[13]

In 1991, a balance of payment crisis—India was close to defaulting on international loans, and foreign exchange reserves were so low that the country could barely afford three weeks' worth of imports—forced the government of P. V. Narasimha Rao to launch massive market reforms and increase the role of the private sector and foreign investment in the economy. Manmohan Singh, then the finance minister, now the prime minister, opened the Indian economy by easing controls on foreign currency, liberalizing restrictions on trade as well as foreign and domestic investment, and raising ceilings on technology licensing. Tariffs on imported goods were greatly reduced, and foreign ownership was allowed, up to a full 100 percent stake, in many sectors. Direct tax rates for individuals and corporations were lowered, and the license Raj was gradually dismantled. By October 2008, only twenty-one products remained on the reserve list, and the government had raised the investment ceiling to over $1 million for high-technology and export-oriented industries.

The 1991 reforms laid the groundwork for India's rapid growth. For the previous four decades, economists had spoken disparagingly of the "Hindu growth rate" of approximately 3 percent. In the first decade of reform, the average annual rate of growth doubled to close to 6 percent. From 2005 to 2008, India sustained an annual average of 8.3 percent growth, although the rate dropped to 6.1 percent in 2009. Simultaneously, India emerged as a software powerhouse. Exports rose from about $4 billion in 2000 to $72 billion in 2009; KPMG, the global tax, audit, and advisory firm, predicts the domestic and exports markets will reach $285 billion by 2020.[14]

The explosion of India's technology industry was the result of the confluence of several serendipitous occurrences: changes in computer architecture, policy decisions made in the 1980s, the communications revolution, and the need for multinational companies to address the Y2K problem—the operating problem computers were expected to face as the year changed from 1999 to 2000. During the 1960s, the government of India adopted a highly protectionist policy toward computers, with high import tariffs and bans on foreign computer companies opening subsidiaries within India. But these policies did little to close the gap between India and the West; IBM and the other producers of mainframes were too big, rich, and technologically sophisticated.

The shift to minicomputers and the growth of distributed data processes—networks of smaller individual computers working on the same problem—gave India a realistic target to chase. Building a microcomputer was affordable, and the market was much less concentrated; the constant stream of small companies developing new models prevented any one company from dominating the market. Since the technological distance between the Western incumbents and their Indian challengers was not as wide as it had been in main-frames, suddenly the goal of self-reliance was attainable.

While IBM's departure in 1977 had the unfavorable outcome of making a generation of foreign investors suspicious of India, it also had the beneficial effect of forcing about 1,200 Indian engineers to find something to do. Government and defense industries were in need of more software, so many of the ex-IBM engineers chose to start their own companies. Indian customers wanted software coded in UNIX, an open-source operating system that had the advantages of being free and highly adaptable; it was soon in high demand from foreign clients.

When I was in India in 2006 and again in 2008, technology entrepreneurs often told me that information technology exploded because the government knew nothing about it and did nothing to support (or regulate) the sector. Although they were largely right, two policies the government of Rajiv Gandhi promoted were important. The 1984 Computer Policy specifically recognized software as an industry, making it eligible for various incentives and relaxed restrictions on the import of intermediate parts and peripherals, while imposing a tariff of 200 percent on the import of a finished computer. As a result, the production of mini-computers in India went up tenfold over two years. The Computer Software Export, Development and Training Policy, passed in 1986, ended the emphasis on self-reliance with respect to software by allowing imports, though with a stiff 60 percent tariff. The policy's goal was to give Indian companies a proper grounding in both the business practices and the software needs of multinational companies.

In addition, widespread English fluency, paired with knowledge of Western business practices, would prove crucial to India's future. When Indian science and technology stagnated in the 1960s and 1970s, engineers and scientists migrated to the United States and worked their way up the corporate ladder. Once American companies decided to outsource software development, Indian managers in these companies could hire old classmates from IIT Bombay and Madras who had stayed in India. The explosion of cheap fiber-optic cable in the 1990s connected the subcontinent to clients in the states, and the 10½-hour time difference meant that Indian firms could work on projects as the day ended on the East Coast. India's success, as one entrepreneur put it to me, was the outcome of "British-given English, and a God-given time difference."

Finally, and most important, Indian companies developed a radical new way of doing white-collar work. As Jerry Rao, who worked at Citibank for almost twenty years before he founded the information technology outsourcer Mphasis, described for me, Indian software did for paper-intensive office jobs what Henry Ford and the efficiency expert Frederick Taylor did for manufacturing. Finance, accounting, customer service, and software coding were treated like the Model T and broken down into ever-smaller components. The parts were standardized, codified, and digitalized and then sent back and forth between India and the United States. In the case of tax returns, American accounting firms scan and transmit W2 and 1099 forms to a secure server at the end of a workday; using the same software, Indian accountants in Bangalore organize and prepare a return to send back the next morning; the American accountant checks the accuracy of the return and submits it to the IRS. The whole process saves money and time.

At the beginning, Indian companies concentrated at the low end, supplying call center support or simple software programming. Today, however, many companies have moved from the periphery to the core of their clients' operations. Wipro sees itself as a "global lab for hire" and provides R&D services for telecom and embedded software, the bits of code that increasingly are present in cell phones, consumer electronics, automobiles, and integrated circuits. M. Divakaran, chief technology officer at the company, told me that

Wipro provides something fundamentally different from services: complex hardware and software products for customers. In some cases, Wipro develops the entire component.

As in China, the Indian science and technology system has been energized by multinational companies building their own R&D centers in India and by the movement of scientists and technology entrepreneurs between India and the United States. Texas Instruments set up the first R&D center in Bangalore in 1985, and there are now approximately 150 foreign R&D centers in India. As in China, multinational companies may have originally come for lower-cost labor but have since discovered that the labor is both low cost and highly skilled. At the beginning, Texas Instruments India primarily did internal work for other divisions of the company, but eventually the company moved more important, high-end design work to Bangalore. The lab has filed for at least 225 patents, and Texas Instruments India now calls the shots in some technology areas.

WANTING THE GOLDEN EGG *AND* THE GOOSE: POLITICS OF TECHNOLOGY

In November 2005, *BusinessWeek* described a budding "love affair" between Cisco and India. Indian companies were increasing their spending on information technology, talent was cheap and plentiful, and the opportunities for Cisco were vast. "Once you spot a market transition, you've got to go for it," the article quoted Rangu Salgame, the head of Cisco India.[15] In the case of Dutt Kalluri (the Indian returnee who was subject of the *Washington Post* article quoted in the previous chapter), his decision to leave Maryland and return to Bangalore was related to a larger trend: technology entrepreneurs, uncertain of the future of the American economy, annoyed with the irrationality of U.S. immigration law, and homesick for their families and culture, moving home to India to take part in a booming market. The stories of both Cisco, a company, and Dutt Kalluri, an individual, echo the dominant theme of globalization as the accretion of uncoordinated, seemingly irrepressible, market-oriented decisions. Although such forces dominate the news coverage of this story, governments also play a role. As previously discussed, decisions by Chinese and Indian policy makers to liberalize their investment laws created the conditions in which foreign multinational companies thrive. Chinese expatriates have been lured home by generous government packages that offer moving allowances and high salaries. In addition, shifts in the movement in technology are not created equal; trade between India and the United States means something far different than trade between Japan and China.

The present century did not start well for China and Japan, with relations between the two as bad as they had been at any time since World War II. Although bilateral trade was growing rapidly, the two countries were increasingly suspicious of each other. Much of the Japanese public worried about Chinese intentions and had tired of what Japan saw as Beijing's constant hectoring over World War II–era grievances. The Chinese military was modernizing at a rapid pace and was clearly more assertive; Chinese "research" ships regularly crossed into an area of the East China Sea that contained a natural gas field claimed by Japan.

The Chinese were equally distrustful of Japan. From Beijing's perspective, closer military ties with the United States—as well as internal debates about becoming a more active global power and revising Article 9, the constitutional clause that renounces war— were all clear evidence of a more assertive Japan. Annual visits by Prime Minister Koizumi Junichiro to Yasukuni, the Shinto shrine dedicated to those killed fighting for the Emperor and, most controversially, honoring the spirits of fourteen "Class A" war criminals, only strengthened the Chinese perception that Japan had not fully confronted its wartime atrocities.

These tense relations took a turn for the worse when anti-Japanese riots erupted in April 2005 in Beijing, Shanghai, Chongqing, and at least ten other cities. Angered by a new history textbook that they believed downplayed Japanese war crimes as well as by Japan's bid for a seat on the UN Security Council, marchers shouted, "Down with Japanese militarism" and other anti-Japanese slogans, and called for a boycott on Japanese goods. Rock-throwing protesters tried to storm the residence of the Japanese ambassador in Beijing. By 2006, according to a survey conducted by Pew, 70 percent of the Chinese population held unfavorable attitudes toward Japan, with almost the exact same percentage of Japanese having negative views of China.[16]

The protests were a wakeup call, a warning that nationalist sentiment could spin out of control, irrevocably damaging a relationship that was of critical economic importance to both sides—by 2009 the amount of two-way trade had reached nearly $267 billion, greater than that between Japan and the United States. Leaders on both sides began looking for ways to rebuild bilateral ties. Some of the bad feeling eased when Koizumi Junichiro left office, and his successors—first Abe Shinzo, next Fukuda Yasuo, and then Aso Taro—sent clear signals to Beijing of their desire to ratchet down the tension by staying away from the Yasukuni Shrine. Abe's first trip overseas as prime minister in October 2006 was to Beijing, and it was followed by Premier Wen Jiabao's visit to the Japanese capital.

In May 2008, Hu Jintao made a highly successful trip to Tokyo, the first for a Chinese president in a decade. During the visit, Hu and Fukuda agreed to promote mutually strategic interests and committed to annual state visits and greater coordination on issues such as climate change. The Chinese side in particular looked to make technology a linchpin of future relations. In a speech to Japanese business leaders, Hu proclaimed his desire to make environmental technologies a centerpiece of economic and trade cooperation, and asked the Japanese to transfer more cutting-edge environmental technologies to China.

Despite what seemed like a natural match between Japanese expertise in clean technologies and China's massive pollution and rising energy demands, Hu's call for closer cooperation was met with some suspicion in Japan. I visited a senior member of the Democratic Party of Japan who did not think much of Hu's plan. Sitting almost knee to knee in his cramped office—surrounded by piles of documents on the floor, interrupted by his assistants reminding him of his next meeting or an incoming phone call—he told me of an invitation he had received to lead a delegation of small and medium-sized enterprises to China to discuss sharing environmental technology. He had eventually decided not to go, even though China was clearly a huge growth market. This politician had heard that the Chinese were interested in buying many of the companies, and he worried that their goal was technology transfer, not technology sharing. "The Chinese," he said, "don't just want the golden egg. They also want the goose."

This politician's sentiment is part of what MIT scholar Richard Samuels described as a larger strategic response to the rise of China as a potential commercial and security rival. During the 1990s, Japanese manufacturers began to take advantage of labor costs in China that were on average only about 5 percent of those in Japan. Much of Japanese investment in new factories and equipment during the decade went abroad—about 80 percent according to numbers quoted by Samuels—provoking a fear of the "hollowing out" and gradual deindustrialization of Japan.[17] Investment in China exploded from $0.8 billion in 1999 to $4.6 billion in 2004 and reached $6.9 billion in 2009. In 2002, Japan's Ministry of Economy, Trade, and Industry, reporting on the flow of investment abroad, warned that "intellectual property is not strategically obtained, managed or utilized sufficiently." As a result "technology is unintentionally draining overseas."[18]

The challenge faced by Japanese policy makers and business

leaders was to turn China from a threat into an opportunity. The strategy, somewhat paradoxically, was to expand the range of activities in China, all the while focusing on global competition. Like their counterparts in Korea, the United States, and Europe, Japanese companies would think of China not just as a manufacturing location but also as an R&D base, though the research and development was primarily for adapting products to the local market. Keidanren, the Japanese Business Federation, described this as part of the shift from *Made in Japan* to *Made by Japan*—"The nation will continue to innovate at home, but it will make full use of technological resources from around the world."[19]

The phrase "innovate at home" is crucial. While Japanese firms planned to embrace China, they also intended to hold some things back. As Samuels noted, when Japanese companies opened their R&D centers in China, they sought to "black box" technology, keeping the most advanced technology in Japan locked away from the Chinese.[20] Toyota, for example, puts the Prius together in Changchun, but core components are delivered in sealed boxes from plants in Japan. Likewise, an executive at Sony told me of how the company maneuvered around the problem of intellectual property theft. For products like digital cameras, Sony does not use joint ventures. The companies are 100 percent Sony owned, and at the final stage of production, the most advanced technology is shipped from Japan as a black box. Sony's plan isn't to thwart the Chinese entirely, but to deter their efforts at reverse engineering by at least one or two years.

An executive from Hitachi was equally frank. There was, he admitted to me, pressure from the Chinese government to set up an R&D facility in China. Hitachi complied with Chinese wishes but spent considerable time thinking about how to manage the facility without transferring any real technology to China. "The Chinese see China as the center of the world, and they have a sense of superiority over Japanese," the executive told me. "It's OK with us, we don't worry about feelings of superiority as long as we maintain financial and technological control."

A LOOK AT INDIA'S FUTURE

Pundits and journalists love to engage in the popular parlor game of guessing who will eventually win the race between China and India. Will China, with its authoritarian political system and its ability to mobilize resources and implement top-down decisions, edge out the chaotic, but democratic Indians? Or might India, with its flexible capital markets, indigenous technology companies, and transparent corporate governance, eventually pull ahead of China, which is too dependent on foreign investment and state-owned enterprises?

While these predictions focus primarily on the competitive race, U.S. policy makers and business leaders need to ask: Will India follow China in implementing a nationalist approach to technology? China has at least a decade's experience and frustration with failing to develop its own intellectual property through opening to global competition. A decade from now, will India be similarly disillusioned? Or will India's experience be different, so that it will continue its less predatory relationship with foreign technology?

India's strong techno-nationalist sentiment, running back to Nehru and independence, was marginalized by the reforms initiated in 1991 and by the success of the information technology sectors. For Nehru and other nationalists, economic power was a prerequisite for military strength and international influence, and science and technology were important components of economic power. State funding was concentrated in the mission-oriented institutes such as the Defence Research & Development Organisation and the Department of Atomic Energy, and India pursued high-profile space and nuclear science programs, which were and continue to be symbols of national prestige and security.

Calls for self-sufficiency no longer have the same political power, though the relationship between India and the multinational companies is critiqued. Prabhat Patnaik, a professor at Jawaharlal Nehru University and vice chairman of the Kerala State Planning Board, claims, "The lack of innovativeness has made the country subservient to foreign technologies and process, reducing it to no more than a glorified processing backyard of the world."[21] When I visited the School of International Studies at Jawaharlal Nehru University in Delhi, I saw a huge poster hanging from the side of the building. Across the top of the poster ran the legend "I Want My Country Back"; below it was a man in a business suit, wearing a red, white, and blue tie and carrying a suitcase labeled "Nuke Deal"—a reference to the U.S.-India nuclear agreement. Inside his hat was "FDI" (foreign direct investment); the jacket was labeled "patents," and the pants "SEZ" (special economic zones, areas with more liberal laws aimed to attract foreign investment). The man, painted white, was kicking another man, painted brown, who was wearing a dhoti, the white handspun loincloth worn by Gandhi as a way of identifying with India's poor. Across the bottom was another legend: "Resist Recolonization."

Beyond such fringe propaganda, there is, so far, no Indian parallel to the popular concern about technology traps that have inspired the Chinese drive for "independent innovation." A more nationalist approach to technology, focused on autonomy and the ownership of intellectual property, may return one day; but with over 300 million people living on less than a dollar a day, the most pressing political issues are poverty and inequality. India leads the world in the number of early childhood deaths, and its literacy rate is as low as 60 percent, even as the ranks of the middle class and super rich swell. Between 2006 and 2009, India dropped from a ranking of 126 to 134 on the Human Development Index, a composite measure used by the UN Development Program that includes life expectancy, education, and standard of living. India's future, in the words of Nobel Prize–winning economist Amartya Sen, "cannot be one that is half California and half sub-Saharan Africa."[22]

Information technology encompasses all the promises and perils India faces. Indian information technology companies lead the world, and the software and technology service sectors are growing at a pace more than twice the rest of the economy. This new prominence on the world stage, and the confidence that came from beating IBM and other world-class companies at their own game, generated what the India expert Matthew Rudolph described to me as an almost messianic fervor. In 1998 and 1999—the long year spanning the test of India's atomic bomb and the listing of Infosys on NASDAQ—political and business elites began embracing information technology as, in Rudolph's phrase, "a form of salvation" for the grave challenges facing the country: technology exports would make the country a software superpower; information technology would increase productivity and reduce poverty; the Internet and mobile phones would unite a divided and fragmented polity and connect the isolated countryside to the world; information technology would increase transparency and solve the problem of corruption; and, through the promise of leapfrogging, information technology would resolve the seemingly intractable problems of poverty and underdevelopment.[23]

At the height of his popularity, Chandrababu Naidu, chief minister of the state of Andhra Pradesh from 1994 to 2004, exemplified all the hopes and grandiose rhetoric surrounding information technology. While in office, Naidu was a vocal and highly visible cheerleader for information technology, leading a delegation to Davos and cultivating contacts with the likes of Bill Gates and Michael Dell. The Western and Indian press portrayed him as more CEO than politician, delivering PowerPoint presentations and sending a stream of emails from his IBM ThinkPad, as one Indian newspaper reported.[24] Microsoft built its first overseas software development center in Hyderabad, the capital of Andhra Pradesh, and investments from Oracle and IBM followed. Government offices were computerized and linked by a statewide area network. In 2000, Naidu, the "czar of Cyberabad," told an interviewer, "I am confident that information technology can bring accountability, transparency and quick disposal of cases and redress of grievances in all the villages. I believe it can alleviate poverty. I see three areas where information technology can be an effective tool: job generation, poverty eradication and wealth generation."[25]

At the national level, the National Democratic Alliance government, led by the Bharatiya Janata Party and Prime Minister Atal Behari Vajpayee, adopted a similar tone. "Technology," according to Vajpayee, "has created a massive growth in productivity. It has also proved to be a revolutionary tool for education, health care, and sustainable development."[26] In the run-up to the 2004 election, the NDA's campaign motto, "Shining India," reflected a sense of confidence and pride in India's rising middle class, the prominence and skill of the software sector, and India's growing international stature.

Both Vajpayee and Naidu lost in separate elections held in 2004. Economics certainly played a role, though poorly run campaigns and shifting party alliances were the more determining factors. Many voters found the "Shining India" campaign offensive, and it served to draw attention to the 70 percent of the population who still live in rural areas and had no link to the booming information technology, pharmaceutical, or automobile sectors. The information technology sector is viewed as India's international jewel, yet it employs only about as many Indians as the national railroad—1.6 million people in a population of over 1.1 billion.

In the 2004 National Election Survey, more than two-thirds of the 23,000 respondents said that they believed economic reforms had benefited only the rich.[27] In Andhra Pradesh, the victorious Congress Party successfully undermined Naidu's leadership, calling into question whether ten years of reform had actually delivered any concrete benefits to voters. This was an effective strategy, as all sections of society defected from Naidu's party, but losses were heaviest among women, farmers, and the poor. These voters told exit polls that one of their most important considerations was Naidu's neglect of rural development and failure to provide irrigation water.

So even if the importance of the Congress Party's strategy is accepted as an explanation for the 2004 elections, the outcome was a sign that "pressure to make reforms relevant to the masses is rising," according to Brown University political scientist Ashutosh Varshney.[28] This pressure, however, has so far not translated into either the wholesale refutation of reforms or a groundswell of support for new reform policies. The economic reforms that might help India's poorest—changes to labor laws, the privatization of state industries, the creation of special economic zones, and reforms of fiscal policy— are the same ones that will inflict the most short-term pain on those at the bottom. In most developed democracies, the poor stay home and the middle class and the rich vote. India's democracy is unique, not only in that it is poor, but in that the voting rate of the lower classes is already relatively high and rising.

Few Indian politicians (or those anywhere else) have either the courage or the ability to inflict short-term pain on potential voters. Instead, the political parties enter into a competitive populism, trying to outdo each other by offering ever-greater subsidies to low-income, low-caste, and rural voters. In the run-up to the 2009 elections, Congress and the United Progressive Alliance introduced a relief package for the agricultural sector that included a loan waiver program for destitute farmers valued at $15 billion. Campaigning to return as head of Andhra Pradesh, Naidu promised increased pensions for the elderly, unemployment payments for jobless youth, free cooking gas for women, free bicycles for students, two acres and a house for members of the lower castes, and free housing, education, and electric power for the poor.

The end result of all of this populism is what the political scientist Varsheny calls "a strong consensus around weak reforms."[29] Political leaders are happy to raid the budget for new social programs and perhaps tinker around the edges with some of the easier policy changes, but they delay on the hard decisions needed to push reforms forward.

Take the Tata Nano, the $2,500 mini car hailed by the press, the public, and the government as a demonstration of "India's technological, intellectual and entrepreneurial ability," in the words of Kamal Nath, who was commerce minister in January 2008 when plans for the car were first announced. The day after the project was announced, the headline of the *Times of India* read, "Tata Reinvents the Wheel."[30]

The road, however, from Tata's announcement of the plan to build the car, to the day the first Nano rolled off the production line in July 2009 was bumpy despite the national enthusiasm for the project. In October 2008, Tata announced that it was halting construction of a $350 million factory outside of Kolkata (Calcutta) because of political opposition and protests by farmers' groups who said they were not fairly compensated for their land. An estimated thirty thousand protesters gathered around the factory, blocking shipments into and out of the plant. Workers were beaten up and equipment stolen. Later in the month, although the state had heavily supported the project with the expectation that the factory could create close to ten thousand jobs, Tata announced it was relocating to Gujarat.

Part of the problem is that India lacks a modern law for acquiring land for development projects; thus, it relies on the 1894 Land

Acquisition Act, which states that lands can be seized for "public purpose" but only vaguely defines that purpose, turning most building projects into loaded political battles. Land seizures are frequently suspect, and opposition politicians take advantage by holding large projects hostage to political protests. In addition to the Nano, political protests were delaying over twenty large projects, including Tata Steel in Chhattisgarh, Posco Steel in Orissa, Reliance in Gurgaon, and several other investments of close to $100 billion in 2009.

While democracy is often cited as an Indian advantage over China, the trend lines for the governance of India do not look good. Corruption is endemic, with at least a quarter of the members of the national legislature facing some criminal charge. The *Wall Street Journal* reports that in the state of Uttar Pradesh over half of the members of the state assembly face criminal charges. According to National Election Watch, an umbrella group of Indian nongovernmental organizations, over three hundred candidates in the 2009 election had assets over 10 million rupees (about $212,000).[31] The professionalism and efficacy of the civil service and the judiciary have been seriously degraded.

Still, Indian entrepreneurs remain highly confident not only that they will continue to skate above the muddle of the politics of India, but also that they will successfully change India itself. Others are less certain. There is much talk about India's potential, of how India will soon become one of the world's most powerful economies. "We no longer discuss the future of India. We say: 'The Future is India'," said former commerce minister Kamal Nath. But as a 2008 Goldman Sachs report put it, "Having the potential and actually achieving it are two separate things."[32] At the least, the inabilities to provide education, build adequate infrastructure, and undertake structural reforms make it much less likely that India will meet its goal of becoming one of the world's largest economies by 2050.

Some developments, especially the rising demands of India's

extraordinarily young population, could present a more fundamental challenge and have a much bigger effect on Indian society and politics than could a marginal change in the growth rate. With more than half of its population being twenty-five years or younger, India does not have China's potential problem of becoming old before it becomes rich. But this strength of youth is also a potential weakness. Hundreds of millions of people will have to be educated and find jobs, and expectations about the future run high. Manufacturing, which will provide many more jobs in the future, has been growing at a healthy rate, but manufacturing as a share of GDP remains at about 17 percent, below the 25 to 30 percent medium-term goal the government set, and well below the 33 percent China boasts. Many Latin American countries in the 1970s and 1980s turned the opportunity of relatively young populations into policy failures, creating large urban underclasses and new foot soldiers for leftist movements.

To create more jobs, the government needs to deregulate labor markets, invigorate agricultural growth, and increase investment in infrastructure—all difficult steps to take politically. The patience of the populace, if the government's ability to deliver continues to lag behind rising demands, is an open question.

The results of the May 2009 election produced some hope that reforms would be pushed forward. The Congress Party won the election with enough seats so that it did not need the communists and other left-leaning parties to form a ruling coalition. Before, the communist and left-leaning parties had blocked lifting restrictions on foreign investment in key industries such as retail, media, and insurance, as well as labor law reform. Soon after the election, Congress leaders signaled they were serious about education reform and promised to tackle tax laws as well. Yet, as of February 2010, it was hard to read victory as a mandate for liberalization and reform; Congress had been forced to put labor reform and farm deregulation on the back burner in the face of public pressure.

In sum, as it stands, the information technology sector is likely to remain divorced from the rest of Indian society and focused on export markets, thus reinforcing much of the inequality in Indian society, which in turn feeds back into Indian domestic politics and maintains the status quo. By contrast, a virtuous cycle would see a strong reform program creating the conditions for a broad-based innovation system.

For much of the last wave of globalization, spanning from approximately 1983 to 2008, we were told that we needed to understand the economic and technological forces driving globalization. And we do. The freedom of multinational companies to move anywhere and the explosion of cheap and near ubiquitous information and communication technologies have, as countless commentators have pointed out, transformed the world. But if we want to understand how technology itself is developed as well as how, where, and why it moves around the world, then simply focusing on the economic and the technical is not merely inadequate, but provides a distorted view of what is actually occurring. We need to expand our focus to consider how the demands of autonomy, security, and equality direct and influence technology.

In addition, we have to realize that the second couplet, the contest between high and low politics, doesn't apply only to Asia—it constantly shapes technology development at home, often to the detriment of our national interests.

Chapter Five

TRADING WITH
THE (POTENTIAL) ENEMY

On the way to a summit meeting in Washington, D.C., with President George W. Bush in April 2006, Chinese President Hu Jintao first made a stop in the other Washington, to tour the Microsoft campus in Redmond. During his meeting with Bill Gates, Hu offered the ultimate praise: "Because you, Mr. Gates, are a friend to China, I am a friend of Microsoft." Hu then added, "Also I am dealing with the operating system produced by Microsoft every day."[1] When Gates goes to China, he is treated like a rock star. The press follows his every move and students ask for autographs. In 2007, he was named a trustee of Peking University and received an honorary degree from Tsinghua University.

This is a remarkable turnaround. Just five years before, the Chinese press was portraying Microsoft as a bully who sued smaller Chinese companies for copyright violations, as a foreign interloper out of touch with the Chinese market, and as a potential security threat. While a majority of government offices installed (probably pirated) versions of Windows, it was widely believed in China that the program had "back doors" exploitable by the U.S. National Security Agency. Managers at Microsoft China came and went with little success, heightening the sense that something was wrong at the company. One departing manager, Juliet Wu, wrote *Up against the Wind: Microsoft, I.B.M. and Me*, a bestseller criticizing the company for failing to understand China.[2] Not content to simply not buy Microsoft products, the Beijing city government actively promoted the use of a Linux competitor.

If the company was unpopular in China, Microsoft's feelings for the country were not much warmer. The theft of Microsoft software was prevalent, with piracy rates for all brands of software at almost 90 percent in China. In several notorious cases, Microsoft sued Chinese companies for installing Windows and Office on their computers without approval, and for churning out thousands of illegal copies of their software. Business was hard, and revenues relatively low. At one point Gates reportedly exclaimed that Microsoft had been "fucked" by the Chinese government.[3]

So how did Microsoft engineer this reversal? The first steps were relatively easy. Microsoft stopped suing local companies for violating its intellectual property. To assuage security concerns, the company shared part of the Windows source code with China and fifty-nine other countries. And Microsoft began pricing software for the local market, offering Windows at prices that Chinese consumers could afford.

The most important move by Microsoft required a more dramatic shift: it began repeatedly telling Chinese leaders that it wanted to help China develop its own software industry, and then it walked the talk. Lee Kai-fu, then manager of Microsoft's operations in China, described this strategy in an internal memo as "contribute first and benefit later." Despite all the challenges of operating in China, Lee argued that "benefits eventually come to those who contribute and help China early and sincerely."[4]

The Japanese call this approach "tickling China's heart"—winning the support of the Chinese leadership (or at least their benign indifference) by helping them accomplish their development goals. One of the most significant decisions Microsoft made was to establish a new R&D center, Microsoft Research Asia, in Beijing. The center was one of the first foreign research facilities built in China and is currently one of the most active in conducting advanced research. The majority of foreign R&D centers, by contrast, do the opposite and concentrate on minor adjustments to products for the local market.

Microsoft also ramped up its investments. In 2006, the company announced a $3.7 billion commitment to its Chinese operations over five years. In cooperation with the National Development and Reform Commission, Microsoft created a software innovation center to encourage innovation and product development among Chinese software companies. In November 2008, the company announced an additional $1 billion investment in research and development. All of this activity, according to Tim Chen, who now runs Microsoft's China subsidiary, has "changed the company's image. We're the company that has the long-term vision. If a foreign company's strategy matches with the government's development agenda, the government will support you, even if they don't like you."[5]

Despite Chen's confidence in this strategy, the detente between China and Microsoft may not last. In December 2008, the two sides came to blows again when a local government in the south of China forced Internet cafes to replace Windows XP with the Red Flag Linux operating system. At about the same time, Microsoft's Windows Genuine Advantage and Office Genuine Advantage, upon detecting a pirated version of Windows, temporarily blackened computer screens, enraging many Chinese PC users. When Hong Lei, the creator of a Windows clone called Tomato Garden Windows XP, was detained by Chinese authorities in 2009, a survey on Sina.com found that 80 percent of respondents supported Hong, with many calling him a national hero, and only 4.4 percent supported Microsoft.[6]

There is nothing inherently malicious about Microsoft's strategy. The company and hundreds of other American technology companies like it are responding to undeniable market pressures. Globalization is their reality, not a choice. Still, with R&D centers in China and foreign scientists training in American labs, the blurring of the distinctions between technologies used in war and those in trade, and the deep integration of the American and Chinese economies, it is nearly impossible for the United States to control technology. As a result, foreign militaries, and the People's Liberation Army (PLA) in particular, have benefited from an ever-greater range of know-how available on global markets.

The American challenge is to develop effective policy that takes into account the new realities of the global situation and, more important, avoids making it worse. Some good policy choices, like using technology to strengthen cooperation between Washington and Delhi, are straightforward. An overzealous policy attempt to slow the diffusion of technology, however, could prove disastrous for the American system of innovation, which is defined by openness. Policy makers would be irresponsible not to attempt to prevent the loss of technology, but policies limiting the United States' access to people or ideas could do more damage to security than any leak of secrets. The United States must continue to lead in the production of new technologies, not doggedly defend whatever edge it currently possesses.

GLOBALIZATION AND TECHNOLOGY CONTROL

In 1955, the U.S. government placed Qian Xuesen, an MIT- and Caltech-trained rocket scientist, on a boat back to China. Qian, who had arrived in the United States in 1935, was one of the most prominent rocket scientists in the country. He was cofounder of the Jet Propulsion Laboratory in Pasadena and instrumental in the design and launch of the U.S. Army's first missiles. Early work Qian did on space travel would eventually influence the design of the space shuttle.

Five years earlier, a few months after Qian had become a citizen, the FBI discovered an American Communist Party document with his name on it. Qian's security clearance was revoked. Unable to find work and worried about his elderly sick father back home in China, Qian declared that he would return there. His announcement created a conflict in the government between those who wanted to deport him as a spy and those who did not want Qian and his knowledge to fall into the hands of the Chinese Communists. Undersecretary of the Navy Daniel Kimball declared, "I'd rather see him shot than let him go. . . . He's worth three to five divisions anyplace."[7]

A few days before Qian was scheduled to leave for China, the Customs Bureau seized Qian's luggage.[8] The government could not decide whether the technical papers stuffed into Qian's bags were proof of espionage. Officials from the Atomic Energy Commission, for example, concluded that the papers were typical of what one of the world's foremost technical scholars in aircraft and missile design would accumulate after ten years of work in the fields. The military and the intelligence community wanted to seize and classify Qian's entire library. On September 7, 1950, officials from the Immigration and Naturalization Service arrested Qian.

Qian returned to China in 1955 as part of a prisoner exchange, whereby seventy-four American POWs from the Korean War were returned. Once on the mainland, Qian began working to make Undersecretary Kimball's worst fears come true. Qian initiated China's ballistic missile program, established the first institute of missile design, and developed a strategic plan that focused on atomic energy, missiles, computer science, semiconductors, and electronics. Qian designed the Dong Feng, China's first intercontinental ballistic missile, and his research served as the basis for the Long March, the rocket that launched *Shenzhou V*, China's first manned spacecraft, in October 2003. The author Iris Chang described Qian's accomplishment as "taking a primitive military establishment and transforming it into one that could deliver nuclear bombs intercontinentally; he initiated and guided numerous projects that brought China into the space age."[9]

Half a century later, at the end of 2002, Fei Ye, a U.S. citizen, and Ming Zhong, a permanent resident, were arrested for the possession of trade secrets stolen from four Silicon Valley companies: Sun Microsystems, the Transmeta Corporation, NEC Electronics, and Trident Microsystems. In June 2006, FBI agents in Silicon Valley raided the homes of Lan Lee and Ge Yuefei and arrested them for stealing proprietary chip designs and software both from their employer, NetLogic Microsystems of Mountain View, and from Taiwan Semiconductor Manufacturing in San Jose.[10] In May 2007, Chi Mak was convicted of giving information about submarine propulsion systems to his brother, who then passed the data to Chinese authorities. Mak, whom prosecutors called the "perfect sleeper agent," had lived in Los Angeles for close to twenty years, working as an engineer for various defense contractors. In February 2010, U.S. District Judge Cormac J. Carney sentenced Chung Dongfan, a seventy-three-year-old engineer at Boeing, to fifteen years for passing data on the space shuttle and the Delta IV rocket to China.

All of this spying, according to David Szady, a former assistant director of the FBI's counterintelligence division, is only a small part of "the No. 1 counterintelligence threat that the United States faces."[11] As a result, the FBI has increased its operations against Chinese activities in the United States. The number of espionage cases involving China has spiked over 50 percent in the last couple of years, with Immigration and Customs Enforcement officials launching more than 540 investigations of illegal technology exports to China since 2000.

Today's cases of alleged espionage, at first glance, would echo those of the cloak-and-dagger 1950s. But today, the movement of technology, on the black market and through legal trade, is more complicated and uncontainable. During the Cold War, American policy makers and their European and Japanese allies generally knew which technologies they wanted to control, where that technology was located, and whom they wanted to keep it from. The United States, Japan, and Europe were the sole producers of most advanced technologies. There was a clear line between military and civilian technologies. The United States, the United Kingdom, and France all had strategic weapons research programs—for nuclear weapons and the missiles, submarines, and aircraft that would deliver them—that were geographically isolated from and had little contact with the domestic economy, much less the outside world.

These countries were in relative agreement about the control of technologies. The United States, most of Western Europe, and Japan were members of the Coordinating Committee for Multilateral Export Controls, which restricted the movement of conventional weapons and dual-use technology items to the Eastern Bloc. Cooperation between the United States and its allies was not always easy during the Cold War. During the Carter administration, for example, the United States blocked the sale of oil and gas exploration equipment as punishment for the Soviet conviction of the dissident Natan Sharansky as well as the harassment of American journalists. The Soviet Union quickly switched to a French supplier. Still, except in those cases where Europe felt that the United States had levied unilateral controls to make political points, there was a general consensus about what technologies should not be sold to the USSR.

Most of these conditions no longer hold. The walls surrounding technology, real and conceptual, have dissolved. It is no longer a given that important technologies will be developed or produced in the West. In a number of scientific fields, including polymers, solar energy, and adaptive mechanics, the United States is one player among several science powers. Advanced commercial technologies are as likely to be developed by Japanese, Taiwanese, or Korean companies as they are by American firms.

Purely civilian technology cannot be reliably distinguished from purely military technology. Technologies that have only a military purpose—say, the stealth technologies used to make the F-117 and B-2 aircrafts invisible—are much rarer today than those whose commercial importance is increasing, like cryptography and space exploration. Much of the technology that could be used to counter American systems is inexpensive and easy to develop. As one Department of Defense official told me, "We buy from Lockheed Martin, Raytheon, and Boeing. Our competitors steal what they need from Radio Shack."

American defense planners are concerned less about the transfer of manufactured goods, a specific chip or flat screen monitor, than about the transfer of the knowledge of how they were made. Knowledge, however, is difficult to corral, as it encompasses the output of many people spread across multiple laboratories around the globe.

Furthermore, the United States cannot easily convince even its closest friends not to sell dual-use technology to China. The Coordinating Committee for Multilateral Export Controls ceased functioning in 1994, to be replaced in 1996 with the Wassenaar Arrangement, a set of guidelines that have no legal binding authority. Practical implementation of the guidelines, the actual decision not to sell a technology, is up to each of the forty individual member states, and few have chosen not to sell dual-use technologies. The difference between the United States and Europe is especially sharp. Simply put, the economic rewards of selling into the Chinese market are high, and European policy makers predict conflict involving China as very unlikely. In addition, Europe, unlike the United States, has no Taiwan Relations Act, the law passed in 1979 as Washington switched recognition from Taipei to Beijing declaring that the United States would see any efforts "to determine the future of Taiwan by other than peaceful means" as a "threat to the peace and security of the Western Pacific area and of grave concern to the United States."

Many in Europe would go further than selling dual-use technologies by seeking to lift the arms embargo that was put into place after the 1989 Tiananmen Square massacre. In January 2004, French President Jacques Chirac called the ban an anachronism, and political leaders in Germany, Spain, and Italy called for its lifting. Today, the embargo remains in place, primarily because of pressure from Washington and as a result of a serious diplomatic misstep by China. Just as the European Union was discussing lifting the ban, Beijing passed an "anti-secession law," which described the conditions under which it would use military force against Taiwan. This law, with its threat of force, effectively pulled the rug out from under proponents of ending the embargo, who had argued that China's rise was destined to be peaceful.

Perhaps the most deeply ingrained reason why the technology trade defies control is that the American and Chinese economies are so greatly interdependent. During the Cold War, ideological competition between the Soviet Union and the United States created two separate and competing economic camps; Soviet-American trade peaked in 1979 at $4.5 billion, representing 1 percent of total U.S. trade. In contrast, the American and Chinese economies are firmly intertwined. Toys, textiles, and machine parts travel east across the Pacific; U.S. investment floods back into China. During January to November 2009, two-way trade topped $331.1 billion, representing 14 percent of total U.S. trade. In many technology sectors, it makes no sense to speak of a separate "Chinese" or "American" industry. The personal computer industry, for example, stretches across the Pacific, involving Chinese, American, and Taiwanese entrepreneurs, designers, managers, and technicians.

America's extraordinary openness to China is a source of both great strength and some concern. As a Commerce Department advisory group report bluntly stated, "Today's United States research enterprise would barely function without the foreign-born individuals, including foreign nationals, who contribute to it."[12] Naturally this openness is a boon to Chinese spies and the Chinese intelligence agencies who seek access to technologies that can advance their military and economic objectives. The "key modality is no longer the spy," according to Jim Richberg, then the deputy national counterintelligence executive, "but the businessman, student, or academic."[13] During the Cold War, the FBI grew familiar with its opponent: agents could trail the military attaché, cultural officer, or Soviet "journalist." Today, as security agencies monitor Chinese nationals in the United States, the FBI must contend not only with language and cultural issues, but also with a far wider array of potential threats, now embedded within business and academia, in addition to the military.

CHINESE MILITARY MODERNIZATION: DIFFUSION AND ACCESS

In June 2005, Secretary of Defense Donald Rumsfeld met with regional security experts at a conference in Singapore and complained that Chinese defense expenditures were much higher than publicly reported. At the time, China's official defense budget was approximately $30 billion, and at the end of 2009 it was approximately $70 billion, while the Pentagon estimated the real spending to be two or three times the reported number. For comparison's sake, U.S. defense spending in 2010 was $680 billion. At the time, China was expanding its short- and long-range missile force and building more technologically advanced weapons. Since "no one threatens China," Rumsfeld wondered, "why this growing investment? Why these continuing large and expanding arms purchases? Why these continuing robust deployments?"[14]

Rumsfeld was probably being willfully obtuse. Beijing's motivation for more defense spending is, in fact, pretty clear. At the top of China's list of concerns is Taiwan. Throughout much of the 1990s, relations across the Taiwan Strait were palpably tense, and the possibility that conflict could erupt was very real. Since the end of the Chinese civil war in 1949, the two sides had agreed that there was only one China, with each side claiming that it was the sole legitimate government—one day the Communists on the mainland would take Taiwan, or the Nationalists would return from the island. During the 1990s, Taiwanese leaders began to suggest first that they were in no hurry to unify with China and then that Taiwan was in fact a distinct country with its own cultural identity. History books were changed to stress Taiwan's separation from the mainland, and Taiwan began campaigning in international organizations to be recognized as a sovereign nation. As Taiwan seemed to be moving toward independence, China massed weaponry aimed across the water. Twice, in 1995 and 1996, China test-fired ballistic missiles that landed in the waters near Taiwan.

Now, in the middle of 2010, conflict across the Taiwan Strait looks unlikely. Economic ties tightly link the two sides; bilateral trade hit an all-time high of $129.22 billion in 2008, with China remaining Taiwan's largest trading partner. One million Taiwanese, or almost 5 percent of the population, live or work on the mainland. The last time I was in Taiwan, when I was reading the newspaper it took me a few moments to realize that I was looking at advertisements for new apartments in Shanghai, not Taipei. Taiwan's president, Harvard-trained Ma Ying-jeou, has sworn off the more provocative moves toward independence of his predecessor, Chen Shui-bian, and in June 2010 signed the Economic Cooperation Framework Agreement, which lowered barriers on trade with the mainland.

Still, these friendly trends are easily reversible. In October 2008, for example, after the Pentagon announced its intention to sell $6.5 billion in weapons to Taiwan, China harshly criticized Washington and quickly cut off exchanges with the U.S. military. In early 2010, when the Obama administration finally approved the sales, Beijing threatened that the deal would harm China-U.S. relations and again ended military-to-military exchanges, which have restarted only recently. Taiwan is expected to request that the United States sell it the Lockheed Martin F-16 fighting aircraft, a sale that would disrupt relations among Taipei, Beijing, and Washington. While circumstances have changed since the 1990s, Beijing remains determined to retain the military capacity to influence Taiwan's political future.

Although the "problem" of Taiwan gives the Chinese military buildup its shape and purpose, Beijing has other motives for modernizing the military. As Director of National Intelligence John Negroponte told Congress in January 2007, "China's aspirations for great-power status, threat perceptions and security strategy would drive this modernization effort even if the Taiwan problem were resolved,"[15] which succinctly answers Rumsfeld's query as to why China increased defense spending. Chinese military planners kept a close watch on U.S. forces in action during the first Gulf War and in Kosovo and, like everyone else watching CNN, saw buildings destroyed as cruise missiles, launched from several hundred miles away, entered through air vents. Chinese defense planners were both awed and worried. Their own military was not too different from Iraq's, equipped with Soviet-era weapons and designed to fight extended wars of attrition.

The People's Liberation Army quickly realized that it risked falling even farther behind the U.S. military if it did not develop and leverage high technology. It began preparing for the most likely next war, not a long, great-power conflict but rather a quick, intense, and destructive regional war. As Lieutenant General Zhang Qinsheng said in 2007, the Chinese military is developing a force capable of "winning the war of the information age."[16]

Also, China not only has to defend one of the longest land borders in the world, but also is engaged in a boundary conflict with India and in territorial disputes with Japan over natural gas fields in the East China Sea and with Vietnam, the Philippines, and others in the South China Sea. China is now the world's second largest importer of oil, and almost 80 percent of its oil travels through the Strait of Malacca, a narrow passage between Malaysia and Indonesia that the U.S. Seventh Fleet patrols. The Chinese are unlikely to want to rely indefinitely on the U.S. Navy for their economic security, and the Chinese navy has taken a more active role in projecting power farther and farther away from the Chinese mainland. Tracking, protecting, and communicating with ships out on the open sea is a new technological challenge for the Chinese navy.

Beijing appears content to become, at least over the next decade, the predominant regional military power. Global power requires aircraft carriers and the ability to move large numbers of troops or material by air or by sea to Africa or the Middle East, none of which China has—yet. Still, outside observers really do not know what China's longer-term aspirations are. I am not sure the Chinese know either. Some think China will act as rising powers always have throughout history: build a military and wield influence. Chinese leaders do seem to be preparing the world for some changes. In March 2009, National Defense Minister Liang Guanglie told his Japanese counterpart, "Among the big nations, only China does not have an aircraft carrier. China cannot be without an aircraft carrier forever."[17] Still, even if China remains a regional power, it needs a more technologically advanced military and is acquiring technology anywhere it can get it.

The Chinese buy some technology as an end product: a more than $13 billion order from the Russians included advanced fighter jets, destroyers, cruise missiles, and submarines. The Chinese are looking to the global market to buy information technology, micro-electronics, nanotechnology, space, new materials, propulsion, computer-aided design, and other dual-use technologies.[18] Few of these technologies are unique to the United States, and the PLA (through front companies in many cases) buys them from suppliers in Europe, Korea, Israel, Taiwan, and Japan.

Not only is the physical technology widely available; the knowledge needed to use, improve, and integrate complex technological systems is also spreading. The National Intelligence Council, the CIA's think tank, explains the process: "The most significant source of diffusion [is] not the transfer of armaments themselves; it [is] the importation or migration of skilled personnel from the 'knows' to the 'know-nots'."[19] The destroyer the PLA buys from Russia might be equipped with sonar from France, radar from Italy, and software from Israel. The challenge—and it has been a challenge for the PLA—is to get all of these different parts to work together. Now that the PLA can draw on the experience of Chinese who have managed and integrated complex projects at large multinational companies, getting the various components to work together ought to go more smoothly.

Globalization has also made Chinese defense industries more efficient. In the past, Chinese defense firms were afflicted with the worst pathologies of the state-owned, centrally planned economy: overstaffing, low productivity, a lack of understanding of final markets, a dearth of management skills, and technological backwardness. Despite early successes in developing missiles and nuclear weapons, they consistently failed to deliver the advanced fighter jets, tanks, artillery, and other conventional weapons the PLA wanted. So the Chinese military was forced to rely on KBP, Rosoboronexport, and other Russian arms suppliers.

Since the late 1990s, the government has invested a great deal of money in the Chinese defense industry, and the technological capabilities of domestic defense firms are slowly improving. The most notable progress, however, has been in sectors such as shipbuilding and information technology where Chinese firms are competing globally, according to a 2005 RAND study.[20] As they move into international markets, Chinese firms often form alliances with other global companies, which give them access to equipment and know-how.

American companies have been involved, at least at a remove, in improving military capabilities through cooperation with commercial Chinese technology companies that have links to the PLA. The Chinese telecom company Huawei, for example, has signed technology development agreements with Intel, Lucent, Motorola, IBM, Texas Instruments, and Sun Microsystems. ZTE, a manufacturer of telecom equipment, partners with Motorola and Texas Instruments, and maintains ties to the China Aerospace Science and Technology Corporation, one of eleven conglomerates that make up the Chinese defense sector. Huawei and ZTE both helped the PLA replace its antiquated analog communication system with digital communications via fiber-optic cable, satellite, microwave, and encrypted high-frequency radio. The end result is that the PLA can better direct forces, observe the enemy, and identify potential targets.[21]

In many respects, however, placing guilt by association on American companies is deceiving. Indeed, Intel and IBM do cooperate with Huawei; Huawei is both an important customer and a sponsor of research and development for the PLA (according to the 2005 RAND report); and therefore, a simple conclusion is that Intel and IBM aid the PLA.[22] Such connections, however, are rarely so simple or direct. The ownership of companies like Huawei has become increasingly complex, and the PLA purchases only between 1 and 5 percent of Huawei's products. Export controls already prevent American companies from transferring sensitive technology to China, and besides, self-preservation would stop American companies from providing their competitors with advanced technologies. Nonetheless, the perception that American companies could be helping the PLA is already driving new regulations.

If Huawei represents the problem of diffusion, circuit boards are at the center of the question of secure access for U.S. defense suppliers. In October 2006, a Chinese submarine trailed the USS *Kitty Hawk* in the waters off Okinawa, surfacing undetected and within firing range of the aircraft carrier.[23] Surfacing near U.S. ships was novel for Chinese subs, an unexpected display of confidence after a decade-long buildup by the Chinese navy of its submarine fleet. According to the International Institute for Strategic Studies in London, China now has fifty-eight submarines, including twelve Kilo-class submarines purchased from Russia. A new nuclear-powered ballistic missile submarine (Type-094) and nuclear-powered attack submarine (Type-093) are expected to enter service soon.

Submarines would play a central role in any potential conflict in the Taiwan Strait. Chinese submarines could blockade Taiwan, sinking (or threatening to sink) commercial ships. Shipping insurance rates would skyrocket, and if the blockade went on long enough, it would collapse the Taiwanese economy. "Submarines," in the words of one Chinese defense analyst, "are the maritime weapons that pose the greatest threat to an aircraft carrier formation."[24] This analyst was thinking not just about any aircraft carrier, but of the USS *Kitty Hawk* (and now of its replacement, the USS *George Washington*) sailing from the U.S. naval base in Yokosuka, Japan, to break the blockade.

During peaceful times (and even more so if a war were to break out), the U.S. Air Force and Navy identify and track Chinese submarines. Sonobuoys, launched into the water by ships or aircraft, play an important role in this strategy, since the U.S. fleet cannot continually search the huge expanses of the Western Pacific for Chinese submarines. Active sonobuoys issue an acoustic signal that helps identify potential targets in the water; passive sonobuoys listen for the noise generated by passing ships or submarines. In both types of the device, the information is radioed to aircraft or ships that can then investigate and, if necessary, engage detected crafts.

Which brings me back to circuit boards, particularly the ones that Sparton Corporation, the only U.S. manufacturer of sonobuoy technology, produces in China. The threat, according to Larry Wortzel, a former army attaché at the U.S. embassy in China and now a commissioner on the U.S.-China Economic and Security Review Commission, is that agents of the Chinese military or intelligence community could tamper with the sonobuoy's circuitry: "Now, I'm not even a computer weenie but if I was in the PLA, I would figure out how to make sure that circuit board wouldn't pick up a submarine."[25]

This is not an isolated problem, affecting only simple components, but reaches to more technologically sophisticated products such as routers and microprocessors. In March 2008, the FBI and Canadian authorities seized counterfeit Cisco routers, switches, and network cards worth $78 million; much of the haul they traced back to factories in Shenzhen. While announcing the breakup of the smuggling operation, Assistant Attorney General Alice Fisher of the Department of Justice warned network administrators from the private sector and the government that they could be using counterfeit goods. Some of the routers and network cards may have been sold to the U.S. Navy, Air Force, and Marines, Raytheon, and Lockheed Martin among others, exposing their networks to failure or penetration by Chinese hackers—not an idle concern given the rise of cyber attacks over the last few years. Attacks, apparently from China, have been mounted on the networks of, among others, the Pentagon, the U.S. nuclear weapons lab at Oak Ridge, the State Department, the White House, and the Department of Homeland Security, as well as Google, Intel, Lockheed Martin, and other technology companies.

Reliance on possibly compromised routers from Shenzhen only increases the United States' exposure to similar attacks.

The microprocessor, the linchpin of U.S. military strength, is also a point of vulnerability. In almost any conflict, the United States expects to have superior information—to know more about the battlefield than its enemies do. To achieve this, U.S. forces depend on superior sensors and information-processing capabilities, which in turn depend on better quality microchips. But if the components of its information systems are compromised, U.S. forces might be vulnerable. After Israel bombed a suspected nuclear reactor in northern Syria in 2007, defense analysts began wondering why Syria's advanced radar failed to provide any warning of the attack. Some speculated that microprocessors in the radar, bought commercially on the open market, had a "backdoor," a few lines of code that let the Israelis send a signal and turn off or, at least, disrupt the chip and thus disable the radar.

With the exception of IBM's facilities, the majority of chip foundries, the production facilities used in the manufacturing of integrated circuits, are located outside the United States. And many, if not most, of the newest foundries are located in China, where market demand is growing fastest and the government offers substantial tax breaks and other subsidies. Since, according to the Defense Science Board, testing or reverse engineering cannot reveal whether a design had been compromised or spyware inserted into a chip, U.S. defense planners cannot learn whether Chinese intelligence agencies have inserted malicious code.[26]

INDIA: BECOMING A GLOBAL POWER

While the United States has struggled to restrict China's access to sensitive technologies, it has worked actively to develop India as a new global power. According to one former U.S. State Department official, "India as a global power is in an early, formative stage. The United States' job for the next 5 to 10 years is to promote, assist, and shape that process."[27]

After the 1962 Sino-Indian war, the United States and India enjoyed a brief period of political and technological cooperation before sliding into mutual mistrust and suspicion for most of the Cold War era. American leaders regarded India's policy of nonalignment in the struggle between the West and the Communist Bloc as downright immoral, and by the mid-1960s, the nonalignment promise was more rhetorical than real, as New Delhi was clearly tilting toward Moscow. Indian leaders leveled no criticism of the Soviet invasion of Czechoslovakia, and India became dependent on the Soviet Union for arms and technology. For its part, New Delhi believed the United States, especially through its support of Pakistan, was attempting to contain India. The opening to China in 1972 was taken as further evidence of Washington's intention to prevent India from exercising its natural rights in South Asia.

In the wake of India's "peaceful" nuclear test in 1974, Washington relied almost solely on sanctions as its foreign policy toward New Delhi. According to Stephen Cohen, a scholar of South Asia at the Brookings Institution, "The primary tools of U.S. policy [toward India] have not been economic aid, diplomacy, or military force, sales, or assistance, but technological embargoes and economic sanctions. These put great strain on the relationship with India."[28] Over the next two decades the Congress, and international agreements such as the Zanger Committee, the Nuclear Suppliers Group, and the Missile Technology Control Regime limited the sale of nuclear and missile-related technologies to India.

The severity of the tension meant that even attempts to cultivate a thaw could end in mutual recriminations. In 1982, President Ronald Reagan and Prime Minister Indira Gandhi signed an agreement providing for the transfer of sensitive technologies to India, primarily for use in a new combat aircraft. At the time, the Reagan administration wanted to balance the aid it was giving to Pakistan; it also hoped to lure India away from the Soviet Union. In the course of the agreement, the Indians put in a request to buy a Cray XMP-24 supercomputer in order, they claimed, to study monsoons. Since that version of the Cray could also be used to design nuclear weapons, the United States made a counteroffer with the Cray XMP-14, a less powerful computer that could be used for storms but not bombs. The request for the XMP-24 was further evidence to the United States that India simply wanted to exploit their relationship to pursue its nuclear ambitions. In New Delhi, the lesser offer of the XMP-14 was proof that American promises were not credible.[29]

With the end of the Cold War, India and the United States made tentative steps to improve their relationship. Controls on some technology goods were lifted, but all forward progress came to a halt with India's nuclear test in May 1998. In response, President Bill Clinton levied new sanctions that included the loss of foreign assistance, bans on sales of defense articles, opposition to any loans by international financial institutions, and the prohibition of U.S. banks from making loans or extending credit to the government of India.

The sanctions hit the Indian scientific community hard. Specific disciplines and departments—physics, engineering, aerospace—were targeted. Prominent Indian scientists were denied visas to attend international conferences in the United States, and American companies refused to provide equipment to academic departments at the Indian Institute of Science. American scientists who were funded by the Department of Energy were not allowed to travel to India and were warned not to have any contact with their Indian counterparts at international conferences. John Peoples, the director of Fermilab, the Department of Energy's high-energy particle physics lab outside Chicago, was told to remove the Indian flag from the research institute's display of world flags in front of the main building.[30]

Immediately after the terrorist attacks of September 11, 2001, India offered the use of Indian airspace and air bases, and President Bush soon waived most of the sanctions levied after 1998. Since then, India and the United States have slowly built a much closer relationship, based in part on opposition to Islamic extremism and on shared foreign policy goals as democratic partners. There is a further reason, however, for the increasing coordination between the two sides, though neither the United States nor India has wanted to say it out loud. "Hovering like Banquo's ghost at the banquet for both the United States and India," according to Robert Blackwill, former ambassador to India, "is the rise of Chinese power."[31] President Bush's goal was to maintain good relations with Beijing while relying on the rise of India (as well as continued U.S. cooperation with Japan) to prevent China from dominating Asia. This policy is likely to continue under President Obama. "Our strengthened bilateral relationship with China," said Deputy Secretary of State James Steinberg in April 2009, "must be accompanied by a vigorous commitment to building on the enormous potential for a new era in U.S.-India relations."[32]

While the nuclear deal with India—which allows India access to U.S. nuclear fuel and reactors for the first time in thirty years—is the most public face of the cooperation, it is part of a much broader reworked U.S.-India technology relationship. Early in the Bush administration, the U.S.-India High Technology Cooperation Group was formed to promote high-technology trade. In January 2004, the United States and India agreed to expand cooperation in civilian nuclear activities, civilian space programs, and high-technology trade as part of the Next Steps in Strategic Partnership plan. With the conclusion of the first phase of the plan in September of the same year, the United States removed the Indian Space Research

Organisation from a Department of Commerce watch list, allowing it to import many dual-use items.

Two years later, Indian companies were no longer required to submit an import certification, a guarantee from the Indian government that the imported products would not be diverted to another user or re-exported to another country. At the fifth meeting of the U.S.-India High Technology Cooperation Group in February 2007, the Commerce Department announced that a number of Indian companies dealing in aerospace, semiconductor manufacturing, and information technology would be exempted from American export controls as part of a "trusted customer program." The outcome of all these policy changes is that few U.S. exports to India continue to require licenses. After the 1998 nuclear tests, almost 25 percent of goods exported required a license; now less than 1 percent do.

NEW WORLD/OLD CONTROLS

Although the world of science and technology has changed radically over the last few decades, the extensive American system of controls on exports dates back to the Cold War, when the United States was the dominant power and had a clear adversary in the Soviet Union and few trade connections with the Eastern Bloc. These controls essentially fall into three categories. First, there is a ban on the export of weapons, or "defense articles or services." The State Department, working with the Defense Department, maintains a list of goods and services that cannot be sold to China and other countries as part of the International Traffic in Arms Regulations. Second, there are already extensive export controls on dual-use items in areas such as satellites, nuclear technology, and computers. Maintaining these is essentially the responsibility of the Commerce Department, in consultation with the Defense and State Departments. Finally, the president has the ability to restrict investment in U.S. companies by Chinese military companies or by businesses connected to the Chinese government. The Committee on Foreign Investment in the United States, under the direction of the Treasury Department, reviews the security implications of all investments from abroad, especially in sensitive industries.

Throughout its second term, concerned about the pace of the PLA's military buildup, the Bush administration expanded the controls on the sale of dual-use items to China. At the same time, the administration expressed interest in working with China as a "responsible stakeholder." Despite growing tensions over trade and the valuation of the yuan, President Bush spoke of China as a partner (or potential partner) in rolling back North Korea's and Iran's nuclear programs, in ending the bloodshed in Darfur, and in developing new green technologies to reduce carbon emissions. In addition, exports of high-technology products to China were the one bright spot in the $226 billion bilateral trade deficit. "Our goal is straightforward," said Commerce Undersecretary David McCormick in June 2006. "China's development [should] be both peaceful and prosperous. U.S. export control policies that facilitate legitimate civilian technology trade while discouraging China's military buildup are critical to this objective."[33]

The Bush administration's first move was to tighten the regulations surrounding "deemed exports." A Chinese engineer at Intel or an Indian postdoc at Georgia Tech who works with technology that is controlled for export is "deemed" an export, and the company or university must obtain a license for that worker or student to use the technology in the lab. In 2003 and 2004, the Defense Department and the intelligence community became increasingly worried that spies were taking advantage of a loophole that defined status by current residence or citizenship, not by place of birth. The business community began hearing stories from contacts in the Pentagon of fourteen Chinese who gained Canadian citizenship, crossed the border, and then found work in sensitive technology sectors in the United States.

In April 2004, the Commerce Department's inspector general recommended two changes to address what the department saw as weaknesses in the existing regulations. The first proposed change, regarding wording, was highly bureaucratic. The second proposed change garnered significant public attention and required that deemed export licenses be issued on the basis of country of birth, rather than of current residence or citizenship. Under the proposed guidelines, a scientist born in Shanghai and naturalized in Toronto— no matter whether the scientist had left China at the age of four or forty-four—would be considered Chinese, not Canadian.

The Commerce Department called for public input on the proposed changes, and the public, especially research universities and technology companies, was, to put it mildly, very unhappy. Academia and industry associations submitted more than three hundred negative comments. The Association of American Universities, the National Science Foundation, and other scholarly organizations argued that the new provisions would provide little security and would impose a high cost on the American economy. In an email to the chairs of physics departments around the country, Judy Franz, executive officer of the American Physical Society, called for a letter campaign to protest the new regulations. The ultimate outcome of the change, according to Franz, would be "the number of Chinese and other foreign national students would decrease markedly as their 'second-class' status on campus became apparent, thus ultimately weakening the nation's science and technology workforce; the administrative costs of research would rise markedly; and national security would ultimately be weakened as a consequence of a loss of leadership in economic and technology development."[34] The Commerce Department eventually withdrew the provisions, but it is still considering ways to respond to the alleged dangers of openness.

The Bush administration's next move came in 2006 as it proposed new regulations on dual-use technologies. This initiative, at least in part, was a response to increasing pressure from Congress. In an exchange with Commerce Undersecretary Peter Lichtenbaum, Representative Henry Hyde argued for an expansive view of the threat: "Even minor components such as traveling wave tubes, wiring harnesses and vacuum hoses in Chinese missiles and attack aircraft help increase the reliability of those systems and that there is a moral question presented when such systems are deployed against U.S. forces or those of our allies."[35]

In July 2006, the Commerce Department introduced for public comment a proposal for new controls on approximately forty-seven items from the chemical, computer, telecommunications, electronics, and encryption software industries, among others. The regulations also called for the creation of "validated end-users": that is, Chinese firms could become trusted customers and import without a license through repeated on-site inspection from Commerce officials.

Not surprisingly, the business community reacted negatively to the proposed new regulations. A report commissioned by the American Chamber of Commerce in China found that China already had access to a level of technology "well above those in the proposed rule." Most of the technologies on the proposed list were already in China, made by foreign companies or the Chinese themselves. Controlling the items listed in the new regulations would, according to the study, "have no impact on Chinese military capabilities but will only serve to inhibit legitimate commercial trade."[36] In deference to this report, the final list was narrower and included twenty distinct products from a list of thirty-one technologies, although the ultimate effect of the regulations on the pace of Chinese military modernization will be negligible. Japanese and European officials informed the U.S. government that they had no intention of restricting the sale of the technologies on the list to China.

Overly restrictive regulations can have no impact on security but still damage other national interests, as was the case when Arizona State University (ASU) won a spot at the 2005 Beijing Science and Technology Week. The university had ambitious plans to get a foothold in the world's fastest growing economy, gain access to excellent students and faculty collaborators, and advance its own international reputation. The 2005 Beijing Science and Technology Week looked like the perfect venue to showcase ASU to the people of China. Science and technology weeks occur annually all over China, but the largest and most prestigious event is in Beijing. These weeks, which are like huge science fairs attended by schools and families, are designed to popularize new discoveries and instill an interest in science in Chinese citizens. Before ASU secured its spot, no American university had ever participated in the event. "If we could pull this off, it could have unprecedented public relations value for ASU, exposing thousands of visitors in Beijing and millions of television viewers and newspaper readers throughout the country to images and text about our university," said Jonathan Fink, who at the time was vice president for research and economic affairs.[37]

From the beginning, however, high politics and security concerns almost derailed the plan. An ASU professor, Phil Christensen, had designed the thermal infrared spectrometers used to send data back from the Mars Exploration Rover, and ASU proposed making a full-scale cardboard model of the Mars rover the centerpiece of its exhibit during the week. The Chinese were enthusiastic; the U.S. government much less so. While NASA originally had been guardedly positive about the plan, the State Department worried the exhibit might result in the transfer of sensitive technology, and gave ASU conflicting messages about whether it could go ahead with the project.

Since the PLA is heavily involved in the Chinese space program, there is constant worry in the United States that any cooperation with the Chinese space agency, even on a civilian project, could have military implications; it might lead to more accurate and reliable long-range missiles. In this instance, however, the Chinese probably had already gained access to more technical data about the rover on NASA's website than they could have discerned from close inspection of a cardboard model.

ASU hired a Washington lawyer to try to make sense of the International Traffic in Arms Regulations, the provisions that control the export of defense-related technologies. With no clear direction from the U.S. government, the opening date fast approaching, and the Chinese organizers assuming that the exhibit would center on the Mars rover, ASU came up with a new plan: replace the full-size cardboard model with a toy plastic model one-tenth the size of the actual robot. The children's model was then anchored to an eight-foot-diameter Mars globe. No one who has bought a toy over the past decade will be surprised to learn that the smaller model was made in China.

Stories like this one are unfortunately all too common with the current U.S. export control policy. In the new world of science and technology, export controls have remained the product of the old world, which no longer exists. The same is true of the incentives for the government officials charged with enforcing them. Officials are rarely rewarded for creatively interpreting and enforcing export regulations, and no one wants to be called by an angry senator to testify about why a router ended up in the hands of the PLA. It is hard to lose your job by stressing security over innovation concerns; doing the opposite is far riskier.

In January 2010, the Obama administration announced its intention to revise the restrictions on some dual-use technologies. "We have too many controls on items readily available around the world," Commerce Secretary Gary Locke told a group of business leaders in Washington.[38] In an environment where innovation is rushing to become global and collaborative, getting these policies wrong is immeasurably costly. Misguided and badly designed policies affect not only American foreign and security policy, but also the United States' ability to innovate at home. The next four chapters guide policy makers and business leaders through this new world where trade, security, and innovation are more tightly interconnected than ever before—a world where, in effect, they have to navigate the software and hardware, high and low politics, and local and global innovation.

Chapter Six

AN OPEN WORLD:
ITS RISKS AND BENEFITS

Chinese businessmen buy a small chip design company in San Jose and then ship technology back to Shenzhen. A large Chinese telecom company with ties to a research lab that does work for the People's Liberation Army (PLA) wants to set up a marketing and distribution office in Silicon Valley. Chinese and Indian graduate students get hired by an advanced aerospace research lab at the University of Michigan, master new equipment, attend conferences around the country, and eventually return home to work. A U.S. technology company sells a supercomputer to a research lab in Bangalore that has connections to the Indian space and missile programs.

There are two ways of looking at each of these hypothetical but entirely possible scenarios. While receptiveness to new ideas and peoples is a fundamental strength of the United States, essential to its dynamism and its economic and national security, it is also a potential source of vulnerability for American economic and security interests.

After September 11, 2001, the United States naturally sought to build higher walls. Higher walls, however, have their own, often unintended, liabilities. As security expert Bruce Schneier argues, "There's no such thing as absolute security, and any security you get has some cost: in money, in convenience, in capabilities, in insecurities somewhere else, whatever. Every time someone makes a decision about security—computer security, community security, national security—he makes a trade-off."[1]

Of course, all policy making is the art of the trade-off, where one chooses among various imperfect courses of action according to their likely effectiveness given limited time, attention, and resources. The decision-making process for technology control is a particularly difficult art to master given the globalization of science and technology: more dual-use technology is in the commercial sector, more of it is developed outside of the United States, and it spreads around the world more quickly than ever before. Decisions have to be made earlier in the technology development process, with less information and few resources at hand to shape outcomes.

Still, for the United States, the hazard of getting the balance between openness and security wrong is dire, but not only in the obvious sense. Critical technologies must not end up in the wrong hands, and labs and companies must be protected against spying. The cure, however, should not be worse than the disease. In pursuit of the illusory security that comes from a further tightening of export controls, we shouldn't damage our own competitiveness. Defending old technology is rarely as important as creating the new, and ideas and people from outside are an important catalyst, speeding America's competitive metabolism. For the United States, the basic equation is simple: economic strength and national security depend on innovation, innovation thrives only with openness, thus policies must defend and nurture openness.

The default policy should be openness, but it is not enough to repeatedly proclaim a commitment to engaging the world. Rhetorical promises of openness must be translated into concrete policy decisions, especially in relation to foreign investment in the United States and to immigration access for scientists and entrepreneurs.

OUTWARD INVESTMENT: INDIA AND CHINA

Politicians and government officials often see the threats inherent in openness more clearly than the benefits. The costs are concrete—country X has bought technology Y that is now operating in factory Z. But the benefits are diffuse, often spread throughout an economy and hard to measure. In addition, the motivations and objectives of the buyers are sometimes opaque, especially in the case of China where the boundaries between market and state are porous. Is a company being acquired for economic reasons or is there something else going on?

Take the issue of foreign investment in the United States, where, despite its largest current account deficit ever and continued dependence on foreign capital, there is skepticism about money coming from abroad, especially from the Gulf States and China. As much as the United States needs foreign money, investment is greeted with distrust. Foreign investment used to chiefly mean investment by rich countries in other rich countries, or by rich countries in the developing world. Even today more than 90 percent of investment in Japan, Europe, Canada, and the United States comes from other developed countries. Still, the world has reached an inflection point, a change in degree and kind: the emerging economies are amassing capital at a record rate, and money from Asia and the Middle East is key to the future of globalization. With each year, China invests more capital around the world. More than ten thousand Chinese companies have invested in 173 countries and regions, according to the Chinese Ministry of Commerce. Outward investment was $55.9 billion in 2008, and in a survey of 100 Chinese executives conducted by the ministry, 70 said they were planning to invest overseas. All of this is a dramatic change from the past three decades, when the Chinese government capped outward investment for the entire economy at $5 billion per year.[2]

So far, the growing hunger of the Chinese economy for energy and raw materials has been the primary driver behind outward investment, and so Chinese companies have focused on acquisitions in Southeast Asia, Latin America, Australia, and Africa. The largest purchases in the last few years have included Sinopec's $7.3 billion deal for Swiss Addax Petroleum, and Yanzhou Coal Mining's $2.9 billion bid for Australian Felix Resources. Now, however, Chinese companies are turning their attention to technology and acquisitions in Japan, Korea, Europe, and the United States. In the first quarter of 2009, Chinese companies spent $13 billion in Europe. Buying technologies abroad is a cheaper and perhaps quicker strategy to boost the competitiveness of Chinese firms, an alternative to spending millions of dollars and dozens of years building technological capacities at home and still facing potential failure. The Chinese are very aware that it took Samsung and LG several decades and hundreds of millions of dollars to build recognized and trusted brand names.

This desire to leapfrog to the next stage was behind Lenovo's high-profile purchase of IBM's personal computer business in 2005. At the time of the purchase, Lenovo was a major player in China, with close to a 30 percent stake in the domestic market, but it was less successful in foreign markets. In addition, intense competition from HP and Dell and a price war in the PC market was squeezing Lenovo's profitability at home, making foreign markets vitally important to the company's future health. Its chief financial officer, Mary Ma, told the *Economist*, "If we just focus on China, we cannot generate returns for our shareholders."[3]

In the years before approaching IBM, Lenovo had set a goal of increasing exports to 25 to 30 percent of sales by 2006. The company's lack of name recognition outside China made expanding its share slow and difficult; exports as percentage of sales hovered around 7 percent. The $1.75 billion deal with IBM was an attempt to overcome this shortfall in one fell swoop, bringing Lenovo a brand licensing agreement, the globally recognized trademark of the ThinkPad laptop, IBM support worldwide for five years, and access to IBM's distribution and customer networks.

It is not clear if the deal has worked out the way Lenovo intended. The merger, at first, did not go smoothly. Mergers and acquisitions are frequently difficult to manage, even for the most experienced multinational companies, and some big customers were worried about Lenovo's ability to maintain an IBM-like level of quality. Lenovo struggled to cut costs and saw its global market share shrink, but sales started to rebound in 2007. The bigger problem is that Lenovo may have bet its future on the wrong product: PCs are a shrinking market owing to the advent of netbooks and the mobile Internet. In May 2009, Lenovo announced a record loss of $226 million.

If the Lenovo-IBM deal was China's coming-out party, India's bash took place with Tata Steel's $11.3 billion acquisition of British-Dutch steel producer Corus in February 2007 and, two weeks later, with the Aditya Birla group's takeover of the U.S. aluminum products manufacturer Novelis for approximately $6 billion. Ratan Tata, chairman of the Tata group, told the *Financial Times* that Tata Steel was forced to pay "very close" to its top price for Corus: "We all felt that to lose would go beyond the group and it would be an issue of great disappointment in the country."[4] With these deals, India's sense of national pride in its global reach peaked: "For India, this deal is not about size—it's the first step towards what we call the Global Indian Takeover," wrote the *Economic Times*, India's best-selling business paper.[5]

While this is boosterism, it is also—as with China—about fundamental economic change. According to the United Nations Conference on Trade and Development, the average annual investment by Indian companies in foreign firms from 1990 to 2000 was a mere $110 million. In 2005, the amount of outward direct investment exploded, totaling $2.97 billion. In 2008, the number topped $17.68 billion, though it slipped in 2009 as Indian firms became slightly more cautious during the global economic crisis.[6]

Natural resources have, so far, made up a smaller share of foreign acquisitions for India than for China, and the majority of acquisitions have occurred in North America and Europe. Indian companies have largely pursued brands and market access as well as specialized technological knowledge. All of the fifteen largest Indian software and related service companies have invested abroad: Wipro acquired the U.S.-based Infocrossing, an outsourcing company, for $600 million in August 2007; Reliance Communications bought a 90 percent stake in U.K.-based eWave World, a telecom operator, in April 2008; and Infosys Technologies announced in August 2008 that it would take over Axon Group, a business software consulting company based in London.

Because they are primarily privately owned companies, the internationalization of Indian firms has not raised the same political concerns as have China's forays abroad. Still, economically, there is no reason not to welcome Chinese money. In fact, there are strong economic rationales for the United States not only to adopt a relatively *laissez-faire* attitude toward foreign investment, but also to do even more to attract money from abroad. Americans do not like to be reminded of the fact that as the world's largest debtor, the United States needs money from abroad. By 2008, the current account deficit was approximately $670 billion, which meant the United States needed to attract $2 billion each day in foreign investment to pay back its creditors. The deficit dropped in 2009 to $380 billion, mainly because of the recession and a sharp cut in spending by American households, but it has trended upward ever since, partly under the weight of a massively expanding federal budget. Until the current account deficit shrinks, the United States will rely on foreign investors purchasing government securities.

Most Americans will not feel or see this investment in bonds and debt, but they are much more likely to be affected by foreign companies investing in American ones. Foreign companies in the United States employ 5.1 million workers and pay higher salaries than domestic firms—30 percent higher on average, according to a study conducted by David Marchick and Matthew Slaughter.[7] That benefits the thousands of Americans now working for Honda in Ohio, Alabama, and North Carolina, and the close to four hundred people working in Lenovo's R&D center in North Carolina.

Foreign companies operating in the United States also have a positive impact on productivity through investment in research and development and physical capital. In 2005, foreign companies spent $31.7 billion on research and development, accounting for almost 15 percent of the amount spent by all companies in the United States.[8] And foreign firms often bring "best practices" in management, production, and marketing, forcing U.S. companies to adapt and adopt in order to remain competitive.

Some of the uneasiness about Chinese money has been tied to one company in particular: Huawei. The telecom giant's founder, Ren Zhengfei, was an engineer in the Chinese military, and the company's relationship with the PLA has been a source of concern for the U.S. and other governments, even raising eyebrows in India. In 2005, Huawei proposed pumping an additional $60 million into its India division in Bangalore. Indian intelligence recommended rejecting the bid, citing Huawei's alleged links to the PLA and to Pakistan. "We do not possess the capability or the technical expertise for building an adequate safeguard to address the security concerns in the sensitive area of telecommunications," reported a senior intelligence official.[9] Nine times, between 2003 and 2006, the Indian government rejected the company's applications for the trading license needed to sell directly to the domestic market.

In the United States, security issues derailed Huawei's joint bid with Bain Capital for 3Com, which develops computer networks for businesses. Although Huawei was the minority partner, with a stake of less than 20 percent and no operational or decision-making power, the deal coincided with rising suspicion about China. Of particular concern was TippingPoint, a subsidiary of 3Com that produces software the Pentagon and other government agencies use to detect Internet intrusions. Given the number of high-profile attacks on government computers by Chinese hackers (including, in June 2007, a successful breach of a Pentagon network), network security was a sensitive topic. Huawei and 3Com offered to spin off TippingPoint, but several congressional leaders—including Ileana Ros-Lehtinen, the ranking member of the House Foreign Affairs Committee at the time—opposed the deal as a threat to national security. After further efforts to address the security concerns failed, Huawei and Bain withdrew their application from the Committee on Foreign Investment in the United States, the intra-agency panel that reviews the national security implications of foreign investment.

While Huawei is an extreme case—a firm with links to the PLA seeking to acquire a company that supplies security software to the Pentagon—even less sensitive purchases by Chinese firms provoke scrutiny because of the continued role of the state in the Chinese economy. Where state authority ends and market forces begin is a gray area inside of China, and to outsiders it is nearly inscrutable.

The popular view of this relationship—that is, the government and state-owned enterprises move in lockstep, a relationship sometimes described as "China Inc."—is not quite accurate. The government does help companies looking overseas for investment opportunities, but it neither effectively synchronizes strategies among the many Chinese companies abroad nor does a particularly good job of coordinating among the companies and the numerous ministries that regulate them. The fact that a Chinese diplomat in Zambia, for example, has no direct authority over a state-owned enterprise from

Hunan Province operating in Zambia's capital makes a coherent political strategy impossible.

The true sticking point for the United States and other nations is transparency, or lack thereof. That there is a relationship between the government and Chinese companies is obvious but how that relationship plays out economically and politically is murky at best. Any company in China big enough to go abroad is likely to be owned in part by the state or, at least, to receive subsidized credit from state banks. The China Development Bank provided Huawei a credit line of $10 billion to support its international expansion, and technology companies are also given the opportunity to participate in Chinese foreign aid programs. ZTE, a telecom company headquartered in Shenzhen, has been involved in several infrastructure projects in Angola and Mauritania. The lack of transparency means that outside observers have no way of judging what interests are being pursued. Are the transactions driven by economic motives or by strategic interests? Is Beijing using a company to pursue power, profit, or some combination of both? One can only guess.

The fusion of capitalist means and state power—what some call "state capitalism"—is visible in state-owned enterprises, and companies like Huawei that skirt the line between private and public, but it is perhaps most clearly evident in sovereign wealth funds, investment funds managed by the government. While these funds are not new—the Kuwait Investment Authority dates back to 1953—they are growing rapidly. At the end of 2009, they were valued at $3.8 trillion, and a study by the bank Standard Chartered predicts that sovereign wealth funds could hold $13.4 trillion by 2020.[10] At issue, again, are the funds' transparency—do outside observers know how decisions are made?—and the degree to which the investment process is strategic—do funds buy companies that may give them access to restricted technology or leverage over the American economy?

China's sovereign wealth fund, the China Investment Corporation (CIC), scores badly on both fronts, with low transparency and a questionable approach to investment. CIC is valued at $200 billion, and some estimate that it could grow to $600 billion.[11] The president of CIC, Gao Xiqing, has repeatedly claimed that the fund "operates on commercial principles," but there have also been calls within China for CIC to acquire "industrial and strategic resources."[12] In a clear example of the use of financial tools to achieve political goals, another Chinese agency, the State Administration of Foreign Exchange, purchased $300 million in U.S. dollar–denominated bonds from Costa Rica as part of a deal under which Costa Rica cut diplomatic ties with Taiwan (after sixty-three years).

Still, Chinese investment should not be seen as a major threat. While the $200 billion set aside for CIC is a lot of money, it is small compared with the amount held by other funds or the trillions held in other, mainly private, financial assets. In addition, a large percentage of CIC funds are focused on domestic investment. Close to $130 billion has been used to shore up the state banks, leaving approximately $70 billion for foreign acquisitions. So the immediate impact of CIC and other sovereign wealth funds is more likely to be political than economic, a weapon in the battle of ideas.

All of these instruments of state capitalism create diplomatic and ideological challenges for Washington. An economically vibrant China presents the developing world with an alternative to Anglo-Saxon capitalism. China's rebounding from the financial crisis of 2008–2009 more quickly than the United States reinforces the sense that the state is now a more powerful engine of economic growth than the market.

Although this ideological battle has been much discussed, China offers other states few practical lessons, and the lesson of the model may be only that China has successfully managed one-party, authoritarian rule and rapid economic development.[13] Moreover, the model's attraction is highly dependent on China's fate over the next decade. A serious economic downturn plus social and political dislocation could easily tarnish state capitalism.

In any case, an effective response to state capitalism requires reform of the American economy and a greater engagement with the developing world; it does not require investment protectionism or restricting foreign capital in the United States. The tools are already in place for deciding whether a proposed foreign investment in the United States threatens national security. If U.S. policy makers fear that other countries will find China a more attractive development model, they need to demonstrate more clearly the benefits of liberal democracy. Also, the United States needs to engage Africa, Latin America, and Southeast Asia in terms that interest them: a change in emphasis, a willingness to listen to local concerns, and an offer of more economic development and assistance, with less military support.

The challenge for the United States is to manage others' perceptions of it—both abroad and at home. Early in 2006, DP World's offer to take over port operations in six U.S. cities provoked a firestorm of protest from politicians because it involved money from an Arab state to manage critical U.S. infrastructure, in a world still wary after the attacks of September 11. Soon after this offer collapsed later in the year, over twenty bills were introduced in Congress, including several that would have restricted foreign investment in significant parts of the American economy. Eventually the protest cooled, and the new legislation was not so drastic: a bill that reformed the review process for foreign investment and required heightened scrutiny of investments by state-owned entities, including sovereign wealth funds. As a result of the new legislation, more deals are being submitted to the Committee on Foreign Investment in the United States, and more face a second stage of investigations. This may have had an effect on foreign investment—it is hard to know about decisions not to pursue deals that are not publicized, but no deals have been blocked as of July 2010.

Still, foreign investors have noted America's change in attitude. Responding to the growing political opposition to China's investments in the United States, CIC's Gao Xiqing said, "Fortunately there are more than 200 countries in the world. And fortunately there are many countries who are happy with us."[14] Even managers of sovereign wealth funds with long histories of investing in Europe and the United States, like the Kuwait Investment Authority, have spoken of the hostile reception they have received and of the possibility that they will seek investment opportunities elsewhere.

In May 2007, President Bush issued a Statement on Open Economies, directed at audiences both at home and abroad: "The United States unequivocally supports international investment in this country and is equally committed to securing fair, equitable, and nondiscriminatory treatment for U.S. investors abroad. . . . My Administration is committed to ensuring that the United States continues to be the most attractive place in the world to invest."[15] In the week before the April 2009 G-20 Summit in London, President Obama wrote an op-ed, published in many international newspapers, promising that the United States would "embrace a collective commitment to encourage open trade and investment, while resisting the protectionism that would deepen this crisis." [16]

At the same time, the United States can work with its trading partners to avoid further politicization of foreign investment. While all states have the right to block some investment that might threaten national security, there are no widely accepted criteria defining which industries are critical to national security. National airlines were once thought critical to security, but today few would argue that foreign investments which help bail out American or Delta are a threat to the American way of life. Telecommunications also are closely related to security, but should foreign investors be kept completely out, or should they be restricted to minority ownership? Can they invest in software but not in hardware?

The international lawyers Alan Larson and David Marchick suggest that the United States should work first with its allies Japan and the Europeans to develop shared norms for national security restrictions.[17] This would not be a binding regulation, but rather an effort to develop common definitions and principles. The development effort would then be expanded to include China, India, and Russia.

Similarly, in October 2008, an International Monetary Fund working group released a code of conduct for sovereign wealth funds—the "Santiago Principles." These voluntary principles strive for greater transparency and for assurances that investment decisions are made on the basis of risk and return, not of political objectives; they call for greater disclosures about the funds' governance structures and operational management so as to assuage concerns about state control. Some like Temasek, Singapore's sovereign wealth fund, already publicly release detailed information. This ongoing process will require sovereign wealth funds to abide by the principles, and the countries receiving sovereign wealth fund investment to strengthen their own investment standards.

In addition, there need to be frank discussions with America's trading partners. The United States, Japan, and the European Union, for example, are entitled to ask Beijing for greater openness in the Chinese market if Chinese firms want to invest and acquire companies abroad. This not only makes sense economically, but also would both promote the goal of transparency—Beijing would have to provide a rationale for any restriction on investment—and limit Chinese government authority in the economy.

SECURITY AND SCIENCE: LIVING BY PARANOIA

If trade and defense specialists often speak past each other when they discuss the costs of an open economy, then scientists and defense analysts are engaged in a dialogue of the deaf. As Admiral B. R. Innman, former deputy director of the CIA, put it, there is a conflict between the "scientist's desire for unconstrained research and publication on the one hand, and the federal government's need to protect certain information from potential foreign adversaries who might use that information against this nation. Both are powerful forces."[18]

This is not a new problem. From the beginnings of the Cold War, there was a tension between security through obscurity—that is, trying to keep secrets out of the view of the Soviets—and security through transparency—trying to outpace the Soviets through exchange and innovation. In 1950, the National Academy of Sciences warned the State Department that excessive restrictions created a "furtive atmosphere" that hampered the spread of information and the progress of science. And for the next four decades, American scientists would periodically criticize the seemingly random and apparently ineffective restrictions placed on their visitors from the Eastern Bloc.

In the mid-1980s, the academic and the security communities reached a strained agreement on the balance between openness and control. The growing Soviet threat created real alarm in the early years of the Reagan administration, and a number of senior officials called for more restrictive controls on academic research. According to William Casey, director of the Central Intelligence Agency from 1981 to 1987, "The Soviets got virtually a free ride on all of our research and development."[19] In several public forums, Defense Department officials reported that the Soviets had acquired both the technology to develop a superior antitank missile and high-speed computers used for designing advanced weapons systems.[20]

At the same time, there was more of a sense that the Soviet Union, owing to its secretiveness and tight control of information, was falling behind the West in science and technology. George A. Keyworth

II, a physicist and science adviser to President Reagan, commented at the time, "The last thing we want to do is ape the repressive Soviet model which stifles technological innovation through its obsession with secrecy."[21]

In 1985, after several years of back and forth, the (qualified) primacy of openness was enshrined in National Security Decision Directive (NSDD) 189, a document that declared the Reagan administration's policy toward academic research: "to the maximum extent possible, the products of fundamental research [shall] remain unrestricted." Although NSDD 189 remains in effect today, the terrorist attacks of September 11 again raised the question of the right balance between openness and security. The George W. Bush administration, concerned that terrorists could gain access to any research that might help them build a chemical or biological weapon, sought tighter controls on universities. Significant amounts of work have been classified as "Sensitive But Unclassified," a less restrictive classification that, though theoretically in the spirit of NSDD 189, has, in fact, dampened research and collaboration.

There was also a scramble after September 11 to tighten visa regulations, with the predictable result that many foreign scientists and engineers whose fields of study appeared on the government's classified Technology Alert List either could not get permission to visit the United States or were unable to get back in after short visits home. Foreign enrollment at American colleges and universities dropped significantly, although it rebounded in 2007 and 2008. Applications from China to U.S. graduate schools fell 53 percent from 2002 to 2004, and applications from India declined 32 percent after decades of growth. One-third of American companies reported long delays in securing visas for skilled employees.

In 2006, only weeks before President Bush's first visit to India, the U.S. consulate in Chennai denied a visa to Goverdhan Mehta, a former president of the Indian Institute for Science; he had visited the United States many times in the past and held visiting positions at American universities. Embassy officials reportedly told Mehta that his work had a potential link to chemical warfare. Mehta was, at the time of his rejection, the president of the International Council for Science, an international organization whose mission is facilitating interaction among scientists from all countries. The Indian public and press were not amused by the irony. To its credit, the State Department has tried to improve visa processing for international students and scholars. In 2003, it took seventy-five days to complete a check on an applicant; by 2004, the time had fallen to fifteen days. Unfortunately, there was another significant breakdown in 2008 and 2009 when science and engineering researchers seeking to obtain or renew visas had to wait for months. This systemic problem has greatly damaged America's reputation.

Along with the attacks of September 11, the rise of China has provided a continuing rationale for the United States to slow the movement of science and technology. Beginning in 2003, the Bush administration began introducing new controls on the sale of dual-use technologies to China and revising and tightening the restrictions on foreign scientists and graduate students who study and work in the United States.

The high number of dual-use technologies already available on the global market suggests that the new controls on dual-use technologies are largely symbolic—a point government officials did not try very hard to deny when speaking with me. Admitting that much of the technology the regulations are designed to control is already widely available in China, one senior Commerce Department official told me, "While availability is an important factor, it is not the determining factor. We are also sending a signal to the Europeans, Japanese, and Chinese about what types of technology concern us. And it is clearly in the national interest not to have a Chinese weapon system enabled by U.S. technology directed at the U.S. military."

Signal sending does not make for good policy. The goal of good policy should be to prevent the diffusion of critical technologies to the PLA without harming the competitiveness of American technology companies. It is fairly clear that the current system of export controls fails on both measures in some critical technology sectors, including space. In 1999, American companies held 83 percent of the commercial satellite market; in 2005, the share had fallen to 63 percent; and in 2006, U.S. manufacturers accounted for 40 percent of sales. The controls currently in place fail to differentiate between critical technologies and widely available components like wires and bolts. European companies such as Thales Alenia Space now advertise their satellites as being free of U.S. components in order to be free of American export restrictions.

Perhaps worst of all, the controls have not significantly impacted foreign countries' capabilities. As a task force at the Center for Strategic and International Studies concluded, "Export control policy has not prevented the rise of foreign space capabilities and in some cases has encouraged it."[22] China's space program certainly has not slowed. In 1999, China launched its first unmanned space ship, the *Shenzhou*. In 2000, the Beidou navigation system began to operate, and China launched a high-resolution satellite. In 2003, the *Shenzhou V*, China's first manned mission, rocketed into space. In 2007, China destroyed one of its own satellites in a test of an antisatellite system and launched a lunar probe. In 2008, the first *taikonaut*, the Chinese term for "astronaut," took a space walk.

U.S. policy makers need to readjust their expectations. Export controls are unlikely to slow Chinese weapons development and at best can be a secondary policy. "Dual-use" is too broad a category; export controls will always overreach if they are geared to technologies from the commercial sector. Instead, the United States needs to concentrate on the biggest dangers and figure out what it can realistically control—technologies that are developed in government labs and classified as top secret. Or as one security expert put it to me, "We have to learn to live with what's out there, and then decide what we are really going to go after." This has typically been a small list of highly specialized technologies, such as stealth and nuclear weapons.

Everything else should move relatively freely. Although free movement has drawbacks, the creation of new technology is more vital than the protection of old: if American companies are to remain at the cutting edge of science and technology, they need to be actively present in foreign markets, especially China. During the Cold War, critical technologies came almost entirely from research sponsored by the Pentagon. The Pentagon, for example, funded almost 50 percent of the research and development in semiconductors from the 1950s until the 1970s. Today most technologies used by the Pentagon are drawn from the commercial sector. According to a 1999 Defense Science Board Task Force on Globalization and Security, the Defense Department relies "increasingly on the U.S. commercial advanced technology sector to push the technological envelope and enable the [d]epartment to 'run faster' than its competitors."[23]

American companies cannot continue to push that envelope unless they are in Asian markets, close to Asian customers. As one Corning manager told me, "We always follow our customers, and our customers are increasingly migrating to Asia." Only by being deeply embedded in emerging technology markets in Asia can American companies influence the future of technology development.

Being closely connected with technology development in Asia is the only safeguard for U.S. policy makers and business leaders against unwelcome surprises. With American companies, universities, and venture capitalists involved there, intelligence agencies should gain a sense of what is happening inside China: what technologies are being developed, what the Chinese have purchased from abroad, how the technologies are being used, and what weaknesses might be exploited. Of course, information will not gather and analyze itself; this will require greater coordination and communication among industry, academia, and the intelligence community as well as some changes in the intelligence community itself.

The CIA and other agencies are ill prepared to analyze science and technology, according to Lily Johnston, a CIA analyst who tracks biotechnology issues. Few analysts speak the language of science and technology or understand its culture. Even officers with a scientific background have difficulty keeping up with the most recent breakthroughs in their fields; they spend most of their days at Langley, not in a lab. Johnston says there must be new channels of information, and suggests that small teams of science and technology experts be created to move back and forth between the intelligence agencies and the outside world.[24]

The same overarching policy objectives should guide the supervision of foreign scientists and graduate students: keep important technology out of the hands of the wrong people, but avoid damaging the open system of science. As Charles Vest, a former president of MIT, says, "[The] openness of our national borders and especially of our campuses to talented men and women from other lands is a major factor in our academic excellence, our cultural richness, our economic success, and, in a strategic sense, our national security."[25]

For the last fifty years, the Indians, Koreans, Chinese, and Taiwanese who have returned home after studying and teaching in American research universities have widely extended the influence of the United States. Kishore Mahbubani, a former diplomat and now dean of the Lee Kuan Yew School of Public Policy at the National University of Singapore, writes,

> One of the big reasons all of Asia should send a big "Thank You" note to America when the modernization of Asia is complete is because U.S. universities have done more to train and educate

Asian elites than any other society. . . . When these students went home, they did not just bring with them specific technical skills learned in American universities, they also brought with them the entire American ethos: the optimistic view of life and the belief that great societies could be created through human intervention.[26]

The American influence has been particularly strong in some of Asia's most prestigious institutions. At Seoul National University, a little more than half of the professors with doctorates received their training in the United States; at the Advanced Institute of Science and Technology, in Daejeon, 84 percent of science professors received their doctorates in the United States, and almost 75 percent of engineering faculty trained in the United States.[27]

An attempt to keep all sensitive technology out of dangerous hands is both too expansive and, as I have said, hazardous to innovation within the United States. In a public hearing in 2006, counterintelligence officers claimed that over the last few years, there were twenty-five arrests of foreign individuals who gained access to sensitive technology, and implied that it was clearly necessary to tighten controls on scientists from China or other countries in academic settings.[28] Nonetheless, to put these numbers in a larger context, let's say that the actual number of people involved in espionage is three or four times the number of arrests. That would be about 100 people out of the more than 140,000 foreign students enrolled in science and engineering disciplines at American universities, which seems like a relatively unimportant threat, especially considering the rewards America reaps from openness.

With American political and diplomatic influence in decline in many areas around the world, science remains a bright spot. The United States derives real soft power from the widespread view of it as a scientifically innovative and dynamic society, demonstrated by a *New York Times* article on the unexpected popularity of physics lectures uploaded to the web. Students who see Professor Walter H. G. Lewin's videotaped physics lectures, provided free online as part of MIT's OpenCourseWare, write to tell him of their love of physics or their new knowledge, and include the United States in the glow. A seventeen-year-old from China writes, "I love your inspiring lectures and I love MIT!!!" "You are now my Scientific Father," writes a physics teacher from Iraq. "In spite of the bad occupation and war against my lovely IRAQ, you made me love USA because you are there and MIT is there."[29] (Lewin was born in The Netherlands and came to the United States in 1966.)

In light of the value of scientific transparency both as a condition of innovation and as a tool of diplomacy, erecting new barriers against research by foreign-born students is a terrible idea, particularly when it categorizes entire fields as a risk. Resources should be dedicated to reviewing students on a case-by-case basis, and zeroing in on individuals who trigger significant attention, because of previous areas of residence and past or present occupations.

IMMIGRANT ENTREPRENEURS

The influx of new people has been critical to maintaining the competitiveness and creativity of the American economy. This is true at the micro level—prominent examples of immigrant high-technology entrepreneurs include Andy Grove of Intel, Sergey Brin of Google, and Pierre Omidyar of eBay—and at the macro level—a 2007 Duke study discovered that one-fourth of the technology companies started in the United States from 1995 to 2005 had at least one foreign-born founder. Companies founded by immigrants produced $52 billion in sales and employed 450,000 workers in 2006.[30]

Despite the benefits these entrepreneurs have brought to the American innovation system, foreign students are being educated here and, once they have completed their studies, are being forced to return home, where they may then start companies that eventually will compete with American ones. "The U.S. has succeeded because the right people have come from all over the world to be here," says Bill Gates. If the United States does not find a way to let them stay, the country "is taking our greatest asset and throwing it away with both hands."[31]

To address the apparent talent shortage in the United States, Bill Gates, Craig Barrett, and other technology leaders have called for an increase in the number of H-1B visas issued. They claim that the shortage of H-1B visas, and of Americans going into science and engineering, makes it likely that their companies will have to locate R&D work abroad. H-1B is a temporary visa given to specialty workers for three years, with the possibility of one renewal. After reaching a high of 195,000 a year in 2003, the number of H-1B visas granted has dropped to 65,000 a year, and congressional efforts to raise the cap have failed. The visas are distributed through a lottery, but the demand is so great that there are not nearly enough available. In 2008, the application process was closed down after a day when 150,000 applications were received.

The number of applications dropped in 2009 during the economic crisis, but the issue of H-1B visas has been as contentious as the debate over the mainly low-skilled, eleven million undocumented workers. Critics of the program argue that these visas are used to bring low-wage workers into the United States and so end up depressing the wages of American technology workers. Workers on H-1B visas are supposed to be paid the prevailing wage, but research by Ron Hira, a professor at Rochester Institute of Technology, shows that the median wage in 2005 for new H-1B computing professionals was just $50,000, less than the wage for an entry-level worker with a bachelor's degree and no experience.[32] Numbers from the Bureau of Labor Statistics reinforce Hira's research: the wages of 85 percent of computer programmers on an H-1B visa were below the median.[33]

In addition, while American companies claim that they need more H-1B visas to fill shortages (because they cannot find Americans with the specialized skills they need), in 2008 four of the top five companies receiving H-1B visas were not American, but the Indian outsourcers Infosys, Wipro, Satyam, and Tata Consultancy Services bringing workers into the United States.[34]

On the other side of the debate, a report by the National Foundation for American Policy, a pro-immigration think tank, found a positive correlation between companies that applied for H-1B visas and new jobs. According to the study, companies increased their employment by five workers for every H-1B visa application. Microsoft claims that it adds "on average four additional employees to support them [H-1B hires] in various capacities."[35] Neither the report nor the software giant, however, specify the skill or pay level of these new support jobs; both are probably lower.

The decrease in the number of visas issued through the H-1B program is a bit of a red herring though, since the United States continues to attract large numbers of talented people and will do so for the immediate future. The real issue is how can U.S. policy target the most productive and talented immigrants and make sure they can stay in the United States if they want to stay?

Gary Becker, winner of the 1992 Nobel Prize in economics, sidesteps the debate over the potential misuse of the visas and proposes gradual phasing out of the H-1B program in favor of permanent admissions for skilled immigrants. Permanent admission, as Becker notes, is better for both the workers and the United States. H-1B visa holders are tied to their employers and forced to accept lower wages or lose their sponsor in the visa lottery. They cannot start a new business, and their spouses cannot work or apply for a Social Security number. Everything about their lives reeks of the temporary. With permanent admission, skilled professionals would "be more concerned with advancing in the American economy rather than with the skills and knowledge they could bring back to India, China, or wherever else they came from," says Becker.[36] It would also allow the United States to compete with Britain, Australia, and Canada, all of which have a point system that gives higher scores to skilled immigrants with advanced education.

Changes need to occur at two steps in the process: when foreign students apply for admission to the United States and when they graduate. The Immigration and Nationality Act of 1952 requires students and scholars to show American consular officers evidence of intent to return home. If the officer does not believe the applicant is going to return home, then the officer must deny the visa. Students in Beijing in the 1990s used to swap (what they thought were) successful strategies to show an intent to return to China: espousing a deep-rooted desire to study bioengineering in order to design limbs for amputees was said to be particularly effective in swaying cold-hearted visa officers. Soon the embassy was besieged with students dedicated to helping China's disabled. The goal of U.S. policy should be to attract the best science and technology talent, so the continued testing of the intent to return home makes no sense. As the National Academies suggests, the focus should be on what the students are studying and whether they have the financial means to complete the course of study.[37]

Once these students finish, those with graduate degrees in science and engineering should be granted work permits and residency status after a background and security check. The chance to become an American citizen would act as a powerful lure for many highly skilled, highly motivated scientists. Today, more than one million "skilled immigrant workers," a category that includes scientists, engineers, and researchers, are competing for 120,000 permanent U.S. resident visas each year, according to a study conducted by the

Kauffman Foundation.[38] The wait to become a U.S. resident can stretch for six years, and for many potential immigrants, especially those from China and India, the economic opportunities at home make living in limbo even less attractive.

A number of venture capitalists and technology experts—Paul Graham, Brad Feld, Eric Ries, and Dave McClure—have suggested a more dramatic reform of immigration policy: the creating of a "founders" or "start-up" visa. While the specifics of the plans vary, the overall idea is the same. If an entrepreneur wants to start a company in the United States, and can attract funding, say, $150,000 from a U.S.-based venture capital or angel fund (a fund composed of wealthy individuals who invest an average of $200,000 during the second round of financing in exchange for some ownership), then he or she is given a permanent resident visa. Graham suggests that ten thousand of these visas could be offered a year. America harnesses the creative and disruptive energy of the new arrivals, and the start-ups create new jobs, first a handful and then, hopefully, larger numbers of local workers.[39]

American unease with foreign investment and immigrant scientists and entrepreneurs ranges from the specific—a focus on Huawei or "sleeper cells" of Chinese nationals embedded within defense contractors—to the more philosophical—debates over the proper role of the state in the market and the investment strategies of sovereign wealth funds. While this disquiet points to some serious policy questions, U.S. officials must always be aware of how their actions can rebound and affect the workings of the American innovation system. They must be prepared to be uncomfortable, to see more technology slipping out of their hands and to have more people floating around university labs than they would like. But since the most effective means to boost U.S. security is to promote the innovativeness of the economy, the primary goal must be attracting capital, ideas, and talent. And, in turn, openness must be a two-way street. U.S. policy makers must ensure that foreign markets are similarly open to American companies and entrepreneurs.

Chapter Seven

ATOMS AND SMART GRIDS: SEEING ASIA AND OURSELVES

If we are to think clearly about U.S. policy and business strategy with respect to China, Japan, South Korea, or India, we need to put aside any notion we have of each being an entity as solid and consistent as, say, a billiard ball. Instead, each country is more like an atom, with constantly shifting fields of competing interests. A country's trajectory clearly matters: we want to know where each country is headed, and whether it will bang into and ricochet off other states. It is, however, equally important to listen to these countries, to understand how the particles and subparticles—interest groups and ruling coalitions ever circling each other and competing for influence—help determine why a country heads in a specific direction, and in what time frame.

The ongoing battles within Asia create opportunities and openings for American policy makers and business leaders. Although the United States cannot determine the outcomes of policy struggles in other countries, it can help nudge them in the right direction by supporting coalitions seeking open technology trade and by undermining those pursuing mercantilistic paths. At the very least, Washington should avoid giving foreign politicians justification for pushing higher trade barriers to protect domestic markets. Advocates for such positions in Asia should not be able to say, "We are only doing the same as the United States."

To play this shifting world to its advantage, the United States needs four policy tools: dialogue, cooperation, the wedge, and the stick. Dialogue and cooperation not only aim to convince another country of shared interests, but also reward it for choosing a common direction with the United States. With the wedge, Washington tries to create space between competing interest groups within a country, notably with respect to intellectual property rights and China. Finally, the United States can wield the stick in ongoing negotiations to further a positive outcome or as sanctions when dialogue or cooperation fails.

Beyond these policy tools, the United States needs to take a good look at itself and maintain a realistic sense of its own future role in Asia. The day will come when it is no longer the biggest science and technology power, but this will not matter much if the United States keeps its friends close, develops broadband and other new technologies, and places more Americans in foreign labs and markets. Strength is not simply a function of size, and so the goal for the United States is to act as a "smart grid," a global network that monitors and manages the creation and distribution of technology.

DIALOGUE

While diplomats love summits, special consultations, frameworks for understanding, and high-level meetings, dialogue as policy is easy to disparage—in some cases, rightfully so. The United States has several dialogues with China about technology that have gone on for many years with mixed results. The U.S.-China Joint Commission on Commerce and Trade, which dates back to 1983, engages China in discussions on intellectual property rights, technology standards, government procurement, and other contentious issues in the bilateral technology relationship. In addition, from December

2006 until December 2008, former Treasury secretary Henry Paulson co-chaired the Strategic Economic Dialogue, cabinet-level talks that he was at pains to describe as focused on long-term strategic challenges, rather than on pressing trade issues, in order to lower the expectations of Congress and the American public about what the meetings might deliver.[1]

The Strategic Economic Dialogue was renamed the Strategic and Economic Dialogue by the Obama administration, but, as the minor change in the title suggests, its purpose remains essentially the same: to talk about the global financial crisis, nonproliferation, and other common challenges the two countries face. At the start of the July 2009 meeting of the Strategic and Economic Dialogue, President Obama declared that "the pursuit of power among nations must no longer be seen as a zero-sum game." During the Bush years, there was criticism of the failure of the Strategic Economic Dialogue to secure concrete commitments from the Chinese on the question of the valuation of their currency, the yuan. China does not allow the yuan to float freely, but ties it to a basket of foreign currencies; Morris Goldstein and Nicholas Lardy at the Peterson Institute for International Economics believe it was undervalued by 25 percent in 2005 and by as much as 40 percent in 2007. In February 2010, economists believed China's currency was undervalued by 25 to 40 percent.[2] A lower price for the yuan makes Chinese goods even cheaper for American consumers, and thus contributes to the massive trade surplus China has with the United States.

Congress was not happy with this situation, about which Senators Charles Schumer of New York and Lindsey Graham of South Carolina were the most vocal. They introduced legislation that threatened a 30 percent tariff barrier on Chinese imports if the yuan did not appreciate against the dollar. In July 2005, China announced that it would allow its currency to float within a narrow band of 0.3 percent. While the yuan gained close to 20 percent against the dollar over three years, it was not enough for many of China's critics. "The current dialogue isn't working," Senator Charles Grassley of Iowa said in August 2007. "China's progress on currency modernization has been glacial."[3]

The currency talks have hoarded the attention, but the Strategic Economic Dialogue also included discussions on innovation, energy, and conservation. These topics were supposed to be less contentious; they were more about recognizing common benefit than pushing for changes in Chinese behavior. Concrete progress on this front is especially difficult to quantify, since the goal is to shape Chinese views of their own objectives and welfare, which are difficult to discern.

In the summer of 2008, I was on a panel with a former senior U.S. official extensively involved in dialogue with the Chinese. The discussion was about China's rise and its role in the world. As we talked about Darfur, Iran, and other areas where the Chinese had been less helpful than the United States might have wished, a few people asked the official some pointed questions about what Washington was actually getting from all of the consultations with Beijing. The official elaborated by describing the frequency with which he met with his Chinese counterparts and the quality and scope of the discussions. Clearly frustrated that he was not getting his point across, he finally said, "Quantity has a quality of its own."

To understand his point, imagine both the decision-making process in China and the debriefing that occurs on the Chinese side after each meeting with American negotiators. As a number of very public reversals demonstrate, policies in China are not the result of decisions made by a few powerful leaders sitting on top of a unified Communist Party but instead are the result of bargaining among different bureaucracies and commercial interests, inside and outside of the country. For any serious economic issue there are a series of mini-debates between those who have a more mercantilistic view of the world, and those willing to pursue Chinese goals through collaboration and open trade. The United States wants this second group to prevail as much as possible.

Those on the other side of the debate gained fuel from a 2005 incident, in which the China National Offshore Oil Corporation (CNOOC) tried to acquire Unocal. The deal died even before the U.S. government had a chance to review its security implications. Once CNOOC announced its intention to acquire the California-based company, the political atmosphere quickly grew negative; the mix of oil, economic security, and the Chinese (or the Chinese communists, as some liked to refer to them) was too potent for many in the press and Congress. Representative Richard W. Pombo, a California Republican, introduced a resolution declaring that permitting the sale would "threaten to impair the national security of the United States."[4] It passed easily, 398 to 15. CNOOC soon withdrew its bid after members of Congress approved another measure that would have required a further security review and delayed the acquisition. Chevron then acquired Unocal.

To be sure, China does the same thing. Beijing itself closely monitors and limits many foreign acquisitions, and companies trying to acquire even a small stake in a Chinese company have to receive approval from several government ministries. For those within the Chinese government arguing for a more liberal approach to mergers and acquisitions, the debate in the United States over CNOOC can only have been bad news. On the other hand, it strengthened those already suspicious of multinational companies or private equity groups buying up Chinese companies. In August 2006, after CNOOC withdrew its offer for Unocal, Beijing introduced its own measure to require government review of mergers and acquisitions that could affect China's "economic security" or involve "key industries" or popular domestic trademarks. The Carlyle Group waited for more than three years for Beijing to approve its $178.4 million offer for Xugong Group Construction Machinery before it finally withdrew the deal in July 2008, and in March 2009, the Chinese blocked Coca-Cola's $2.4 billion bid for Huiyuan Juice Group, a Chinese juice manufacturer.

Expectations for meetings between China and the United States must be tempered. As I indicated, when an administration tells Congress that it is entering into a dialogue to address a major irritant in a bilateral relationship, Congress expects something concrete to come out of those talks. At some point, senators and representatives will lose patience with the prospect of developing common interests through dialogue, and will be more than willing to try to force concessions on their own. In addition, the American people are going to wonder what, with American-made goods so hard to find on the shelves at Wal-Mart, is still up for debate. Thus, only a really strong president—or, as in the case of President Bush, one who faces so many other challenges that he can convince Congress that the United States has enough problems without a trade war with China—will be able to rely on a policy of slowly shaping interests over the long term.

COOPERATION

If selling dialogue and negotiation is difficult, promoting science and technology cooperation as a foreign policy tactic is too easy. Everyone can get behind something that obviously benefits everyone. Common sense and history suggest that having more smart people tackle the most difficult issues makes everyone better off, as happened in the 1960s when the Ford Foundation cooperated with the Indian government during the Green Revolution. Through the import and spread of a new variety of rice, yields per hectare went from two tons in the 1960s to five tons in the 1990s, and famine in India became a thing of the past.

Today, so the argument goes, the most pressing problems such as climate change must be addressed through international cooperation and technological collaboration. As Secretary of State Hillary Clinton told reporters en route to her first official visit to China in February 2009, "I'm very positive about the kind of cooperation that we can achieve together on behalf of really serious issues like clean energy and climate change and nuclear proliferation, as well as the economic crisis."[5]

China recently passed the United States to become the world's largest emitter of greenhouse gases, and the two countries together account for over 40 percent of the world's greenhouse gas. Both countries will probably have to deal with severe weather, the disruption of water supplies, and the disappearance of coastal marshes. The development of clean energy technologies would reduce the growing dependence of both countries on foreign oil—China is the world's second largest importer of oil, and in 2009 the United States sent $265 billion to the oil exporters.

There is already broad engagement on environmental and energy technologies. China, the United States, and the world's other large energy consumers participate in several multilateral projects focused on the hydrogen economy, technologies for the capture and storage of carbon, next-generation nuclear energy, and renewable energy. On the bilateral level, the U.S. Department of Energy is involved in more than a dozen areas of cooperative research and development with China, including projects to extract coal mine methane, the creation of climate datasets, and the joint deployment of solar, wind, biomass, geothermal, and hydrogen energy. The state-owned Huaneng Group has signed up to participate in the U.S. Energy Department's FutureGen project to work on carbon capture and storage.

The private sector is also deeply involved. In clean technology areas, American venture capital had deals in China totaling more than $80 million in 2006. In 2008, Intel Capital, the chip maker's venture capital fund, bought a $20 million stake in the solar energy firm Trony Solar. American universities are busy developing joint research projects with their Chinese counterparts. The University of Tennessee has established, with the Chinese Academy of Sciences, the China-U.S. Joint Research Center for Ecosystem and Environmental Changes, while the University of Florida and Zhejiang University have plans for a Joint Research Center of Clean Sustainable Energy.

So, given the desire to "save the planet," it might seem petty to talk about the protection of intellectual property and the drive for technological autonomy, but it is unavoidable. Beijing has extremely ambitious plans for renewable energy; it expects to source 15 percent of its energy needs from wind, biomass, solar, and hydropower by 2020, up from 7 percent in 2007. Not surprisingly, Chinese leaders prefer that the companies developing the solar panels, biofuel engines, new turbines, power grids, and transmission lines be Chinese, using Chinese-owned and Chinese-developed intellectual property. To this end, they implemented domestic content requirements that require new wind turbines, for example, to include 70 percent local (that is, Chinese) content. In 2009, under pressure from U.S. negotiators, Beijing agreed to end the domestic content requirement. One trade official told me that the Chinese complied "because we asked them to." It was easy for Beijing to be magnanimous, however, after Chinese producers had already increased their share of the market from 20 percent in 2004 to 75 percent.

In the run-up to the December 2009 United Nations Climate Change Conference in Copenhagen, there was a good deal of maneuvering over technological transfer and who would pay for adopting and diffusing carbon-neutral technologies. For most of the decade, China's view, which was shared by India and others in the developing world, was that the West was responsible for most of the pollution and should bear the lion's share of the burden dealing with it. Since no one asked the West to limit itself when it was growing economically, no one should expect the developing countries to restrict their use of oil and coal now that they are dramatically uplifting the lives of their citizens. Besides, even though the total amounts are rising, the per capita emissions of China and India are still well below America's.

India and China therefore, so the argument continues, should be compensated for whatever costs they incur in cleaning up the mess. Indeed, as the Copenhagen summit drew closer, many thought that any agreement on reducing carbon emission would require the creation of a board that would oversee and implement technology transfers, and a multilateral fund that would make payments to developing countries so they can purchase the necessary technology as well as give developing countries the ability to engage in compulsory licensing—the transfer of patent rights to companies by order of the government. In 2008, right before the meeting of the United Nations Framework Convention on Climate Change in Poland, Premier Wen Jiabao explicitly called for the rich countries to transfer technology to China.

The United States was of two minds about technology transfer. While Secretary of Energy Steven Chu championed international cooperation as critical to reducing greenhouse gas emissions, American companies, worried about their competitive position in the Chinese market, were more circumspect. In March 2009, Dr. Chu told reporters, "It's like all countries becoming allies against this common foe, which is the energy problem." He continued, "By very collaborative, I mean share all intellectual property as much as possible." Told of Chu's comments, Steve Fludder, the head of the Ecomagination division of General Electric, strongly disagreed: "Why would we invest $1.5 billion a year in innovation that just slips through your fingers? I mean, why would anybody invest in anything that they would have to just give away?"[6] In June 2009, the House of Representatives passed an amendment to the Foreign Relations Authorization Act to establish a new U.S. policy "in opposition to any global climate change treaty that weakens the intellectual property rights of American green technology."[7]

The Copenhagen summit ended with no binding accords, no target year for peak emissions, and no concrete technology transfer agreement, though there was a great deal of anger and recriminations about whether Beijing or Washington was to blame for the failure. Still, Washington at least tried to appear optimistic about the future. "Clean energy may be the greatest economic opportunity of the 21st century," said Commerce Secretary Gary Locke in January 2010, "and the development, production, and deployment of American clean energy and energy efficiency technologies can be one of the most beneficial areas of cooperation in the history of U.S.-China relations."[8] It is good to hold out hope, but it is also worth noting that Locke stressed the development and deployment of American technology. The United States must cooperate with China with its eyes open to everyone's primary interest: China wants both to reduce carbon emissions and to develop its own technology; the United States wants to reduce carbon emissions without hurting its own companies through uncompetitive practices.

THE WEDGE AND INTELLECTUAL
PROPERTY RIGHTS

In some instances, aiming for dialogue and cooperation can be like yelling into the wind. Some positions may be so divergent that finding common interests is impossible. Or, the domestic position of potential allies of U.S. policies may be so weak that they have no real impact on the creation or implementation of policy. If a country has a bitter dispute with the United States, any effort to influence domestic politics may actually undermine potential allies within that country. When the push for open markets cannot get enough traction, it is best to adopt a wedge strategy or, to borrow the language of Maoism, to "heighten the contradictions." China's failure to protect intellectual property rights may be a particularly prime area to drive a wedge through a range of competing interests.

Mass-scale intellectual property theft in China is old news. Almost every visitor to Beijing or Shanghai has a story of being accosted by hustlers on the street selling DVDs of new movies the day after their premiere in Los Angeles. Filmed in theaters in the states with handheld cameras and sent to China over the Internet, movies are boxed, wrapped, and displayed in stores. A week before Microsoft released Vista in the United States, it was on sale in Beijing for a little more than a dollar. The International Intellectual Property Alliance, a coalition of software, entertainment, and publishing companies, estimates that the piracy rate is 90 percent for music, 79 percent for business software, and 95 percent for games and other entertainment software, for a total cost to U.S. businesses of close to $3.5 billion in 2009.

The problem is not the lack of laws. The U.S. Trade Representative, the U.S. Chamber of Commerce, and the International Intellectual Property Alliance all concede that China has made significant progress in revamping its legal system and creating a comprehensive set of laws required to protect intellectual property rights. The problem is implementation; as a report from the U.S. Trade Representative puts it, China has had "little success in actually enforcing its laws and regulations."[9]

This implementation failure stems from many sources: a lack of transparency and coordination among Chinese government agencies, local protectionism, and corruption. One of the most important factors is the absence of credible criminal and administrative penalties. When pirates are caught, few go to prison, and the punishment is not harsh enough either to stop them from returning to their business or to deter others from entering the pirate's life. In a notable exception, in December 2008, a Chinese court sentenced eleven people for pirating Windows XP, Windows Vista, and Office 2007 to terms ranging from a year and a half to six and a half years. In general, the bar for criminal offenses is set unrealistically high. In 2004, for example, only 1 percent of copyright and trademark cases was turned over to the police, and in 2007, a couple in Qingdao Province were fined only $2,600 for selling 2,900 pirated DVDs and possessing 19,000 more.

At root, intellectual property rights theft flourishes because local government officials have strong incentives to encourage development and trade in their cities and provinces, even if it is illegal trade. One party vice secretary in Chongqing told Cornell political scientist Andrew Mertha, "I believe that intellectual property and economic development are both important, but I consider economic development to be the more important of the two."[10] Since piracy can generate significant revenue, taxes, and employment, and local officials are promoted according to the rates of economic growth and the level of social stability in their regions, they turn a blind eye to (or even actively support) companies involved in piracy.

While a very senior Chinese official in the Ministry of Science and Technology once told me that the intellectual property rights problem was essentially America's fault—"Who buys the pirated DVDs when they visit China?" he asked me, and answered, "American tourists"—Chinese leaders now seem to take the protection of intellectual property rights more seriously, especially as they pursue the development of their own intellectual property. In 2003, Beijing created the Leading Group on intellectual property rights, a high-level group to coordinate enforcement across several different departments under the direction of Vice Premier Wu Yi. The appointment of Wu Yi, a woman dubbed the "iron lady" by the media and widely respected for her ability to get things done in the Chinese bureaucracy, signaled the importance the central leadership attached to the issue. Local officials were told that they would also be evaluated, come promotion time, on the basis of how many intellectual property rights violations occurred in their regions. In 2008, the Chinese again rolled out a new strategy for tackling these issues, and Wang Qishan, vice premier of the State Council (the Chinese equivalent to the American cabinet), wrote an op-ed in the *Wall Street Journal* entitled "No More Chinese Knock-Offs."[11]

This renewed attention to the problem of intellectual property, at least at the very top of the Chinese leadership, fits a widely held view that the failure to protect intellectual property rights is in part a symptom of China's stage of development. Or as former secretary of state James Baker III put it in a speech to the U.S.-China Business Council in June 2007, "Views on intellectual property rights and foreign investment, for instance, will surely converge as China turns more to technological innovation and herself becomes a major direct investor abroad."[12]

If China were to develop robust protection of intellectual property rights, it would be traveling a well-trodden path. Developing countries historically have had no problem with "borrowing" intellectual capital. When it was a developing country, the United States actively stole from Britain, France, and Germany. The historian Doron Ben-Atar writes that in the decades after American independence, "technology piracy became the premier tool to industrial development."[13] In his *Report on the Subject of Manufactures*, submitted in December 1791, Treasury Secretary Alexander Hamilton called for Congress to offer money and other inducements to British engineers, German mechanists, and others to move to America in order to increase the "extent of valuable acquisitions to the population, arts, and industry."[14] Only after the United States had reduced its dependence on Europe for technology, and American companies had their own technologies to commercialize, did the United States develop a robust system of intellectual property protection.

Japan followed a similar course. After an interview with a Sony official who made several pained comments about the theft of intellectual property in China, I wandered around the museum in Sony headquarters dedicated to the triumphs and breakthroughs of the company. Visitors can view the artifacts of the consumer electronics revolution: the small, cheap transistor radios that were Sony's first big success, along with the Trinitron color television set, Betamax VCR, and Walkman personal stereo. There are also copies of the Iwama Reports, which date back to Sony's initial agreement in 1953 (when the company was known as Totsuko) with Western Electric to manufacture transistors in Japan.

In January 1954, Iwama Kazuo, a Totsuko general manager, traveled to the United States to learn the manufacturing process. Western Electric would not provide specifications for the manufacturing equipment, but engineers and managers were happy to give Iwama tours of the factory and to answer his numerous questions. At the end of the day, Iwama returned to his hotel room and scoured his memory for what he had heard and seen, putting sketches and technical details into seven letters sent back to Japan. With the help of the reports, and copies of *Transistor Technology*, "the transistor bible" brought back from an earlier trip to the United States by Sony's cofounder Morita Akio, Sony engineers constructed their own equipment. By the time of Iwama's return to Japan, the company had manufactured its first transistor.

China is unlikely, however, to move along the same historical trajectory. Anne Stevenson-Yang, an American entrepreneur and technology analyst in Beijing, and Ken DeWoskin, a former professor of Chinese studies at the University of Michigan, argue that intellectual property theft in China has little to do with its stage of economic development.[15] Rather, it is the result of the government's continued control of the economy and its drive to create Chinese intellectual property—a by-product of the drive for indigenous innovation. State funds are given to companies and scientists to develop technologies that have already succeeded on the international market, and they are expected to crank out Chinese versions of the technology in three to five years, the attention span of the typical bureaucrat. In essence, companies are paid by the government to copy.

As long as the Chinese state continues to intervene in large parts of the economy, the outlook for improving intellectual property rights is poor. And the reliance on state-owned enterprises is actually increasing according to recent research by MIT's Yasheng Huang.[16] State-controlled firms make up at least half of the economy, and one of the outcomes of Beijing's stimulus package was to further blur the line between state and private firms. While the outside world has little ability to force Beijing to withdraw from the economy, the United States should try to create a wedge that exploits the multiple economic interests that coexist within China toward that end.

American officials and businesses need to work with and change the incentives of the local officials who often have the real power in the Chinese system. In their relentless quest for economic development, provinces and municipalities are constantly competing with each other for foreign investment, often resulting in an arms race of escalating subsidies and tax breaks. During the 1990s, for example, the central government allowed cities to offer high-technology companies a three-year tax holiday, followed by another three years of taxes reduced by 50 percent. By the time it was all over, some local officials had bid themselves up to a ten-year tax holiday in their attempt to lure companies to locate to their cities.

The U.S. government and businesses should make the effective protection of intellectual property an element of the competition at the local level, praising officials and funneling foreign investment to those areas that offer adequate protection, and shunning those that make no progress. This means not only working with local officials to build their capacity to implement Chinese laws on intellectual property rights, but also developing benchmarks that would allow for foreign investors to compare the effectiveness of protection across regions. The U.S. Chamber of Commerce recently signed a memorandum of understanding with the Jiangsu Provincial Intellectual Property authorities, which includes collaboration on education, training, and benchmarking. The Commerce Department and U.S. Trade Representative have also announced a benchmarking process at the provincial level—they maintain an open, annually updated record of the level of intellectual property rights protection and prosecution of violations.

THE STICK AND BENCHMARKING

Benchmarking will also play a supporting role in the fourth strategy: the effective use of sanctions, or the stick, especially for cases taken to the World Trade Organization (WTO). On intellectual property cases, U.S. trade officials want to play hardball with China yet are often frustrated with the attitude of U.S. businesses operating in China. American companies loudly complain about the high rates of piracy, but in any intellectual property rights case against China, no one wants to be named as the complainant. Daniel Chow, a law professor at Ohio State and former counsel to Procter & Gamble in China, explains that "you have multinational companies in China—I used to work for one, so I know—who are afraid of retaliation against their business so they often praise the Chinese government."[17] Few want to alienate the central government in Beijing, and many fear reprisal from local government officials, who levy fines for spurious safety and labor violations, refuse new building permits, or subsidize their competitors.

Through benchmarking, individual companies avoid the burden of individually confronting China on the failure to protect intellectual property rights and are thus less susceptible to local government pressure. Benchmarking would allow U.S. trade officials to collect data from relatively objective sources in order to threaten or actually bring an action to the WTO, which has, in the past, had noticeable success. As I described in chapter 4, China backed down from its support of the WAPI technology standard in April 2004 after the United States threatened to pursue the case at the WTO.

In July 2004, China backed down again. The United States made it clear that it planned to file its first WTO case against China over a value-added tax (VAT) on semiconductors. The tax was designed both to foster domestic integrated circuit production and to lure advanced producers to the mainland from Taiwan, the United States, Europe, and Japan. Domestic manufacturers received a rebate of all but 3 percent of the 17 percent VAT on their locally produced integrated circuits. Beijing imposed the full 17 percent VAT on imported integrated circuits, unless they were designed in China. The tax was working. In two years, from 2000 to 2002, China's semiconductor industry attracted $3.6 billion in new investment. In March 2004, the United States announced its intention to file a case. "The bottom line is that China is discriminating against key U.S. technology products, it's wrong, and it's time to pursue a remedy through the WTO," said U.S. Trade Representative Robert Zoellick.[18] Soon after the announcement, China ended the tax.

In 2005, Washington, along with Japan and Switzerland, requested statistics and information from Beijing on its enforcement of intellectual property rights in preparation for a possible case at the WTO.

At an April 2006 meeting of the U.S.-China Joint Commission on Commerce and Trade, China made important concessions on intellectual property: it restated a commitment to neutrality on mobile telecommunications standards; took action against fourteen factories producing illegal optical disks and pledged to increase enforcement in the future; required the preloading of a legal operating system software on all computers produced or imported into China; and obliged government agencies to purchase computers with preloaded software.

In June 2009, the Ministry of Industry and Information Technology announced that all new computers sold in China would be required to have the "Green Dam-Youth Escort" Internet filtering software preinstalled. The official purpose of the software was to help parents protect children from "smut" on the web, but independent studies found that it had broader censorship functions—it had a list of sensitive words that could be continually updated to block surfing—and made PCs vulnerable to hacking. After a month of protests from the U.S. government and the European Union, PC makers, and Internet users within China, Beijing announced that it would delay the implementation of the regulation. One month later, in August 2009, the ministry completely withdrew the requirement that Green Dam Internet censorship software be preinstalled on computers, although it was still required to be installed on computers at Internet cafes and universities.

Quiet diplomacy is widely believed to work best with China. Public denouncement and pressure backfire because of issues of face and because the government can never allow itself to be seen as giving in to foreign demands. Yet, as each of these cases demonstrates— when China has clearly violated a principle to which it has publicly committed, and the pressure is multilateral and not just from Washington, when governments and businesses speak with one voice— pressure works.

THE UNITED STATES AS A "SMART GRID"

If the United States is to match means to ends, it needs to be clear about what it wants. As Asia rises, the relative decline of the United States as a science power is inevitable. Yet even as the United States will not be the sole technological superpower, it will remain, as I have said, an important driver of innovation. The United States has no interest in trying to prevent the technological rise of other states. Such a goal would be not only impossible to achieve but also prohibitively expensive and damaging to America's self-interest, generating resentment and anger in the rest of the world. Besides, this country should be confident and clear-eyed enough to see that the rise of scientific and technological capabilities in other places will also benefit the United States. When I have a headache, I am happy to have aspirin available, even if a French chemist first prepared acetylsalicylic acid and the German firm Bayer first patented and brought it to the mass market.

As with every other area of foreign policy, we must pair with multiple partners to address specific science and technology issues, cooperating with China on carbon sequestration, for example, and Japan on robotics. We must consider the type and functionality of our connections to the rest of the world. Are we getting as much as we can from all the networks that connect us to scientists and entrepreneurs throughout Asia, or do they need to be upgraded and revitalized? Are we a traditional grid or a smart grid?

The traditional power grids that connect power plants to houses are unresponsive; energy is sent down the line according to fluctuating demand. Electric companies have no way of monitoring how much power is being used, and since electricity cannot be stored, they tend to oversupply. Power is wasted, and unexpected surges in demand can cause shortages and blackouts. Smart grids, in contrast, use fiber-optics and high-tech sensors to provide real-time usage updates, so a power company can regulate supply and a consumer can adjust demand. According to their supporters, smart grids also allow for "distributed generation," or the integration of locally generated power sources, such as solar panels on homes and backyard wind turbines. During the day, a homeowner could rely on solar power and sell any extra power back to the grid, then by night plug back into the larger grid.

In issues beyond electricity, the United States needs to stop functioning as a dumb grid and reinvent itself as a smart grid. A smart grid in a world of globalized innovation monitors both what is going out—what technology is flowing from the United States to Asia and how it is being used—and what and who flows in—what is coming into the United States from Bangalore and Beijing. It means not alienating friends (and potential friends); developing the infrastructure and the incentives for innovators anywhere in the world to plug into our grid; and putting people in place to take advantage of the new world of decentralized innovation (distributed generation).

ACCOMMODATION, NOT ALIENATION

Since the United States needs access to other countries' domestic innovation systems, it should not needlessly estrange its friends. In 1994, for example, the United States pushed very hard, despite the opposition of many developing economies, to conclude the Trade-Related Aspects of Intellectual Property Rights (TRIPS) Agreement at the Uruguay round of the General Agreement on Tariffs and Trade (GATT, or the precursor to the WTO) negotiations. The TRIPS Agreement requires member countries to establish uniform minimum standards for several types of intellectual property, including copyrights, geographical indications (champagne must be from the Champagne region, Camembert from Normandy), industrial designs, patents, and trademarks. Developing countries were given extra time to implement the treaty and develop the appropriate protections. China ratified the TRIPS Agreement in November 2007; India signed it in 1995 and passed new patent laws ten years later.

While TRIPS calls for patent protection to last for twenty years, it also allows for national variation: states can limit the power of patent holders and define the criteria for granting patents differently. Under the terms of the 2001 Doha Declaration, states are also allowed to break drug patents and produce cheap generic drugs to protect public health. The 2005 Indian Patent Law, for example, controversially grants patent protection only to "new chemical entities," not to "incremental innovations." After TRIPS went into effect, Indian pharmaceutical companies could no longer simply reverse engineer a proven product and produce cheap generics, but the Indian government also wanted to reduce "ever greening," or the practice of making small changes in an existing product simply to extend patent protection. In August 2007, a Chennai high court ruled against Novartis, which was claiming that the Indian government had violated the TRIPS Agreement by denying patent protection for Gleevec (also known as Glivec), a cancer drug that the patent offices had ruled was not a significant innovation from an earlier known drug. A month later, Novartis canceled plans for a $500 million investment in India.

Despite the fact that national exceptions are built into the TRIPS Agreement, American negotiators have insisted that countries, especially smaller, weaker ones, adopt a patent system resembling that of the United States.[19] A bilateral trade agreement with Thailand, for example, reportedly insisted that the Thai government prolong the patent protection on American drugs and limit its right to break patents. While harmonization of patent systems across national borders might reduce the costs of patenting—there would be only one application and fee—this trend seems especially misplaced given the current maladies of the American patent system. The American system has become bloated by expanding the definitions of what is eligible for protection, by lengthening patent terms, and by diluting the standards for the granting of patents.

Patent trolls, companies that buy up old patents not to develop new technology but to extract payments from other firms, are the most conspicuous example of what has gone wrong with the American system. In 2006, the developer of the BlackBerry, Research in Motion, paid more than $600 million to NTP in order to avoid a court-ordered shutdown of its email service, despite the fact that the U.S. Patent Office had ruled NTP's patents invalid and the company did not provide email or other services to compete with Research in Motion. Huge litigation costs are another symptom of a system that slows the diffusion of research and inhibits the pace of innovation.

Pushing our own flawed patent system on others does nothing for our image abroad. Trade partners see the drive for harmonization as a cynical effort either to protect the profits of our pharmaceutical companies or to make other countries less attractive to patent filers. Foreign critics of harmonization note that the rate of filing has risen outside of the United States, and that, unable to reform our own system, we are trying to drag other countries down. The demand to raise the standard of patent protection also produces collateral damage, generating resistance to free trade agreements. Opposition in Brazil to a possible bilateral trade agreement as well as to the region-wide Free Trade for the Americas stems in part from the United States pushing an agenda that demands patent standards higher than those in the TRIPS Agreement.

The more productive course of action is, as trade lawyer Keith Maskus puts it, an agenda that "involve[s] accommodation by the United States at least as much as the other way around."[20] The

United States should abandon pressuring developing countries to render patents more restrictive on medicines used to treat deadly and contagious diseases. The goal remains to draw other countries into an international system of intellectual property protection, but insisting that only the United States knows how that system should be organized is counterproductive. Washington needs to show empathy for local concerns, especially when it comes to patent protection for drugs used in the treatment of HIV/AIDS and other epidemics.

BROADBAND AS A FOREIGN POLICY ISSUE

Despite the United States' need for interconnectivity, the rollout of broadband Internet access here has been slow, uneven, and expensive. The United States ranks low in terms of access to broadband and has slipped, according to the Organisation for Economic Co-operation and Development, from fourth out of thirty countries in 2001 to fifteenth in 2009 in broadband penetration.[21] The United States lags behind most of Scandinavia and developed Asia; the fastest download speeds in the United States are half those in Korea, and over 80 percent of Japanese households have access to "ultra fast" connections of up to 100 megabits per second. In Japan, the average Internet user fee is far lower than those in other developed countries—just six cents per 100 kilobits per second; South Korea follows closely with eight cents, and deep in the pack is the United States at forty-nine cents.

The Japanese and Korean lead over the United States in wireless, mobile phone–based Internet access is even more striking. In Seoul and Tokyo, payments for the subway, vending machines, and convenience stores can be made by phone. A witness to a crime in Seoul can record and send video to the police in real time.

Many observers have lamented the widening gap between the

United States and Asia in broadband access and predicted dire consequences for the American economy. Without more access, there is a fear that Americans will miss out on the next generation of web and mobile phone applications. Rapid upload and download times, for example, are critical to driving innovation in Web 2.0 applications—social networking sites and sites heavy in user-generated content like YouTube and MySpace. In addition, according to a report from the Brookings Institution, "roughly one-third of households in rural America cannot subscribe to broadband Internet services at any price."[22] President Bush, during the 2004 election, promised "universal, affordable access" to broadband technology by 2007. President Obama's 2009 economic stimulus package of $787 billion included $7.2 billion to improve Americans' access to broadband.

Addressing the problem requires creating competition as well as infrastructure. The phone and cable companies dominate the delivery of broadband—controlling more than 98 percent of the residential and small-business markets—which means higher prices and little incentive to build the system. At the beginning of the Bush administration, there were thousands of Internet service providers. Now competition has been severely reduced, with only two providers in many large markets, and limited access in poor and rural regions.

Borrowing an idea from Switzerland, Free Press, a nonpartisan group pushing for media reform, suggests using a tax incentive to push the phone and cable companies to actively compete. In a given house or building, if the big companies install only one fiber line to deliver their own services, they get nothing. If they connect two or three lines that others can rent, then they get a large tax credit.

The best solution to the challenge of improving the delivery of broadband through fiber to Americans may be to sidestep the problem through the expansion of wireless capabilities. According to the Federal Communications Commission, the use of smart phones expanded by 700 percent from 2005 to 2009, though, as anyone who has had a call dropped or waited for a program to run knows, wireless networks have their own set of problems.[23] Currently the distribution of wireless spectrum and access to the airwaves are highly inefficient; only 10 percent of the airwaves is allocated for commercial use, and at any one time, 90 percent is empty.[24] Much of the airwaves are coming back to the government during the shift to digital television. Wireless networks and others should be allowed to bid on that spectrum, and entrepreneurs could then compete to provide better Wi-Fi and wireless service.

While the primary focus of these debates and policies has been domestic, greater diffusion of broadband is a twofer—it is essential to innovation at home and to ensuring that America remains connected to the world. Not only will more bandwidth foster greater efficiency and innovation at home, but also it will allow the chip design company in South Dakota to be more tightly tied to partners in Shanghai. Of course, these links may well encourage sending more jobs offshore, as the South Dakota chip design company may find it easier to locate an engineer in Hyderabad, but that isn't a reason to avoid building infrastructure that is essential to American competitiveness.

PUTTING AN AMERICAN SCIENTIST IN AN INDIAN (KOREAN, JAPANESE, OR CHINESE) LAB

As innovation spreads over the globe, ideas will explode in unconventional places. When this happens, the links to Asian innovation will need to be more than virtual. If U.S. policy makers and business leaders expect to be able to track and exploit this new model of distributed innovation, they can't simply sit at a desk with broadband connections. People have to be on the ground.

Getting there requires a new mindset about how the United States conducts science diplomacy. Historically, bilateral science agreements were usually sideshows, gifts to a government the United States wanted to support or a symbol of the friendship of the American people. Rarely did U.S. policy makers think they could actually learn anything from an agreement: the science in the other countries so clearly lagged behind the Americans'. The lead has evaporated, and attitudes will have to change. Science relationships must be pursued as real competitive opportunities, not as public relations ploys.

The government has begun to address the challenge of tracking science in Asia. The State Department now has a science and technology officer in the embassies in Delhi and Beijing. The National Science Foundation has long had an office in Tokyo and, in May 2006, opened one in Beijing. It is considering opening an office in Delhi. The National Institutes of Health has two staff posted in China, one from the National Institute of Allergy and Infectious Diseases and one from the National Cancer Institute. In India, one person from the National Institutes of Health/Office of AIDS Research is posted in New Delhi, and a senior National Institutes of Health contractor in Chennai.

This handful of people on the ground is clearly not enough. While more government scientists should be stationed abroad, relying on government officials will never suffice. Only a presence that includes scientists, technology entrepreneurs, and students can truly interface with innovation in Asia, both in the lab and on the street. This type of multilevel, multi-actor collaboration is clearly more complex than government-to-government cooperation. Yet, because most of the participants in these collaborations are focused on common interests, their ties are more robust, less susceptible to swings in political relations. In fact, participants in cooperative projects seem completely unfazed by the possible political difficulties. Often at conferences, after listening to a scientist rhapsodize about opportunities in China, I mention Taiwan and security concerns—only to be met with a look of pity suggesting that I am missing the big picture.

Students, undergraduate and graduate, will have to be better prepared for an international world of research and development. In the 1990s there was a broad push for interdisciplinary work. Programs such as the National Science Foundation's Integrative Graduate Education and Research Traineeship revolve around "real-life" problems with complex solutions that span several disciplines. The program on assistive technology at Carnegie Mellon is just one of 125 interdisciplinary projects across the country; students working on robotics, human-computer interaction, and language technology cooperate with colleagues in the departments of occupational therapy, bioengineering, and communication science and disorders to develop new technologies to give greater independence to people with disabilities.

Building on interdisciplinary efforts, the push in this decade and the next should center on international work. The National Science Foundation, the Department of Energy, and the National Institutes of Health should develop programs that provide more international experience, not just short trips but preferably extended sojourns in foreign labs. The National Science Foundation's East Asia and Pacific Summer Institute currently provides approximately 185 U.S. graduate students in science and engineering with firsthand research experience over the summer in Australia, China, Japan, Korea, New Zealand, and Taiwan. The National Institutes of Health has a program that sends about twenty-five students interested in international health and clinical research to several sites in the developing world, including India and China. The Department of Energy should adopt similar programs, the number of summer participants in all of the federal programs should at least be doubled, and students should have the opportunity to find longer visiting fellowships in Asia. The future dividends of investing in such programs will be incalculably valuable.

Similarly, internships and cooperative research will also have to be "internationalized." Today, numerous schools have programs that match engineers with industry, giving them the opportunity to learn about product design, layout, commercial production, and management techniques. These programs need to include time abroad so students can better understand the changing demands of Asian markets. While Georgia Tech, Purdue, and Virginia Tech have set ambitious goals for the numbers of their students spending time abroad, Worcester Polytechnic Institute is probably the farthest along in developing these programs. More than half the junior class goes abroad, not to enroll in a foreign university, but to work on focused projects, such as developing solar energy in Thailand or effective fertilizer application techniques in Costa Rica.[25]

Finally, no matter how much the United States reforms immigration law, scientists and engineers will return home, some right after graduating and some after working for a few years. Some will go because of economic opportunity, others because they are homesick or want to raise their children steeped in their own cultures and surrounded by extended families. American universities and companies will need to actively maintain links with these people, so they can act as nodes in the science and technology networks of this new global world.

In this era of collaborative and globalized innovation, companies and countries are inextricably dependent on ideas and talent from the outside. "The world is our lab now," says John E. Kelly III, director of IBM Research. In a 2009 letter to the head of America's science agencies explaining priorities for the 2011 budget, Peter Orszag, director of the Office of Management and Budget, and John Holdren, director of the Office of Science and Technology, called for each agency to take advantage of today's open innovation model and "become highly open to ideas from many players, at all stages." [26] Policies that balance security and openness at home and that ensure access to foreign markets by American companies and scientists are therefore essential to the viability of our innovation system. Whatever happens abroad, however, will matter little if we do not respond at home. The current has to flow in two directions on the smart grid; we have to generate fresh companies, ideas, and talent so we can stay connected to vital nodes as they emerge and flourish.

Chapter Eight

PROMOTING INNOVATION AT HOME

Over the last several decades, Americans have become accustomed, reluctantly at times, to the mobility of manufacturing, which began in the 1970s and was in full swing by the 1990s. First, relatively low-cost, labor-intensive factories left the United States, then more highly skilled capital-intensive work left. Yet, even as the manufacturing of textiles, shoes, toys, televisions, and cars went to Japan and South Korea, then to China, and on to Vietnam and Cambodia, there was a widespread belief that research, design, and other parts of the production process dependent on specialized knowledge would remain in the United States. Computers might be built in Shenzhen, but the next generation of microchips, so the argument went, would surely be designed in San Jose.

The endless global hunger for new markets, ideas, and talent has undermined this assumption. In January 2007, Cisco announced plans to triple its research staff in India to six thousand by 2010. In Bangalore, the company built Globalisation Centre East, which houses all of Cisco's primary functions, including sales, business development, marketing, and engineering. Wim Elfrink, Cisco's chief globalization officer, moved with his family from Silicon Valley to India, and 20 percent of the company's senior management is expected to be working in India by the end of the decade. Cisco's new investments in India will eventually total more than $1 billion, 70 percent of which will be in research and development.

Cisco is an exemplar of a new wave of global businesses that IBM's CEO, Sam Palmisano, has called the "globally integrated enterprise."[1] Operating in international markets is nothing new for American companies. But in the past, doing business internationally meant operating in separate and distinct foreign markets: there were the European, Latin American, and Asian markets, which had little in common except that they weren't American. IBM set up a branch in Europe to serve European markets and to avoid high tariffs, and then basically copied the strategy for Asia. The European branch of IBM had little or no contact with IBM in Asia. Research and development almost always stayed in the United States, and the exceptions were Canada and Europe, not China and South Korea.

The corporation of today, according to Palmisano, no longer thinks of producing and selling in separate regional markets— supercomputers for Europe, software services for Asia. Instead, the corporation embraces the global market; products are designed and produced along chains that stretch across the United States, China, and Vietnam for consumers in Shanghai, Seattle, and Stockholm. Research can go anywhere there is talent: of all of the new projects announced in Asia between 2002 and 2004, 75 percent (723 out of 885) were in China and India, according to the United Nations Conference on Trade and Development.[2]

Universities are also jockeying for position in global markets. American universities have always had strong international connections, with heavy enrollment of foreign students and collaboration with international faculty, but they are seeking to push further. Yale has declared its intention to become a "truly global university," and its strategic plan for internationalization lists three institutional objectives for its engagement with China: to become "the school of choice for the most outstanding students in a country with 20 percent of the world's population"; to provide "better support and create new opportunities for collaborative projects in China"; and, by working with the Chinese, to contribute "to China's emergence as a modernized and increasingly open society."[3]

Success in the Asian market will be as critical for universities as it has been for technology companies. The brains, the customers, and the competition are all in Asia. By 2025, Asia will dominate the global demand for international higher education, representing some 70 percent of total demand (China and India alone account for more than half of the worldwide demand), up from 21 percent in 2000.[4]

So while there has been a great deal of worry about how the United States will cope with the strains of globalization, universities and American multinational companies have adjusted just fine. Eighteen of the world's fifty best universities are American, and profits from U.S. corporations more than doubled between 2000 and 2008. *Innovation in Global Industries*, a 2008 report from the National Academy of Sciences, found that American technology companies have retained their ability to innovate ahead of competitors, even as they have moved skilled manufacturing and research and development offshore. "Many industries and some firms within nearly all industries retain leading-edge capacity in the United States," the report concluded.[5]

Although this is reassuring, at least in the short term, what does it mean if American companies remain leaders by moving more research and development abroad? Are we now witnessing a divergence between what is good for Cisco (or Microsoft, Intel, GE, or any other large American technology company) and what is good for the United States? As the large technology companies become more global, they are becoming less national, less American. "China will become the center of the IT world . . ." according to John Chambers of Cisco. "What we're trying to do is outline an entire strategy of becoming a Chinese company."[6] The interests of the American economy, however, remain geographically bound: we want to create good paying jobs within the United States.

To be sure, universities cannot move with the fluidity of Cisco or IBM. They educate American students, they have brick and mortar in the United States, and they are dependent on state and federal money, with Washington providing over $25 billion in support for research and fellowships every year. As American universities enter the global contest for students and prestige, tension is nearly guaranteed. Representative Dana Rohrabacher of California rejected the idea that universities should embrace globalization, and put the issue bluntly in a 2007 congressional hearing: "The people of the United States paid for our universities. This is not a public service for foreigners. Billions of dollars spent by the American people for the education of our young people, to provide skills for our young people, and we have no apologies to make about that."[7]

In order to narrow the gap between the diverging interests of the technology companies and the American economy, as well as to ensure the United States' competitive position in the global economy, policy makers need to open up new entrepreneurial opportunities for small start-ups. As they consider which policies are most effective, they should avoid the false dichotomy that characterizes the debate over economic policy. The question of whether the market or the government should lead is simplistic: both, to state the obvious, have their pluses and minuses. Government stimulus spending can cushion the blow of the recession and supports basic research. But too much government intervention squeezes out the private sector, and high taxes undermine incentives to invest in new businesses.

Rather than putting government and markets on opposite ends of the spectrum, policy makers must treat the two as partners, using the power of the government to encourage new types of entrepreneurship and then giving small start-up companies space to grow. Much of the initiative must be local. Cities and regions need to think about where their comparative advantage lies, and how they can best develop collaborative networks that support innovation. And while no single overarching strategy can be applied across the country, the federal government has a large role to play through the use of research support, tax incentives for venture capital investments, collaborative R&D schemes, and the joint development of intellectual property.

PROXIMITY AND COLLABORATION

To promote growth and realign business and national interests, nothing can deliver like small businesses. As is often noted, small companies (those with fewer than five hundred employees) generate about half of total employment in the United States; according to the Small Business Technology Council, they also employ more scientists and engineers than do large businesses, and more than universities and federal labs combined. Yet, as a recent study by the Kauffman Foundation shows, saying that small businesses create new jobs is not exactly correct. Job creation is truly the domain of small, new businesses—since 1980 nearly all net job creation in the United States occurred in firms less than five years old, and since 2007, these created two-thirds of the jobs.[8]

Before we can help small start-ups, we have to grasp that innovation, despite the hype of globalization, remains highly dependent on collaboration and proximity. The popular image of scientific discovery and innovation by the lone scientist in the lab or the entrepreneur in the garage has always been largely a myth. Discovery and development have always been a group activity. In fact, since 1990, the whole process has become even more collaborative: teams of scientists working together write more papers than individuals do, these papers are more likely to be cited at least a thousand times, and the number of group-authored papers has nearly doubled over the last decade.

In the private sector, research and development is so costly and risky that even the largest companies do not want to undertake it alone. Market demand, consumer tastes, and the science behind new products move too quickly for any one company to stay on top of it all. A recent survey conducted by the Information Technology and Innovation Foundation found that over the last thirty-five years, fewer commercial innovations were the product of large firms acting independently; collaborations produced approximately two-thirds of the award-winning innovation recognized by *R&D* magazine in 2006.[9] In addition, independent corporate labs working on "blue sky" questions (that is, futuristic projects with no known commercial use) are disappearing. In August 2008, Alcatel-Lucent announced that Bell Labs—responsible for six Nobel Prizes as well as the invention of the transistor, the laser, and numerous other communication and computer technologies—would no longer conduct basic research in material physics and semiconductors, but instead would focus on more commercial applications, such as networking, high-speed electronics, wireless, and software.

Technology companies now cooperate with a wide network of suppliers, customers, university labs, and sometimes even competitors to develop new products. In November 2004, Toshiba, IBM, and Sony introduced their new "Cell" computer processor. Ten times more powerful than conventional chips and able to handle multiple tasks at the same time, the Cell was the result of three years of collaborative research among hundreds of scientists. Engineers from all three companies worked together at a development site in Austin, Texas. IBM and Toshiba invested billions of dollars in the project; Sony, which used the chip in its PlayStation 3,

invested $2 billion. IBM posted the architecture of the micropro-
cessor online to allow programmers and game players to write new
software for the Cell, and ten thousand copies of the developer's
guide were downloaded.[10]

As research has gone collaborative, the locus of innovation has
expanded from individual universities and corporate labs to ecosystems made up of networks of technology firms, capital markets, and
research universities. Although globalization would seem to make
regional economies an anachronism, in fact the globalization of science and technology has reinforced the importance of place. Distance is not dead; proximity remains critical.

Innovation is rooted within specific places as it becomes truly
global. Look at the Apple iPod. It is an exemplar of the global product, with manufacture and design spread across the globe and involving companies from the United States, Japan, Taiwan, and Korea.
But Apple, PortalPlayer, Samsung, Toshiba, Inventec, Broadcom,
and the other suppliers of the components inside the iPod are situ-
ated in geographical hot spots dense with other technology players:
Hyderabad, San Jose, Hsinchu, and Daejeon.

Business and government leaders across the world have seized
on the innovation ecosystem as a panacea. Looking at technology
clusters, they see that they share common characteristics: a flow of
people and ideas; a concentration of start-ups and venture capital;
strong universities and other research centers; and a culture of risk
taking and a tolerance for failure. Since history and chance play a
large role in determining how ecosystems come to life, there are
noticeable differences across clusters. Northern Virginia, for example, lacks a major research university (George Mason is now trying
to fill that gap), but federal research institutions and government
technology contractors are dynamic substitutes.

Over the last several decades, a number of new innovative
regional economies have emerged in different parts of the coun-

try. San Diego's transformation to technology dynamo started in the 1960s, when the city was primarily known as a navy town and a tourist destination. Although the city had a strong research base with the University of California, San Diego (UCSD), a dense concentration of defense contractors, as well as the Scripps Research Institute and the Salk Institute, the private sector was standoffish. Business leaders saw the university as bureaucratic and difficult to work with, though that situation changed with the arrival of Richard Atkinson, UCSD's chancellor from 1980 to 1995. Atkinson, who had been director of the National Science Foundation and a professor at Stanford during Silicon Valley's early years, had a vision of the university taking an aggressive role in the city's development.

In 1985, CONNECT, a regional nonprofit organization, was created to facilitate university-business interaction at UCSD, and it eventually became one of the country's most successful programs linking entrepreneurs with technology, money, markets, management, partners, and support services. From 1985 to 2003, CONNECT helped companies raise almost $6 billion. At least forty-one communications and telecommunications companies (including Qualcomm) were either founded by students or faculty or spun off from firms with ties to the university.

Money was key, but so was community. In the words of Mary Walshok, one of the founders of the program, "The higher the risk, the more important is trust and mutual respect. Why would you enter into a high-risk relationship with a perfect stranger? And so a lot of what CONNECT did was create a community where people felt comfortable with one another. They knew one another."[11]

The same sense of community was important for Research Triangle Park in North Carolina. Anchored by Duke, the University of North Carolina, and North Carolina State, this innovation ecosystem is the outcome of strong leadership from two governors and the business and university communities. The park's development benefited both from good timing—a committee to promote industrial research was formed in 1956, the year before the Sputnik crisis—and from unique characteristics of North Carolina. Because no one city dominated the state and there was a tradition of statewide civic action, it was easier to build political and economic support for the park. By most measures, the park is a huge success. In 1980, there was no biotechnology sector in North Carolina. Now the state ranks third in the country, with 520 companies employing more than 56,000 people.

THINKING LIKE A COUNTRY: INNOVATION CLUSTER IN ARIZONA

Arizona's leaders would be happy if they could replicate North Carolina's or San Diego's development experience. For Arizona, one of the biggest challenges has been the success of its old model. The state's population exploded from about 1.75 million in 1970 to over 6.5 million in 2008. Metropolitan Phoenix is the fastest growing and already the fifth largest city in the United States.

Much of this growth has been built on Arizona's cheap land, new jobs, and abundant sunshine. The job growth rate has been impressive, but the majority of jobs have been in low-wage sectors like construction and services. The average wage in the first quarter of 2007 was $857 per week compared with $944 around Austin, Texas, and $1,258 around Atlanta, Georgia, according to the *Arizona Republic*.[12] The state's tax base is narrow. Housing accounted for one of every three dollars generated in Phoenix, and the real estate market is volatile; by 2009, housing prices fell by 50 percent from the peak in 2006. Phoenix's identity, according to Grady Gammage Jr., an attorney and author in the city, is built solely on growth. "The city is not based on anything else. It's about how we can get as many people as possible to move here," Gammage told *NPR*. "This has been the social consensus of what we are about. It's attracting people and getting them to move here."[13]

Beginning in 2002, business, academic, and government leaders started reimagining Arizona as a hotbed of innovation. In February, more than fifty community leaders met to discuss what would be needed to turn Arizona into a world leader in biotechnology. They set two goals: to convince the International Genomics Consortium (IGC), a nonprofit medical research organization focused on exploring the human genome, to establish its headquarters in Phoenix; and to build a companion research institute from the ground up.

In May 2002, they achieved their first victory when the IGC announced it was moving to Phoenix. And in less than a year, a task force raised $90 million from the state and private foundations for a genomics research institute. Today, the Translational Genomics Research Institute (TGen) is a nonprofit organization focused on the genetic components of cancer, diabetes, and other complex diseases. In December 2004, TGen and IGC moved into their new headquarters, a $46 million building owned by the city that anchors the Phoenix Biomedical Center, a bioscience and medical research campus in downtown.

Bioscience is a central pillar of technology development in Arizona, but the push on science is broader, with new institutions being built to support innovation across a number of areas of technology. One of the most creative and important is Science Foundation Arizona (SFAz). Founded in 2002 by three business groups from Phoenix, Tucson, and Flagstaff, SFAz is a nonprofit organization dedicated to promoting and investing in local science and innovation. As one prominent business leader involved in SFAz explained to me, the state universities were near the bottom in the level of support they received from the National Science Foundation and the National Institutes of Health, and a strong libertarian and antigovernment sentiment in the state makes raising taxes difficult, if not impossible. Investment would have to come from alternative sources.

The three leading business groups raised operating funds from public and private sources for the first five years of SFAz's operation. In 2006, Governor Janet Napolitano and the state legislature appropriated $35 million for the Arizona 21st Century Fund, which then invested in SFAz. Money has been targeted at promising young researchers, collaborative grants between academia and industry, "seed" investments in research and development with high commercial potential, graduate fellowships, and research internships for high school science students. There is an explicit effort to keep innovation local. New companies that receive seed investments must stay in the state for at least five years, and the collaborative grants are meant to bring local companies together to exploit "Arizona intellectual property."

Other local private groups and foundations have stepped up with promises to fund SFAz or other bioscience programs in the state. In 2006, the Virginia G. Piper Charitable Trust announced a $50 million grant over five years. In 2007, Scottsdale real estate developer and philanthropist Jerry Bisgrove donated $25 million as part of a matching state grant of $100 million over four years. This public-private partnership was crucial. As one local business leader told me, "It is a miracle Science Foundation Arizona ever happened. It really goes against the grain in a state where the attitude toward government is, 'Protect us from our enemies and then stay the hell away.'"

In 2006, the board of SFAz hired Dr. William Harris, an American who had been running Science Foundation Ireland, as president and chief executive officer. As Harris describes it, Ireland embraced innovation to achieve a distinct goal: to make sure its young people didn't have to leave the country to find jobs. Since Ireland's only natural resources are its people and its beautiful environment, the Irish decided to make strategic investments in bio- and information technology. To get things done, Ireland needed business, academia, and government to push in the same direction, to commit to creating comparative advantage out of nothing. "After I finished in Ireland, I was going to write a book," Harris told me. "Then I came to Arizona and met all these people with the same ambition."

Perhaps the most ambitious of these people is Michael Crow, president of Arizona State University (ASU). Crow arrived at ASU in July 2002 from Columbia University, where he was the vice provost; he had participated in several working groups involved in remaking Arizona before he took the job.

In the academic world, Crow's reorganization of several departments and emphasis on real-world problems have garnered attention. A "problem-focused," interdisciplinary approach to research and education fit Crow's mission to remake ASU into an engine of local economic development. New research centers such as the Biodesign Institute, which combines work from the fields of biology, genetics, chemistry, and applied engineering, are, according to Crow, more closely linked to real-world challenges, such as the need for renewable energy, low-cost vaccines, and disease treatment and detection, than more traditional departments.

Like former UCSD president Richard Atkinson, former Georgia Tech president G. Wayne Clough, Jared Cohon of Carnegie Mellon, Susan Hockfield of MIT, and other university administrators, Crow is pushing his university forward as a major engine of the local economy. "We have made our commitment to place," says Crow. Before his arrival, the Office of Economic Development at ASU had a staff of one and was buried in the Department of Public Relations. That office was closed, and Crow and others around him began thinking about how the university could work with local companies to drive the innovation economy. A study done soon after Crow's arrival asked local companies what research and development they needed. The answer, for most, was none; most companies had little or no demand for technology and little contact with ASU. "If we wanted to partner," Rob Melnick, who headed the Office of Economic and Research, told me, "we had to create our own partners."

ASU contributes to the local economy through initiatives in Tempe, Phoenix, and Scottsdale. ASU Technopolis is a training program for technology entrepreneurs at the early stages of development; so far five hundred entrepreneurs have gone through the program. SkySong, a research park and commercial development, sits on the site of a former mall in Scottsdale and has attracted twenty companies from Canada, China, Germany, India, Ireland, Japan, Singapore, and Turkey, mainly in the area of wireless and mobile applications. ASU's Polytechnic campus in Mesa enrolls more than eight thousand students pursuing technical or professional degrees and, when finished, will have over three million square feet of research space. ASU's technology transfer office has been reorganized and moved from the Office of Research to the edge of the university bureaucracy. Renamed the Arizona Technology Enterprises, and established as a subsidiary of the Arizona State University Foundation, the office has launched the ASU Innovation Fund to help faculty bring their discoveries to market. "We are focusing on the software of innovation," Mariko Silver, who worked in Crow's office and then went to work as Governor Napolitano's policy adviser on innovation, higher education, and economic development, told me. "That's where the real value is. Most places have not figured it out. We are pushing on social networks and breaking down barriers between departments within the university and between organizations—between ASU and the rest of the state."

Business and academia in Phoenix have had important allies in two governors—Jane Dee Hull and Janet Napolitano. Napolitano, in particular, made the development of Arizona as a knowledge economy one of her signature issues. Before she left to become head of the Department of Homeland Security in 2009, Governor

Napolitano managed to maneuver the difficult issue of taxation and science funding in one of the most conservative states in America by building a coalition of centrist Republicans and Democrats. For a number of controversial issues, Napolitano managed to find the sweet spot that would appeal to moderates on both sides of the aisle, promoting all-day kindergartens while cutting business property taxes and declaring a state of emergency to free up money to protect the border from illegal immigrants while opposing Proposition 200, which prevented undocumented aliens from receiving state welfare benefits.

Napolitano visited Science Foundation Ireland early in her administration, and everyone I spoke with involved in Arizona's technology initiatives described her as "getting it" right away. Soon after returning from Ireland, Napolitano convened a series of dinner meetings at a local business leader's house, where around fifteen people from all walks of life came together to begin laying out strategy for the state. This early cross-pollination of people and ideas was important because of the considerable rivalry and competition among Flagstaff, Tucson, and Phoenix. Business leaders in Tucson, for example, had to be convinced that a new medical school in downtown Phoenix would benefit not only Phoenix. "We realized," one of the business leaders present at these meetings told me, "that we had to do more than think about state-wide plans. We had to think like a country, think big, and take responsibility for what we do and the resources we need. We want Arizona to have a seat at the table, even if the United States does not have one."

HIGH RISK, HIGH RETURN

The lessons of Maine (discussed in chapter 1), Arizona, San Diego, and North Carolina are clear. Local leadership is critical, as are partnerships and a steady supply of talent and ideas. There has to be a willingness to subsume narrow interest to the greater vision or, as a board member of SFAz put it, "people who realize that what goes on around you can make you better." Business, government, and academic leaders have to tell the story of what they want to accomplish but without overselling the potential benefits, or underselling how long it might take until those benefits are realized.

Culture matters. While a number of people I spoke with in Phoenix decried a lack of urgency rooted in the sense that growth (and the real estate market) always bounces back, they also praised Arizona's relative youth, the culture of the frontier, and the region's openness to new people and ideas. When Jerry Bisgrove decided to leave New Jersey, he considered moving to Arizona and North Carolina. "In North Carolina I would always be a Yankee," he told me. "Two weeks after I arrived here, I went to the banks and the editorial board of the *Arizona Republic* and told them what I wanted to do. I could get those types of meetings here."

Building the software of innovation is a ground-up experiment that must involve public and private forces. William Miller, who has a long history in Silicon Valley as a professor of computer science and management, as vice president and provost of Stanford, as venture capitalist, and as president and CEO of the nonprofit R&D organization SRI International, described what works: "What is effective are 'people and place' policies." He continued: "Policies that support the education and training of the workforce, that support research combined with education, that support a modern infrastructure, and support the development of institutions that facilitate collaboration between business, government, and the independent sector will have lasting effects of building capacity that does not diffuse away."[14]

Not all are in favor of what is happening in Arizona, especially at ASU. Academic departments have been merged and eliminated, and Crow has been involved in disputes over tenure and free speech

on campus. Some decry Crow's willingness to *"MikeCrow"* manage. Asking the Arizona Board of Regents to hike tuition has not
made him particularly popular among students or their parents. The
handling of the decision not to grant President Obama an honorary
degree and ASU's reputation as a party school made good material
for Jon Stewart and *The Daily Show*. Many wonder how the university can grow past an enrollment of 100,000 and still maintain
quality; the state's budget crisis—in the spring of 2009, ASU eliminated five hundred jobs—has heightened the tension between the
goal of creating nationally ranked research programs and the need
to expand access to higher education across the state.

While support for innovation policy in Arizona is broadening, the
process remains driven by a few prominent personalities. When I
visited Phoenix in September 2008, many thought that Napolitano
would go to Washington if Obama won the election. Biotech supporters feared that without her protection, fiscal conservatives in the
legislature would succeed in cutting funding for scientific research.
They were right to be scared. In February 2009, after Napolitano
left to become secretary of homeland security, legislators voted to
use $22.5 million from the 21st Century Fund Competitive Initiative
Fund to help close a $1.6 billion budget gap. Without support from
the fund, SFAz could not support research at several institutes and
universities, and so the research was halted or canceled. In May 2009,
SFAz sued the state of Arizona for promised but unpaid funding, and
in June 2009 a Maricopa County Superior Court judge issued a ruling against the state on behalf of the foundation, but also found that
the court did not have the authority to make the state pay.

In November 2009, the legislature restored the funding, but all of
the uncertainty was bad for business and science. A number of new
firms, unable to find venture funding locally, left for San Francisco,
including one founded by TGen's deputy director for discovery
research. And Crow himself will probably move on eventually.

Arizona's plan is a high-risk one. Biotechnology especially is a long shot: it requires a heavy concentration of talent and companies, and the industry has been profitable for only one year during the last forty. The emergence of any technological ecosystem seems to be more art than science, as much the result of luck and local cultures as of specific policy decisions. It took several decades for technology clusters to coalesce in North Carolina and San Diego, and Phoenix is entering the game late. While the Arizona legislature was cutting funding, Massachusetts was approving a life science initiative that included $500 million in capital funding, $250 million in granting authority, and $250 million in tax credits.[15] And there are countless examples, especially in Europe, of governments that have dumped money into a region in the hopes that the next Silicon Valley will emerge, only to find stasis and failure. The World Bank estimates that Singapore's Biopolis, a $300 million bet on biomedical research, has only a 50 percent chance of succeeding.[16]

Given the weather, solar energy may be the better bet for Arizona. In April 2009, SFAz announced the Solar Technology Initiative, a collaborative effort with industry and the University of Arizona and ASU to develop renewable energy sources. In July 2009, the state legislature passed a bill offering tax breaks to makers of solar and other alternative energy equipment for building new manufacturing plants in Arizona, and in November 2009, Suntech, a Chinese company, one of the world's largest manufacturers of the materials that convert sunlight into electricity, announced that it would open its first American factory in Phoenix. The company was drawn to Arizona for the tax incentives, the proximity to the California market, and personal connections—the founder had gone to graduate school with two professors at ASU. Also, a sense that all the solar players—the universities, the start-ups, the established firms—knew each other and were willing to work together seems to have influenced the decision.[17]

Even with these comparative advantages, the results are uncertain. While one member of SFAz's board thought they would know whether they were gaining any traction in the next two or three years, another predicted a long wait: "All involved in this process know one thing for sure. We will not know the outcome."

FUNDING SMALL BUSINESSES: THE VALLEY OF DEATH

While these regional development strategies depend on local actors, the federal government, if it is careful, can also play a strong role in boosting innovative start-ups. The challenges for small businesses are legion—of the more than 500,000 new companies founded each year, a high percentage will fail—but raising money for science-based start-ups is particularly difficult, especially during a recession, when there is less investment capital and consumer confidence is low. At the same time, this is not a knot that the government is particularly well suited to untangle. Government support can be heavy-handed and hard to tailor, and we do not want officials to get into the business of trying to predict which technologies are going to be the next "new thing." Instead, we want government policies that help create favorable conditions for entrepreneurship—the Obama administration went part of the way when it took $30 billion from the stimulus package and made it available through the Small Business Administration to local banks to loan to small businesses.

Making the banks make the loans, however, has been difficult as banks continued to slash credit during the recession in order to reduce their own exposure. Even when money is flowing more freely, technology entrepreneurs face the additional challenge of what many call the "valley of death" stretching between the lab and the marketplace—that is, the gap in funding between the early stages of development and the commercialization of the final product, a gap that kills many start-ups. A study found that 90 percent of new entrepreneurial ventures fail within three years if they do not attract venture capital.[18] To survive, companies rely on the three F's ("family, friends, and fools"—who usually invest seed capital of between $100,000 and $200,000), on angel investors (wealthy individuals who invest an average of $200,000 during the second round of financing in exchange for some ownership), and at the end, if they are lucky, on venture capital, which comes in the later stage, usually in the range of $1 million to $2 million.

While there is a great deal of venture capital money in the United States, it cannot meet all of the demand. From 2005 to 2008, the venture capital industry averaged approximately $30 billion in investments, according to the National Venture Capital Association. In 2009, investments dropped to $17.7 billion. And of the hundreds of thousands of new companies founded every year, only a small portion—less than four thousand—receive any investment from venture funds. More important, over the last ten years, venture capital has slowly moved away from start-up funding into later-stage development and expansion. Of the 3,808 investments made in 2008, only 29 percent went to early-stage and seed capital, though this was an increase over the 25 percent in 2008.[19]

So despite its association with technological innovation, venture capital traditionally does not fund exploration and research. Federal money can play an important role plugging this hole, as long as the money is spent wisely. The Small Business Innovation Research (SBIR) Program addresses funding issues at the earliest stages for small technology companies and is one of the government's more successful technology programs. Qualcomm, Amgen, Biogen, Genzyme, and JDS Uniphase all received SBIR support at an early stage of their development.

In 1979, Gary Hendrix, who until then had been a researcher in artificial intelligence at SRI International, applied for funding to develop an idea he had for a "microcomputer-based natural language understanding"—software to allow database users to ask questions in English rather than cryptic operating system commands. An SBIR grant of $100,000 provided several months of operating expenses and, most important, acted as a stamp of approval. Once SBIR's evaluation committee accepted Hendrix's business plan, he found it much easier to recruit twelve additional scientists and engineers from academia and eventually to land $3.5 million from the venture capital firm Kleiner Perkins Caufield & Byers. The database software was marketed as "Q&A Software" and would become Symantec's first successful commercial product. Symantec now has revenues over $6 billion and 17,400 employees.

The Small Business Administration oversees and coordinates the SBIR grants, which are awarded by eleven government departments and agencies, including the Defense Department, the National Science Foundation, NASA, the Department of Energy, and the Department of Homeland Security. The Small Business Administration also administers the Small Business Technology Transfer Program, which operates like SBIR but focuses on collaborative projects—to apply for the grants, small businesses partner with a university, nonprofit research organization, or federal R&D laboratory—and so makes the program even more effective supporting and building the ecosystem of innovation by fostering collaborative networks.

As part of the SBIR program, the Department of Defense, the National Science Foundation, and other participating agencies are required to set aside some of their R&D budgets for awards to small businesses. Each of the agencies relies on an outside group to review the commercial potential of the new technology and on a separate academic committee to judge scientific potential—important steps in ensuring that the money goes to a broad range of promising technologies and is not hijacked by failing firms. Grants are $100,000 for a six-month start-up phase and $750,000 for a two-year period, during which the company conducts research and development and considers how to commercialize the product. Until 2006, agencies were not allowed to make grants in the third phase, the commercialization stage. That year, the Department of Defense instituted a commercialization pilot program that bridges the gap between the last stages of development and the ultimate goal—acquisition by the department.

Like any government program, SBIR has its problems. There is no consistent definition of funding goals: sometimes the goal is research and development, sometimes technical merit, and other times commercial potential. Still, a recent study by the National Academy of Sciences found it among the most successful government efforts to support small firms, link universities to commercial markets, and generate new knowledge.[20] The fact that the program is not permanent, but has to be reauthorized every several years, creates unnecessary uncertainty. The scale of funding is too small, and inflation has shrunk the real value of the awards. Little more than 2.5 percent of federal R&D dollars, or $2.3 billion, goes to the SBIR program. Support should be increased.

The government can also use tax incentives to nudge the private sector to do more for start-ups. In 2009, the Colorado House passed, and Governor Bill Ritter Jr. signed, the "Colorado Innovation Investment Tax Credit," which gives angel investors a 30 percent tax break for putting money into new technology companies. Arizona has an angel tax credit allowing investors to claim an income tax credit of up to 35 percent of the investment amount over three years. Similar programs should be adopted in other states and at the federal level. In addition, entrepreneur and consultant Sramana Mitra offers an interesting idea worth pursuing: a tiered tax structure to encourage more risk taking. Investments in early-stage companies would earn lower capital gains taxes for venture capital, but would face higher rates for later-stage deals.[21]

ECOSYSTEMS AND COLLABORATIVE NETWORKS

Once start-ups get up and running, policy makers want them to become a part of a vibrant ecosystem made up of collaborative research networks. Small companies tap into these relationships as they grow, and large companies look for them when they are making decisions about where to locate R&D facilities. While popular wisdom holds that companies go to China and India for cheap labor, in fact, intellectual capital and university collaboration are bigger draws, according to a 2006 Kauffman Foundation study.[22] Collaborative networks are an important comparative advantage for the United States, and the right policies can help develop and extend them.

Policy makers should revive the idea—suggested in 1998 by Robert Atkinson and Jane Fountain—of using federal money to support and bolster university-industry alliances.[23] In Atkinson and Fountain's scheme, the federal government would match grants for research alliances that met specific criteria: consortia would have to include at least five companies; the firms would have to develop a "technology road map" that identifies common technology to be developed over the near term and shared among all the members; and the funds raised would have to be invested in a federal or a university laboratory.

Corporate tax policy is another important tool for reinforcing collaboration. An easy step is to expand and make permanent the R&D tax credit, which allows a break of up to 10 percent of R&D spending against corporate taxes (companies claimed about $6 billion in credits in 2009). The credit has been renewed many times since it was first passed in 1981, but the political debate that occurs every time it needs extension creates uncertainty for long-term R&D

planning. Both parties and President Bush supported renewing the credit in 2006, but their efforts failed when the provision was tied to a bill that included the much more politically contentious issues of the minimum wage and estate tax. The R&D credit was finally extended to 2009 as part of the Emergency Economic Stabilization Act of 2008, and in June 2009, Senators Orrin Hatch of Utah and Max Baucus of Wyoming introduced yet another bill to make the credit permanent, but it did not pass in time to prevent its expiration on December 31, 2009. As of March 2010, the credit had not yet been extended or made permanent.

Besides being made permanent, the R&D credit should also be used to forge ties among industry, universities, and government. Research consortia involving three companies or investments in collaborative research at a federal research laboratory or an American university could be offered a tax break equal to 20 percent of their R&D spending. More than a decade ago, California expanded the tax credit from 12 to 24 percent for business investments in university research, and Norway, Denmark, the United Kingdom, and Japan all provide more generous tax incentives than the United States for companies investing in research and development at universities and public institutes.

Perhaps the most important step would be to facilitate the joint development and licensing of intellectual property between universities and industry. One of the great strengths of the U.S. innovation system has been the Bayh-Dole Act, the 1980 law that allows universities to patent the results of federally funded research and to license that intellectual property to companies for commercial use. In 2002, the *Economist* called it "possibly the most inspired piece of legislation to be enacted in America over the past half-century."[24] Through this legislation, also known as the University and Small Business Patent Procedures Act, some universities have prospered wildly. Stanford and the University of California, San Francisco earned millions from patents related to recombinant DNA, and Emory University's stake in Emtriva, an antiviral medicine used to treat AIDS, was worth around $320 million.

Recently, there has been, if not backlash against the act, some serious questions about its impact on collaboration. As declining operating budgets have made universities more dependent on licensing revenues, they have become, technology companies complain, overly protective of their licenses and thus inhibit cooperation. By centralizing the transfer process in technology transfer offices, the universities have bottled up innovation in bureaucracy. Technology transfer offices also have a tendency to go for home runs, even if hitting it out of the park—the sale of Lycos Internet search patents that bought new buildings at Carnegie Mellon, for example—is a rare occurrence. According to a 2003 study, only 15 of 191 surveyed institutions received more than $20 million in licensing revenue. And swinging for the fences in search of the next home run often results in missed opportunities to collaborate on a smaller scale. Donald Kennedy, who was president of Stanford and editor of *Science* until 2008, wrote that to those who worried that the legislation would be used to bottle up an ever-larger body of scientific knowledge behind restrictive licenses, Bayh-Dole "looks like a bad deal."[25]

As universities maximize their revenues from licensing inventions, their relationship with companies flips from partners to competitors. The end result, according to R. Stanley Williams of Hewlett-Packard Laboratories, is that "large United States–based corporations have become so disheartened and disgusted with the situation they are now working with foreign universities, especially the elite institutions in France, Russia and China, which are more than willing to offer extremely favorable intellectual property terms."[26]

How widespread and deep the damage is can't be judged yet. Without a doubt, companies are self-interested in arguing that the universities are not sharing enough intellectual property with them.

But some of the load needs to be taken off Bayh-Dole, and alternative channels of interaction developed between academia and industry. Robert Litan, Lesa Mitchell, and E. J. Reedy suggested a new model, one that pays less attention to the number of patents and licenses and instead emphasizes the number of innovations and the speed in which they move from university to market. They argued that more ideas can be commercialized through three pathways: faculty members negotiate licenses themselves and then turn over a portion of their profits to the university; several universities within a region form consortia and contract independently with companies; and companies and professors find each other through Internet sites.[27]

New creative ideas about how to revitalize the university-industry nexus have emerged from the companies themselves. Intel has built a network of "lablets," or collaborative research projects, at University of California at Berkeley, Carnegie Mellon, and the University of Washington. These lablets usually don't handle research tightly connected to products and commercial applications, though motes, wireless sensor chips the size of confetti developed at Berkeley, may be an exception. Rather, the lablets focus on exploratory research, looking at new technologies that could eventually disrupt Intel's business, or create entirely new lines of business. In order to prevent worries about licensing interfering with cooperation, all the lablets are run under an open and collaborative research agreement: both Intel and the university actively collaborate, and all intellectual property is nonexclusive and widely shared. Students and faculty are encouraged to publish, and a number of students have done their entire dissertation research in the labs.

In Intel's view, physically locating the lablets next to the universities was imperative. Lablets, as David Tennenhouse, former director of the program, told me, were designed to tap into universities as "idea switches," locations through which all new ideas pass at some point. Collaboration, in his mind, was still tightly tied to specific places and face-to-face contact. Intel is tapping into everything going on at universities across the country. "Everybody is going to come through Berkeley," according to Tennenhouse.

Policy makers need to encourage technological entrepreneurship and use the power of the government to reinforce networks and collaborative relationships, especially with universities. Funding and research are necessary but not sufficient. In fact, the results of basic research funded by the federal government are available to all, and as a result, are mobile. In addition, companies can develop and exploit the findings of basic research to create high-wage jobs outside of the United States. By contrast, a strategy that includes research and collaborative networks narrows the gap between the interests of the American economy and American technology companies. It grounds innovation locally.

This disparate set of policies—regional development strategies, research funds for small firms, and collaborative networks—when united form a very persuasive argument that innovation is an inherently social process. This same focus on the collective nature of innovation should guide our approach to training the next generation of scientists and entrepreneurs. Funding is important, but it is more essential to ensure that young scientists feel they are part of something larger, that they are tapped into collaborative communities of other scientists and entrepreneurs.

Chapter Nine

COMMUNITIES OF INNOVATION

In a low-key ceremony in the Oval Office on August 9, 2007, President Bush signed the America Competes Act. The legislation, which had strong support from both Democrats and Republicans, increased federal research funds, doubling the budgets of the National Science Foundation, Department of Energy, and National Institute of Standards and Technology laboratories, and expanded the pipeline of talent in math, engineering, and the sciences by providing greater incentives for individuals to pursue a career in science—more scholarships, fellowships, and research grants. It also provided millions of dollars for science and mathematics teaching at the K through 12 level. By the time Bush left office in January 2009, most of the provisions remained unfunded. In September 2009, President Obama introduced a "strategy for American innovation" that picked up most of the themes and programs from the America Competes Act, and the president's 2011 budget proposed funding at levels necessary to meet the goals of the act.

Supporters of the legislation were motivated by fear that the United States faces a severe shortage of scientists and engineers that will only worsen. This possibility was presented prominently in *Rising above the Gathering Storm*, a report released in October 2005 by the National Academy of Sciences, and then repeated widely in the press.[1] India, according to the report, graduates 350,000 engineers a year, and China 600,000, and these numbers are growing. The United States graduates only 70,000 engineers a year, and that number is shrinking. Americans, as the report and the press noted, are generally uninterested in science, and ever-fewer undergraduates leave school with a degree in science, engineering, or math. The decline in the number of American students at the graduate level is particularly stark. In 2007, foreign-born students earned nearly a quarter of the master's degrees and a third of the doctorates in engineering and technology fields. In addition to these trends, the imminent retirement of baby-boom scientists and engineers reflects a real talent crisis.

Writing in the *Washington Post* about six weeks after the report was released, Norman Augustine, former CEO of Lockheed Martin and chair of the twenty-member committee that produced the *Gathering Storm*, argued that "the U.S. educational system is failing in precisely those areas that underpin our competitiveness: science, engineering and mathematics." The solution, he continued, included "establishing 25,000 competitive science, mathematics, engineering and technology undergraduate scholarships and 5,000 graduate fellowships." Less than a week later, columnist David Broder bemoaned "a steady erosion in investment in the kind of brainpower that keeps a nation competitive—and a consequent decline in American inventiveness." In the *New York Times*, Thomas Friedman described the recommendations as "the new New Deal urgently called for by our times." In March 2007, Bill Gates told a Senate committee that the United States was facing a "critical shortage of scientific talent."[2]

While the notion that the United States is facing a shortage of highly skilled workers is popular, both the diagnosis and the solutions offered miss the mark. As I discuss in this chapter, the numbers thrown around regarding how many scientists there are here and abroad have been very soft, and predictions of the numbers of scientists and engineers the United States will need have been consistently wrong over the past six decades. Moreover, the single-minded focus on increasing the absolute numbers of scientists is distracting from the real work that must occur. Building collaborative communities of scientists and entrepreneurs is as important, if not more so, than upping the raw numbers. These communities increase the chances that students expressing an interest in science or math will pursue a career in those fields, and draw more women and minorities into the sciences. They also make it much more likely that the new scientists will be innovative themselves—networks tap new scientists into a steady flow of ideas and possible partnerships and in turn allow their own ideas to enrich the larger group. They create the conditions for cooperation and competition. Federal spending on scholarships plays a role in this process, but much of the work is bottom-up, involving university presidents, professors, mentors, and local business leaders.

DOES THE UNITED STATES HAVE ENOUGH SCIENTISTS AND ENGINEERS?

Let's first look at the claims of shortage. As some observers have noted, *Rising above the Gathering Storm* inflated the size of the science and engineering workforces in China and India. A Duke study found that the title of engineer means having different skills and doing different types of work in different places, and that many people with the title of engineer in India or China had only a two-year degree. The researchers from Duke concluded that the United States produced 137,437 engineers with at least a bachelor's degree, while India produced 112,000 and China 351,537. Cong Cao of the Levin Institute in New York and Denis Fred Simon of Penn State found even fewer engineers in China. After subtracting those with degrees from two-year schools, people who entered other careers, and those whose skills did not meet market demand, Cao and Simon whittled the number down to 207,000.[3]

Of even greater relevance, both the Duke group and Cao and Simon argued that the quality of American engineers remained much higher than that of engineers in either India or China. American engineers were much more likely able to apply scientific knowledge to higher-level problems, to work in teams and across cultural boundaries, and to translate jargon into everyday language. Managers at multinational companies in Beijing and Shanghai consistently describe their engineers as being among the best in the world for solving a defined problem; they will work for days on end and eventually come up with a solution no one has expected. But they are not generating on their own the new problems that need to be solved next, and surprisingly, given the clichéd assumption that Eastern cultures are more collectivist, these engineers do not work well in teams. The relentless competition in China's education system encourages an everyone-for-himself ethos.

On the other side of the coin, the situation in the United States is not as dire as many critics have supposed. Michael Teitelbaum, vice president of the Sloan Foundation, pointed out that these forecasts are often made at the same time as engineers and scientists are being laid off, as new doctorals become frustrated with their limited job prospects, and as salaries for the already employed are further depressed. Of the current claims, the picture of a widespread shortage is "largely inconsistent with the facts," Teitelbaum wrote;[4] salaries for scientists have remained flat; and, in the first quarter of 2009 the unemployment rate for engineers and workers in computer occupations was higher than for all other professionals.[5] While some highly specialized areas may have shortfalls in personnel, this is not the same as widespread shortages. A 2007 report by the Urban Institute nicely summed up the situation: "the United States is not at any particular disadvantage compared to most nations, and the supply of

S&E [science and engineering] graduates is large and ranks among the best internationally."[6]

One area where shortages are likely is in the defense industry, where jobs require security clearance. But this shortage is likely to be remedied as much by a change in clearance and vetting policies as by training more American-born scientists. The fact is that creating more scientists is never easy. Predicting market demand for particular skills is especially difficult. There can be a lag of ten years between the decision to fund fellowships and the time people finally enter the job market, which could be very different by then. Many of the industries that drive the debates about talent shortages, especially biotechnology and information technology, are also susceptible to boom and bust cycles. What looked like a widespread scarcity of talent in 1997 and 1998 in the computer sciences, for example, became a glut after the Internet bubble burst in 1999.

We should be wary of rushing to produce more scientists through government funding. When we tried it a decade ago, it created some surprisingly bad outcomes. From 1998 until 2003, the budget of the National Institutes of Health (NIH) was doubled, from $13.6 billion to $27.3 billion, in order to fight disease and support the U.S. biotech industry. Yet data compiled by Paula Stephan, an economist at Georgia State University, shows the doubling has had a negative effect on the careers of young life scientists.[7]

This is what happened. Many university administrators, seeing the NIH budget double and wanting a piece of the action, began to build new buildings. They often managed to convince state legislatures to get into the act, adding even bigger buildings with more lab space. But the buildings were finished, and the labs staffed with new faculty, postdoctoral researchers, and medical and doctoral students, just as the NIH budget was flattening. Now everything had to be paid for and supported. New faculty members were told they needed to raise funds for research as well as several years' salary.

Fundraising was not a new demand on young faculty, but one or two research grants had been the norm in the past, not the three many institutions were now expecting. Under increased pressure to raise funds, scientists often submitted multiple applications to the NIH.

Once the NIH stopped growing, a far larger population was chasing a constant, if not slightly shrinking, pot of money. As Ira Mellman of the Yale University School of Medicine said, "The doubling built the momentum. Then the momentum came crashing to a halt."[8] This situation resulted in an intense competition for support that has had an adverse effect on young scientists. The Research Project Grant, the RO1, is the basic grant for independent research submitted to the NIH, and is a key marker in a young scientist's career, a sign that he or she is pursuing an independent, sustainable line of research, not just furthering the work of a mentor. The success rate for RO1—the chances that a life scientist's application will be funded—has declined from about 29 percent in 1999 to 12 percent in 2008; the success rate for first-time applicants declined from 29 to 25 percent over the same time period.

In addition, promising young scientists have seen their funding opportunities narrow. According to Harvard economist Richard Freeman, the percentage of NIH grants going to scientists under the age of thirty-five dropped from 23 percent in 1980 to 4 percent in 2002; in 2006 more seventy-year-olds received grants than those under thirty.[9] When the chances of landing the grant needed for a successful academic career shrank, droves of young people left academia. One woman, who was a research scientist at Harvard and left for a job in private industry, explained her decision to me: "I was facing competing with tenure-track faculty members as a new investigator. Knowing how low the current funding rate for RO1 was, I was completely daunted. Although I had received a National Research Service Award, a competitive award from the NIH in which I placed in the top 45 percent early in my postdoc career, I kept thinking that

I would have had to be in the top 5 to 10 percent to receive an RO1. I didn't want to bet my future on such low odds." Those who do stay on the academic track spend more time in postdoctoral fellowships, which rarely pay enough to support a family in any large city. In light of these numbers, the journal *Nature* argued (in an editorial entitled "Indentured Labour") that "too many graduate schools may be preparing too many students, so that too few young scientists have a real prospect of making a career in academic science."[10]

For foreign-born students, paltry postdoc salaries and significant career insecurity have formed less of a deterrent. Salaries, even if low by American standards, are higher than at home, and experience in an American lab is essential to a foreign scientist's resume. Thus, the implicit goal of doubling the NIH budget was not achieved: more money did not increase the share of American-born scientists. The foreign-born share of postdoctoral appointments in biological and medical sciences actually rose from 48 percent in 1995 to 54 percent in 2005.[11]

Today we know enough to avoid this course of action in other fields. Over the last twenty years, spending on the physical sciences has been flat. The total budget on biomedical programs, more than $29.5 billion in 2009, is almost five times more than all of the federal spending for physics, chemistry, engineering, and geology.[12] Carrying over commitments made in the America Competes Act, the Obama administration has said it will double the National Science Foundation budget, which was $6.5 billion in 2009, over ten years. This growth, more gradual than the growth in the NIH budget, should provide a consistent flow of money and reduce incentives for universities to overbuild research capacity.

There is a larger issue, however. What it means to be a scientist must be expanded, and the range of skills a scientist develops broadened. There must be new pathways to careers in science.

Part of the problem is the doctorate itself. For undergraduates interested in a career in science, the only option is to pursue a doctorate. Job opportunities for someone with a bachelor's degree in science are little better than those open to a lab technician; but a doctorate discourages many young people because of the time commitment, which is becoming more burdensome as the average time to completion gets longer. Moreover, as Michael Teitelbaum of Sloan pointed out, there is a skills gap.[13] Few companies actually want to hire science Ph.D.s since they often lack many of the skills businesses need today: a broad understanding of the discipline, flexible research interests, and basic business expertise as well as experience with interdisciplinary teamwork, project management, and the ability to communicate clearly with nonexperts using everyday language.

In addition, an interest in science does not necessarily equate to an interest in becoming a professor. In a 2009 survey of one thousand young scientists at University of California, San Francisco, only half wanted to be academics. The others expected to pursue careers in public policy, government, high school education, industry, or law.[14]

The Alfred P. Sloan Foundation now helps universities develop a professional science master's degree, which includes two years of graduate-level coursework in math and science, interdisciplinary research, and classes in business management as well as the fostering of communication, teamwork, and entrepreneurship skills. Feliza Bourguet, for example, wanted to work in the sciences but did not want a Ph.D. Instead of entering a Ph.D. program and then dropping out after receiving a master's, she enrolled in the applied bioscience program at the University of Arizona. Before she graduated, she had a job as a biomedical scientist at Lawrence Livermore National Laboratory in California.[15]

Professional science degree programs can also be integrated into regional development strategies like those in Maine and Arizona.

Biotech companies in New York, Connecticut, and Massachusetts, for example, employ graduates from the University of Connecticut's program in applied genomics. And as a two-year degree, programs can be geared up or down to meet the fluctuating demand for scientists in specific fields. Over one hundred professional science degrees are now offered at sixty universities, with approximately 2,100 graduates. Money from Washington should be used to support and expand such programs.

A SHARED SENSE OF COLLECTIVE PURPOSE

A large part of the push to create more scientists has involved tweaking individual incentives: making a career in science less financially burdensome through scholarships, doubling the size of graduate school stipends, and providing better funding for postdocs. To be sure, these can be and are effective. From 1999 to 2005, for example, the number of applicants for the National Science Foundation Graduate Research Fellowship Award nearly doubled as the value of the grant increased from $15,000 to $30,000. But a career in the sciences is never going to be based simply on short-term payoffs. According to Richard Freeman, lifetime earnings for biological scientists, for example, are close to $3 million less than for doctors and $1.8 million less than for lawyers.[16] Unless job markets change drastically, smart people will always find jobs that are equally rewarding, pay better, and do not require spending most of their twenties and thirties hidden away in a lab.

So to attract young people to science, there has to be a greater lure than money. As Daniel Goroff, vice president for academic affairs and dean of the faculty at Harvey Mudd College, put it in his written testimony to the House Subcommittee on Research, Committee on Science, "Besides dollars, what makes people persist in their fields is a shared sense of collective purpose and mutual support." There are good policies that increase fellowships, and there are better policies that address the collective nature of science and engineering.

Later in that testimony to the subcommittee, Goroff elaborated, linking the shared purpose that brings people to science to the point that being part of something larger also *encourages* innovation:

> It is not just individual winners, but whole communities that are important enablers of STEM [science, technology, engineering, and mathematics] progress. The number of research papers or patent applications with multiple authors has been exploding relative to the number from lone geniuses. It takes teamwork, communication, as well as interactions within and between fields to make discoveries. Rather than flashing from the sky, think of scientific energy as coursing around networks. Scientists are at the nodes of these networks, and I am all in favor of increasing their numbers, but it is the strength, density, reach, and interfaces of their networks (STEM cells?) that promote the innovation and invention we seek.[17]

Goroff's point is critical. The most effective track—not only to draw more people into science, but also to make them more productive—is to build flexible networks that support scientists and innovation.

Let's put it another way. Much of the responsibility for adjusting to the globalization of science and technology has been thrust on the individual American. High school students are told to learn more math and science (as well as Mandarin); university students, to major in physics and then go on to graduate school; and older workers, to upgrade to the new skills that will be in demand in the global economy. The onus is on these folks to become more competitive individually, on the assumption that the United States will eventually become more competitive as a country. While individuals do need to know more, they also have to know how to think as part of a group, a network, and society. As the interaction of networks makes the United States more competitive as a whole, that outcome will in turn make Americans more competitive individually as well.

Two related challenges illustrate the importance of investment in collaborative communities: How do you get people with an interest in science to graduate with a degree in science? And how do you increase the number of women and minorities in the sciences? To meet both, there has to be a sense of collective purpose and mutual support. And as with much of innovation policy, it is a ground-up, local effort that needs to involve business, academic, and community leaders.

MAJORING IN SCIENCE

Despite the hype about young Americans' apathy toward science, more than a third of freshmen surveyed by University of California, Los Angeles plan on majoring in science, mathematics, or engineering when they arrive on campus.[18] With the recession battering the prospects in law, finance, and consulting and with more students expressing interest in public problems like climate change and terrorism, many more people can be expected to at least seriously consider a career in the sciences.

Yet only about half of those who say they plan to major in the sciences follow through; one-third shift to another major outside of technology fields, and one-fifth drop out altogether. The reasons include large, impersonal introductory courses; a culture of weeding out the "weaker" students (summarized in the probably apocryphal story, repeated on every campus in America, of the professor who stands in front of the class on the first day and says, "Look to your left, look to your right, only one of you will be here at the end of the semester"); the teaching assistant with a less-than-perfect command of English; and grades that are systematically lower than grades in other disciplines. But the overwhelming majority who leave—over 80 percent of respondents in one study—cite poor teaching.[19]

"Science majors are not being created in college," Carl Weiman, winner of the 1995 Nobel Prize in Physics, told Congress in 2006. "Rather, they are primarily the few students that, because of some unusual predisposition rather than ability, manage to survive their undergraduate science instruction."[20] At many research universities, professors regard teaching undergraduates as a burden and a distraction. Since promotion depends on research and publications, not on undergraduate teaching evaluations, professors invest their interest and energy accordingly. Teaching assistants, many of whom receive no formal teacher training, do much of the teaching in the introductory biology, chemistry, and physics classes. Any interest that a student has in science is squashed by the end of the first year, and only those with a high tolerance for pain, a deep love of the topic, or some other "unusual predisposition" remain.

Before we offer scholarships to more students to study math and science, a policy agenda both Republicans and Democrats support, we have to make sure that students will actually enjoy science and math classes. Changing the incentive structure, especially for university administrators, certainly would have some impact on how science is taught or, at least, would influence graduation rates. Stanford economist Paul Romer suggested that universities and colleges compete for federal funds based on their success in increasing the fraction of their students who graduate with degrees in science, engineering, or mathematics.[21] Since the major research universities are heavily dependent on federal support—a school like Stanford can draw 40 percent of its budget from federal agencies—universities could be expected to improve the retention rates in these fields.

At the student level, making science education more than a question of survival is no mystery, though it does take time, attention, and leadership from the top. Numerous studies show that individual research projects, small classes, and hands-on apprenticeships with industry improve both the teaching of science, technology, engineering, and mathematic disciplines and the likelihood that students will stay in these fields.[22] Harvey Mudd College, a liberal arts college of science, mathematics, and engineering in Claremont, California, does much of this very well. Collaborative research projects between faculty and students are an important part of the educational experience, with students presenting their findings in fifteen-minute presentations over two days every year.

Other students are involved in solving real-world problems that can have immediate commercial or scientific use. The Aerospace Corporation, for example, came to the Clinic Program at Harvey Mudd, asking students to design a digital camera and GPS add-on board for a microsatellite. Technology start-ups, large companies, and the national laboratories sponsor projects at the Clinic Program and retain the rights to the intellectual capital. The student-designed add-on board, which had to be radically engineered to withstand extreme temperatures and stress, was eventually used on two satellites launched from the Space Shuttle *Discovery*.

Harvey Mudd can boast of the latest equipment, computers, and instrumentation available and a research budget of $2 million annually, as well as of a president who longboards across the campus (Maria Klawe). Fancy hardware matters, but in order to thrive, students must also feel that they are part of a larger community. Simply providing more scholarships for math, science, and engineering degrees is not going to be enough—institutions that build and support community are the ones most likely to raise retention rates and foster more innovation.

SCIENCE AND THE
"UNDERREPRESENTED MAJORITY"

Predicting the skills the market will require a decade from now is an imperfect science, but one eventuality is clear: minorities and women will make up a larger share of both the university population and the workforce. By 2010, women will earn more degrees than men at every level of higher education. Between 2010 and 2015, the number of university students will grow by over two and a half million, of whom two million will be people of color. Yet while women and minorities currently make up about two-thirds of the workforce, they are an underrepresented majority in the areas of science and engineering, holding only one-fourth of the jobs in science and technology fields.[23] Universities and colleges need to begin to adjust to the shifting demographics of the workforce. At a minimum, even maintaining the scientific workforce at current levels will require that it become more diverse.

Again, money makes everything easier, but manufacturing more science and engineering students will take more than just scholarships. African-American students express the same interest in majoring in science and engineering as do their white classmates, but they leave these fields in disproportionate numbers. Along with poor teaching, minority students and women have to deal with academic and social discrimination.

As with improving teaching, what actually works is already pretty well known. Successful programs in the field, such as the Meyerhoff Scholars Program at the University of Maryland, Baltimore County (UMBC), could be expanded nationally. UMBC, a predominantly white undergraduate institution, is one of the largest pipelines for African-American science and engineering doctorates in the United

States, trailing Howard University, Spelman College, and other historically black colleges and universities. The program's overall retention rate in science, engineering, and mathematics is higher than 95 percent. Of the 550 students who have passed through it, about half of them are doing graduate work in the sciences, and dozens have completed medical degrees.

UMBC's president, Freeman Hrabowski III, cofounded the Meyerhoff program in 1988 and pushed it from the top. The program includes mentoring, training, and academic and career advising, as well as financial support for room and board, tuition and fees, and book allowances. Hrabowski, who marched as a child in civil rights protests in Birmingham, Alabama, is often described as exuberant and charismatic, a "magnetic force" according to the headlines of a feature in the *Washington Post*.[24] The faculty responded to his leadership by developing new grassroots programs in many different academic departments. Professors injected original research and more group work into their introductory classes.

Community is central. The summer before their freshman year, students meet for a "bridge semester," and once school starts, they live together. They work collectively, with the expectation that seniors help juniors, juniors help sophomores, and sophomores help freshmen. The underlying premise, according to Earnestine Baker, executive director of the program, is that with a "high concentration of high-achieving minority students in a tightly knit learning community, students continually inspire one another to do more and better."[25]

Hands-on research is also an integral part of the program. Chianna Paschall, who went on to earn a Ph.D. at the University of Pennsylvania, modeled the first key component of the AIDS virus's structural proteins; her work was featured in a cover story for the *Journal of Molecular Biology*. Chelsea Stalling, who has an M.D. and Ph.D. from the University of Pennsylvania, coauthored a paper published in *Science*. Other UMBC students have published in *Nature* and *Structural Biology*.[26]

What was done at UMBC can also be scaled to the regional level. To counter the obstacles minorities wanting to study science face at all stages of education and career, the University of North Carolina at Chapel Hill and seven historically black and Native American colleges developed the Partnership for Minority Advancement in the Biomolecular Sciences. The program offered research internships, ran professional development workshops on grant writing and negotiations, and developed both specialized undergraduate courses to help students "navigate the specialized world of biomolecular research" and a science laboratory in a converted bus that brought technology and teaching tools to high schools lacking science resources. Unfortunately, the program ended in August 2006 when funding ran out.

America's most prestigious research universities bear a particular responsibility for developing homegrown talent. Having attracted the best and brightest from around the world for decades, they must now redouble their efforts to reduce undergraduate attrition in technical majors and sustain American graduate enrollments in the fields of physical sciences and engineering. Other models—Georgia Tech's success in producing African-American engineers through mentorship and research programs; Carnegie Mellon's ability to increase the number of women in computer science—demonstrate what can be achieved.

While the call for increasing the proportion of minorities and women in science-based careers goes back to the 1960s, the rationale for it, as the president of Rensselaer Polytechnic Institute, Shirley Jackson, noted, has changed.[27] In the 1970s and 1980s, underrepresentation was considered primarily a social or moral issue—a question of affirmative action. Today, it is also seen as a competitiveness issue. Only by tapping into emerging demographics, so the argument goes, will the United States be able to address the structural imbalance between the number of scientists the United States needs and the number it produces.

Aside from the argument about quantity, there are other reasons for drawing more people from more diverse backgrounds into science: it would benefit both the culture of innovation and the United States. Studies by Scott Page, an economist at the University of Michigan, show that under the right conditions, diversity leads to better outcomes. By bringing people together who have different perspectives and ways of solving problems, firms and universities have a greater chance of cracking the most difficult problems. Multiple approaches are more effective than a single approach, and thus Silicon Valley outperforms other technology hot spots, according to Page, because of its diversity—smart engineers, scientists, and entrepreneurs from different parts of the world, each with their own viewpoints and life experiences.[28]

SCIENCE AS OPPORTUNITY

The framework for educating, training, and funding young researchers and scientists first emerged during World War II and was formally institutionalized by Vannevar Bush, an engineer and the first science adviser to a president (no relation to the presidents Bush). Before the war, federal funding for research and development had been minuscule, the government did little research of its own, and there were few institutional links between government and industry or between the federal government and the universities. The Second World War changed everything. During the war years, funding for research and development grew by a factor of twenty, large federal laboratories were founded, and, for the first time, federal money went to universities for research—to dramatic effect. Science contributed hugely to the war effort through the development of synthetic rubber, radar, the radio proximity fuse, guided missiles, and the atomic bomb, to list just a few of the most notable inventions.

Fearful that the government's commitment to science would collapse after the war, Bush, Director of the Office of Scientific Research and Development, delivered *Science—The Endless Frontier* to President Harry Truman in July 1945. In his report, Bush offered an extended justification for the government's continuing to play a large role in the creation of scientific knowledge after the war. Private industry almost always underinvests in basic research, since it is what economists call a public good: companies may not actually capture all the benefits of investing in research and development and may also have to share it with others who do not contribute. The United States, Bush argued, could not afford to underfund scientific knowledge since it was essential to national security, to the battle against disease, and to job creation. In the past, "Yankee ingenuity" had been enough as the United States could build on the discoveries of European scientists. That was, according to Bush, no longer an option: "A nation which depends upon others for its new basic scientific knowledge will be slow in its industrial progress and weak in its competitive position in world trade, regardless of its mechanical skill."

Bush wanted the government to fund basic research that would lead to new knowledge but have no immediate commercial applications. Some of this research would be conducted in university labs, where scientific talent could be discovered and trained. Industry would benefit from the creation of all of this knowledge and from a steady supply of engineers and scientists. Bush, in effect, forged the connections among industry, the universities, and the government that have driven science and innovation in the United States over the last seven decades.

Science—The Endless Frontier is, however, about more than the triumvirate of university, industry, and government, about more than funding and organizations. For Bush, pushing these "new frontiers of the mind" was essential not only "to our security as a nation, to our better health, to more jobs, to a higher standard of living, and to our cultural progress." It was also the responsibility of "this constitutional republic" to provide an opportunity to individual Americans to better themselves. The U.S. government had throughout its history, in Bush's telling, created new opportunities by developing the frontier: it had "opened the seas to clipper ships and furnished land for pioneers." By 1945, these physical frontiers had all but disappeared, so now the United States needed to open new horizons of exploration. The "frontier of science remains," wrote Bush. "It is in keeping with the American tradition—one which has made the United States great—that new frontiers shall be made accessible for development by all American citizens."[29]

Although Bush crafted his report with an eye to ensuring political support for his proposal, he was, by framing science as opportunity, making the important point that the institutions built to support innovation require a wider legitimacy. If the nation's riches were going to be used to support the search for scientific knowledge, all citizens had to feel that they had a stake in, and could pursue their own opportunities through, the science and technology system. So while people like Scott Page are correct in arguing that diversity and open access make the United States more innovative, Bush was also right that the stability of the system demands that all have the ability to tap into it. Or as President Obama stated in his inaugural address over sixty years later, "The success of our economy has always depended not just on the size of our gross domestic product, but on the reach of our prosperity; on our ability to extend opportunity to every willing heart—not out of charity, but because it is the surest route to our common good."[30]

For those interested in science policy, *Science—The Endless*

Frontier has become talismanic. A summary of an academic conference series held at Columbia University to commemorate its fiftieth anniversary referred to the report's "biblical status" and described itself as a "Vatican Council for science policy," convened to interpret, revisit, and clarify dogma.[31] But as noted at the conference, the political and economic context in which Bush wrote and delivered the report has changed dramatically. We live in an age of globalized innovation Bush never imagined.

Instead of simply seeking, as much of the public debate has suggested, to increase the funding for the institutions that Bush helped design nearly seven decades ago, we should think about what we want to build next. While the shape of the next generation of institutions may still be murky, we have a pretty good idea of the values that should animate them. That is, no matter what comes next, we must continue to foster a culture of risk, creative destruction, user-driven innovation, and open architecture.

Chapter Ten

THE FUTURE OF INNOVATION

As I conducted interviews across India and China, I would often reflect on the current state of panic at home, based on the prevalent fear among many pundits and politicians of the almost inevitable decline of the United States as a technology power. Occasionally, my interviewee would take the opportunity to probe and categorize America's weakness, but in most cases the person I was speaking with would push back, declaring that reports of America's demise had been greatly exaggerated. Sitting in the lobby of a hotel in Mumbai, responding to my persistent questions about whether America was losing its edge, Jerry Rao, the CEO of Mphasis, observed, "There is no competition between the United States and Asia. The issues at stake are very different in America. It is the only society that constantly grapples with the full set of questions about how technology interacts with what it means to be human. America defines all the interesting questions and provides all the important answers. Maybe thirty years from now China will do that. But until then, America remains the most important place." Addressing a 2008 conference on science, technology, and innovation in China, India, and the United States, C.N.R. Rao echoed the same sentiment: "America—whether you like it or not, however much you complain, howl and cry—continues to be the center of science and innovation."[1]

We often forget that the United States is well positioned—perhaps better than any other country—to take advantage of globalized innovation. Only American society can currently muster all of the skills needed to face globalization—the ability to conduct cutting-edge, interdisciplinary research; recognize new markets and consumer demands; manage across time, distance, and culture; tolerate risk and support entrepreneurship; and welcome new ideas and talent no matter what their origin or social standing. The United States has strengths that are the envy of many, and the cultural, social, and political barriers to innovation in Asia are real and hard to overcome. In a November 2009 poll conducted by *Newsweek* and Intel, 81 percent of Chinese, compared to 41 percent of Americans, believed that the United States was staying ahead of China in innovation.[2] Perhaps we should be more confident of our future.

A lack of confidence is pervasive in the worries about whether the United States is losing the race to develop alternative energy sources. Clean energy technologies, we are told, are the "new Sputnik," but the space race metaphor is misguided. Right now, the United States, like everyone else, benefits from China and India lowering the cost of solar panels and wind turbines. The cheaper these alternative energy sources become, the more quickly and widely they will be adopted, and the more rapidly carbon emissions will be reduced.

Even if we insist on seeing this as a contest, it is far too early to assume that the Chinese are going to eat our lunch. The Chinese are investing significantly in exploration and development and have ambitious plans for reducing their dependence on oil and coal. Chinese firms like Suntech Power and Goldwind Science and Technology are world leaders in the manufacture of solar and wind equipment. Not only do pundits see China moving ahead in R&D investment, but some, such as Thomas Friedman, see China's top-down authoritarian political system as an advantage over the United States'. Chinese leaders can pick a goal and mobilize massive resources, which allows them to "just impose the politically difficult but critically important policies needed to move a society forward in the 21st century."[3]

Yet the game is far from over. So far, Chinese firms have managed only to replicate what they achieved with computers, DVDs, and cell phones: lowering costs while allowing foreign firms to continue to control R&D, design, and high-value services. Low labor and land costs as well as government support have built manufacturing strength, but Chinese firms have not mastered technologically difficult processes like managing wind and solar energy fields and connecting them to the grid. Moreover, as *China Greentech Report 2009* finds, China's top-down method has limitations: poor incentives, lack of competition, higher costs, and market inefficiencies.[4] Once the United States begins to set real prices for renewable energy, the decentralized, high-risk model found in Silicon Valley, Austin, and Phoenix is likely to shift into high gear.

Yes, there is much work to be done, and it is inevitable, and desirable, that the structures of science, technology, and innovation change over the next decade in the United States. Science and innovation are not immune to the same flattening of hierarchies, decentralization, and rapid pace of change that the explosion of cheap data storage and near ubiquitous communication technologies created in so many other areas of activity. As Michael Nielsen, one of the pioneers of quantum computation, observes, the Internet is not only making it easier to share data and findings through online databases like GenBank where biologists can deposit and search for DNA sequences, but also increasing the scale of research through wikis— websites that allow for collaborative work—and other social software.[5] The same technologies are reshaping the role venture capital plays in the growth of new companies, especially for firms planning to provide services over the web. The ability to rent equipment as well as to store and process huge amounts of data and deliver content through servers provided by Amazon and others has greatly reduced start-up costs. As a result, many entrepreneurs, according to Robert Hendershott, a professor of private equity and entrepreneurship at Santa Clara University, will never need to go to a venture capital firm, choosing instead to rely on their own savings or on friends and family. [6]

The combined effects of the web and globalization will mean that the American innovation system will shrink in absolute terms (share of the world's research and development, number of doctorates, number of patents, and production of scientific papers) but become more nimble and flexible. The demands placed on the system will be serious—solutions to the challenges of energy dependence, climate change, and health care reform are expected, at least in part, to spring from technological innovation—and the international competition will ratchet up in intensity. In many ways, the American system will actually end up less "American"—not only as technology companies and research universities globalize, but also as the innovation systems of China and India begin to look more, at least from the outside, like the American system. Yet the U.S. system will also be more community-driven, as cities and states tailor the pieces to fit their own specific needs. The brunt of the responsibility for creating innovation ecosystems will rest not with Washington, but with local business, academic, and community leaders.

While we cannot know which specific institutions will be best suited to cope with the demands of globalized innovation in the future, we can ensure that whatever we create will be resilient and responsive by keeping six design principles, drawn from the previous chapters, in mind:

THE SOFTWARE OF INNOVATION MUST BE OPEN AND
COLLABORATIVE.

In the language of software development, *open source* refers to the ability of many people to access the software's code—code is changed and improved through decentralized collaboration—as opposed to *proprietary software*, whose owner sets limits on its use, modification, or republishing. The hundreds of developers, activists, and fans who have developed the Mozilla Firefox browser for the Internet, for example, have improved security, stability, and usability. By contrast, Internet Explorer is owned and developed by Microsoft; independent coders and hackers have no access to the code and no right to modify.

For the United States, the software of innovation should strive for the openness and collaboration of open source. Since policy makers want the best and the brightest to take the code and modify it on their own, the United States must remain the place where the most talented and skilled still yearn to come. To this end, the country needs to improve visa regulations, welcome highly skilled immigrants, and clear the path to citizenship. Those who excel in school or start their own businesses should be encouraged to stay in the United States.

The United States needs to remain open to the flow of money and ideas. Foreign investment into the United States is essential to its economic health and innovative capability. Sovereign wealth funds, and other instruments of state capitalism, are political challenges, not economic threats. The United States already has a fairly robust system in place to evaluate the security risks of foreign capital; it must respond through a political defense of liberal capitalism and by performing better, not by restricting the flow of capital into the United States.

Strengthening the software means improving the ability to work across platforms. Within innovation ecosystems, policies need to encourage collaborative work, sometimes through research grants, other times by tax incentives, and still others by programs such as the North Star Alliance Initiative in Maine that funnel the efforts of business, academic, and local government leaders into common innovation goals. Universities and industry have to be flexible about technology licensing, shifting focus from the "home run" to the "fire hose approach," pumping as much technology into the community as possible.

There has also been a big push over the last several decades for multidisciplinary work at the nexus of biology, physics, computer science, and mathematics. This is one of the true centerpieces of the American innovation system, and federal money should reinforce the networks and organizations that bring together people with disparate backgrounds and expertise. At the same time, funding and promotion decisions must reward work drawing from several different branches of the sciences, drawing insights from design, psychology, economics, anthropology, and other fields.

THE SOFTWARE OF INNOVATION MUST BE SECURE AND STABLE.

As with any software, policy makers want to make sure that the software of innovation is both secure and relatively stable. A program that is constantly hijacked by malware, or that continually crashes and freezes, will soon be discarded for new software.

Security is an unavoidable issue. While openness undoubtedly exposes the United States to threats, it is such an integral part of the operating system that any attempt to restrict the flow of information, people, or technology must seriously consider the cost-benefit trade-off. Too much security and the system loses flexibility; needless security protocols slow the system down and erode the user's trust in it.

In this age of global science and technology, attempts to control the movement of ideas or talent will not only fail but also damage America's ability to innovate. Export control policy is at best a secondary measure. Openness is indispensable to innovation, which in turn is essential to U.S. security. The creation of new knowledge is far more important to the security of the country than the defense of any technological lead, real or imagined, it currently possesses.

RISK REMAINS ESSENTIAL.

The reputation of risk must be rescued after its unfortunate association with credit default swaps and ninja (no income, no job, and no assets) loans. Hasty, irresponsible risk is bad for the economy, but being too conservative and risk averse can be equally disastrous: witness Detroit and the Big Three automakers. While risk takers drive change and growth, it is not risk for risk's sake that makes their contribution so important. Rather, it is that risk takers generate new knowledge and companies.

Money has to flow to early-stage start-ups. Getting funded is tricky enough when times are flush; it is like getting blood from a stone when credit is tight and the future uncertain. The government can play some role in this through programs like the Small Business Innovation Research program, but it also needs to help create the conditions—through tax relief, loan programs, and aid to community banks—under which entrepreneurs can access capital and private investors are willing to take up risk again. At the more macro level, a dynamic financial market, initial public offerings, and other forms of exit are needed for entrepreneurs who found and build companies.

Hard times make scientists more conservative, but now more than ever they should embrace big-thinking, forward-looking failure. Driven by the need to secure funding, scientists can become "serial grant-writers," according to a white paper produced by the American Academy of Arts & Sciences, writing proposals that extend what they already know, not striving toward something new.[7] To counteract the tendency to stay in comfortable territory, more money should be directed to early-career grants and to support well-designed failures—that is, "paradigm breaking" ideas that, despite their high chance of failure, push the envelope. Lee Smolin, a theoretical physicist, suggests that funding agencies reward scientists who attack the really "hard" problems and penalize those who tread well-worn ground.[8] Likewise, a proliferation of prizes has tapped into innovators' competitive and entrepreneurial spirit. Among these are the $10 million Ansari X Prize for private-sector manned spaceflight; Google's $30 million Lunar X prize for the first privately financed team to put a rover on the moon; and the Virgin Earth Challenge, which promises $25 million for a commercially viable process to remove a billion tons of greenhouse gases from the air every year.

THERE ARE NO GRAND STRATEGIES, JUST LOCAL FIXES.

One of the strengths of open-source software is that users develop new code to fit their own needs. Innovation is decentralized to a distributed community of users and developers. This community can tweak and modify as it sees the need; some users can make as dramatic an impact on new products as the inventors.

Clearly the federal government will continue to play a critical role in innovation, along with the big companies and research universities. Many new projects in basic research will require a scale that only the triumvirate of government, industry, and academia can manage. But we should be looking more to our backyards and communities of makers and tinkerers than to Washington. We need chaotic experimentation, an explosion of new ideas in an ecosystem tolerant of failure. We need an upsurge of small start-up companies to re-energize the economy and to ground innovation locally, as the big technology companies become more global and less national.

Cool ideas, risk, and community—regional economies are critical platforms for new start-ups. Some places are lucky enough to already have a strong base of excellent research institutes or existing technology firms. Other places will have to scramble to put the pieces together, fostering partnerships among government, businesses, and universities, like Maine and Arizona did. The point will not be to re-create Silicon Valley locally—there is no single universal strategy. The work will be slow and from the ground up, as each region discovers what it does well and where its comparative advantage lies. To ensure a competitive advantage, a community will have to act more like a country, taking its destiny into its own hands.

This decentralization of responsibility and initiative is also central to how the United States should conduct science diplomacy. Science issues—climate change, alternative energy, and infectious disease—are of vital importance to the bilateral relationship with China, Japan, India, and many others. The U.S. government is doing more to track and shape technology development in Asia, with the National Science Foundation and the National Institutes of Health, for example, expanding their offices and sending more staff abroad. But since there will never be enough government officials for the job, the source of dynamism in relationships across the Pacific is American society, not the government. The competitive strength of the United States, especially compared with Europe, is the aggregate of graduate students, venture capitalists and technology entrepreneurs, foundation officers, and professors and research scientists who have extensive personal and institutional ties to Asia. The trick for policy makers will be not only to try and keep abreast of developments, but also to influence them so they reinforce larger American political and strategic goals.

AMERICANS MUST ALL FEEL THEY HAVE A STAKE IN "USER-DRIVEN" INNOVATION.

Before individuals and communities build a decentralized system of innovation, they have to feel they hold a stake in it. Many have felt left out of and ill treated by the most recent wave of globalization. As former secretary of the Treasury, and now head of the National

Economic Council, Lawrence Summers wrote in 2006, "What the anxious global middle is told often feels like pretty thin gruel. The twin arguments that globalization is inevitable and protectionism is counterproductive have the great virtue of being correct, but do not provide much consolation for the losers."[9] Trade produces winners and losers, as capital and labor get reallocated to the sectors in which countries excel. Since the winners win more than the losers lose, openness is to the nation's overall benefit—even though the autoworker in Ohio who was put out of work after his factory closed may not share in that benefit.

The consolation, in the standard argument made by economists, arrives when the winners compensate the losers. Such compensation has not, however, been happening, and while American companies have been doing just fine, the American workforce has suffered. Traditionally incomes go up with corporate profits, as companies create new jobs and drive up demand and wages. Yet for many Americans, even those with college degrees, incomes have not kept pace with inflation. While corporate profits have doubled, wages have barely moved since 2000. Inequality has gone up—the share of income going to the top 1 percent of families doubled from 8 percent in 1980 to 16 percent in 2004, and rose again to 22 percent in 2006[10]—as hedge fund managers, bankers, and management consultants took advantage of their excellent position in the game of globalization.

Almost all policy makers, business leaders, and academic leaders agree that the United States must revamp its innovation system. The support for increased spending on research and development and better science education is broad and bipartisan. But as Senator Mark Warner forcefully argued at a conference on the innovation economy in December 2009, these issues have no "political saliency" because the vast majority of Americans "do not believe what we are talking about is relevant to their lives."[11] The solution is to demonstrate how these policies actually improve lives and to spread the pain of adjusting to change. There are a wide range of cost-sharing policies: expand trade adjustment assistance and wage insurance, fund greater investment in on-the-job training and worker retraining, fix the system of health insurance and make it portable. Although these may seem at first glance to have little to do with research and development and technology, they are in fact directly connected to the software of innovation. It is much easier to start a new company if an entrepreneur is not worried about what happens if he or she gets sick and incurs onerous health bills.

THE UNITED STATES MUST BE TIGHTLY LINKED TO SCIENCE AND TECHNOLOGY HOTSPOTS IN THE REST OF THE WORLD.

The United States spends more on research and development than the next seven largest spenders combined. While the scale and scope of the American innovation system give it a great deal of sway internationally, its true strength lies in its links to innovation systems throughout the world. A vast web of collaborative research, corporate alliances, foundation grants, personal ties, alumni networks, and government-to-government contacts tie the United States to established and emerging centers of scientific excellence. In 2005, for example, scientists in the United States were the most popular partners for Chinese and Japanese scientists in every field—chemistry, physics, engineering, environmental technology, and biology—but one: material science. And in that field, they were the second most popular choice for both their Japanese and their Chinese colleagues.[12] The goal, then, is to make sure that the country does not become complacent about these relationships, and that it turns them into a smart grid for the global system of innovation—a combination of hardware and software networks that monitor and adapt to the creation, distribution, and use of science and technology.

The methods for building this grid parallel much of what the United States does in more traditional foreign policy arenas— strengthen international organizations, work with allies and avoid needlessly antagonizing others, and identify and cooperate with emerging centers of power and influence in Asia. President Obama has recognized that "science, technology and innovation proceed more rapidly and more cost-effectively when insights, costs and risks are shared."[13] The State Department has increased the number of science officers in a few embassies around the world and in November 2009 appointed three science envoys who will travel to countries in North Africa, the Middle East, and South and Southeast Asia.

As they engage these newly emerging centers of science and technology, policy makers will have to maneuver between the poles of hardware and software, high and low politics, and local and global innovation. U.S. policy must be fine-tuned to developments on the ground in Asia, and sensitive to the political and strategic objectives that states pursue through seemingly economic means. Autonomy, geopolitics, and rising inequality—these are the roots of the tree slowly pushing up through the sidewalk, warping what is traditionally pictured as a flat world. With each of its trading partners, the United States must make its way across shifting ground, ready to adjust, adapt, and deploy dialogue and cooperation, or the wedge and the stick, depending on the circumstances.

Inevitably, more science and scientific discovery will occur abroad, in new government and university labs in China and India and in the corporate labs of Japanese and South Korean companies. While we have grown accustomed to science flowing west across the Pacific, our true shift in consciousness will not be realized until we internalize how much we can learn and gain from collaboration with Asia by meshing our software advantage with Asia's emerging hardware strengths.

While stopping short of denying that America still had many advantages in science and technology, an executive at IBM once argued with me that he would prefer to be in Asia's position: "I'd rather have growing pains than the aches and pains of an old man." Yet one of the great strengths of the United States has always been its ability to re-create and renew itself, especially when confronted with a crisis. Alexis de Tocqueville, the great French historian and observer of America, put it well: "The great privilege of the Americans does not simply consist in their being more enlightened than other nations, but in their being able to repair the faults they may commit."[14] There is much that is dysfunctional in the United States, but there is also a great deal to be optimistic about. Across the country, numerous regions, companies, and universities are experimenting with new ways to promote and structure innovation, launching bottom-up efforts to create collaborative communities. These efforts are grounded in our comparative advantage—an open and flexible culture and a web of institutions, attitudes, and relations that move ideas from the lab to the marketplace. As long as we actively maneuver between hardware and software, high and low politics, and the local and global, we will prosper and play a dynamic role in the new world of globalized innovation.

Acknowledgments

This book is about the importance of community and collaboration, and I have benefited immensely from both. I am very fortunate to work at the Council on Foreign Relations (CFR), and I thank Richard N. Haass, the president of the Council, for all of his support and for making CFR such a vibrant, stimulating, and collegial place to work.

James Lindsay, senior vice president and director of studies at CFR, helped make this book what it is when he pushed me to write broadly on Asia, not just China. He read a complete draft when he was no longer under any obligation to do so, and has continued to promote the project enthusiastically. I am very grateful for his friendship and insight. I also thank Janine Hill, Amy Baker, and Patricia Dorff for making the burden of the book lighter.

I wish to express my thanks to Irina Faskianos, vice president for national programs, for all of her support and for sending me out on the road. I am grateful to CFR members in Seattle, San Diego, and San Francisco who read and commented on some very early chapters and to members in New York and Washington who took up the challenge of reading and commenting on the entire book: Keith Abell, Christopher G. Caine, Michael Christenson, Richard Foster, Thomas D. Lehrman, Rodney Nichols, Daniel Sharp, William R. Sweeney, and Frederick Tipson. Jana Gasn Beauchamp, deputy director of member relations, was always quick to set up interviews in Silicon Valley and China, Japan, Korea, and India. Michelle Baute and Leigh Gusts fed me a steady stream of useful reports, articles, and data. The advice and good cheer of Steven Cook, Michael Levi, and Shannon O'Neil made coming to the office a real pleasure.

I gratefully acknowledge CA Technologies, the Starr Foundation, and the Ewing Marion Kauffman Foundation for generous financial support of my research.

Over the course of my research, close to two hundred people in the United States and Asia gave their time and expertise. Many spoke off the record, all deserve thanks. My deep gratitude goes to a few who were especially generous in providing feedback, insight, introductions, and logistical support along the way: Ajit Balakrishnan, Joseph Choe, Francisco D'Souza, Brooks Entwistle, Jonathan Fink, William Fontana, Tim Graczewski, Carl Green, Joe Hellerstein, Shantanu Jha, Kohno Michinaga, Manjeet Kripalani, Roger McDonald, Karen Mills, Laura Parkin, Ramkumar Ramamoorthy, the late Dr. N. R. Rao, Matthew Rudolph, Richard Samuels, Sunami Atsushi, Tada Akihiro, Jimmy Wang, Watanabe Ikuyo, Ambassador Frank Wisner, and John Yochelson. Dan Breznitz and Richard Samuels gave very helpful comments on an early draft of the entire book—both are great company and good fun.

Maria Guarnaschelli, my editor at W. W. Norton, has been an enthusiastic promoter of the book and me since the day we met. I thank her for her vision of what the book could be and for guiding it to that point. Phoebe Hoss and Aaron Lammer did fantastic work in closing the gap between policy and popular writing and massaging the all important transitions. Mary Babcock did an excellent job of copyediting.

Lisa Adams and David Miller of the Garamond Agency are agents extraordinaire, extremely helpful from beginning to end, and I am especially grateful to David for his critical engagement with the ideas of the project and for suggesting the book's title. Though I never really had to unleash him, I thank David Shapiro for legal advice.

I was ably assisted by several research assistants, all of whom have gone on to greater things. Cobb Mixter and Andrea Crandall helped at the beginning, Joseph Torigian arrived in the middle and was around until the beginning of the end, and then Woojung Chang came and stayed through the end. All did excellent work, Joseph and Woojung did a monumental amount of research in several languages, and Woojung did all of the drudgery of updating data and tracking down sources. To all, I say thank you.

My colleague Liz Economy deserves a special note of gratitude. While she has read and shaped every part of this project, her help extends way beyond this book. Since my first day at CFR, she has been a trusted adviser, ready collaborator, and closest friend. Rawi Abdelal and I started a conversation almost two decades ago over lunch in the Big Red Barn that is still going on today, although the discussion may be in fits and starts as we struggle to keep the campfire going or watch the kids in the pool. He is an indispensible sounding board and thoughtful critic. As the makers of Laphroaig say, "We take our time to make friends, but when we do it's for life."

My daughter, Lily, has been asking since I started the book if her name would be in it. Here it is, sweetheart: Lily Segal. Noah, of course, is also in the book—hello, Noah Segal. I look forward to the day when you both read this book and submit me to an endless procession of whys and whats. Once again I am grateful to my in-laws Richard and Cecile Sheramy for all their cheerleading and help on the home front. The same should be said about Jonny and Ali Segal, my brother and sister-in-law. About every three months my wife, Rona, would look at me and say, "Tell me what I can do to help you finish the book." And then she encouraged, critiqued, improved, and took care of many things at home at the same time as expertly managing and excelling at her own work. I am indebted to her for making my life so much richer.

Finally, I dedicate this book to my parents, Freya and Anthony Segal. I thank them for the many beautiful days in the Berkshires that were a welcome distraction from writing, for the help that meant I could return to writing when I needed to, and most of all for unwavering love and support.

Notes

CHAPTER 1: GOING NANO

1. "Shopping for America," *San Francisco Chronicle*, December 22, 2006.
2. Remarks by President Barack Obama at the National Academy of Sciences Annual Meeting, National Academy of Sciences, Washington, DC, April 27, 2009, available at http://www.whitehouse.gov/the_press_office/Remarks-by-the-President-at-the-National-Academy-of-Sciences-Annual-Meeting/.
3. National Academy of Sciences, National Academy of Engineering, and Institute of Medicine, *Rising above the Gathering Storm: Energizing and Employing America for a Brighter Economic Future* (Washington, DC: National Academies Press, 2007); Judith Estrin, *Closing the Innovation Gap* (New York: McGraw-Hill, 2008); Thomas Friedman, *The World Is Flat* (New York: Farrar, Straus and Giroux, 2005); John Kao, *Innovation Nation* (New York: Free Press, 2007).
4. Barrett quoted in Richard J. Newman, "Can America Keep Up?" *U.S. News & World Report*, March 19, 2006.
5. Liu Aixiang, "Tsinghua Develops Artificial Bone with Nano Technology," Tsinghua University News, April 22, 2003, available at http://news.tsinghua.edu.cn/eng__news.php?id=379; see also http://www.smalltimes.com/Articles/Article_Display.cfm?ARTICLE_ID=268840&p=109.
6. Jason Kelly, "Nanotech Lures Bankers, VCs with Promise of $1 Trillion Market," *Bloomberg.com*, July 27, 2006.
7. Rachel Parker, "Nanotechnology, Science-Led Development, and Technological Leapfrogging in China," American Association for the Advancement of Science Annual Conference, Boston, February 17, 2008.
8. Scientist quoted in "Leading Nanotech Research Center in China," *Asia Pacific Nanotech Weekly* 2 (2004), available at http://unit.aist.go.jp/nanotech/apnw/articles/library2/pdf/2-23.pdf.

9. "Dr. Mihail C. Roco: Founder and Key Architect, National Nanotechnology Initiative," *Nanotech Briefs* 1, no. 1 (October 2003): 5–6.

10. *International Science and Engineering Partnerships: A Priority for U.S. Foreign Policy and Our Nation's Innovation Enterprise*, National Science Board, February 14, 2008, available at http://www.nsf.gov/nsb/publications/2008/nsb084.pdf.

11. Palmisano quoted in *Innovate America: National Innovation Initiative Summit and Report*, Council on Competitiveness, 2005, available at http://www.compete.org/images/uploads/File/PDF%20Files/NII_Innovate_America.pdf.

12. *Quadrennial Defense Review Report*, Department of Defense, February 6, 2006, available at http://www.defense.gov/qdr/report/Report20060203.pdf.

13. Lieutenant General Michael D. Maples, Director, Defense Intelligence Agency, Testimony before the United States Senate Armed Services Committee, March 10, 2009, available at http://armed-services.senate.gov/statemnt/2009/March/Maples%2003-10-09.pdf.

14. Brian Grow, "Dangerous Fakes," *BusinessWeek*, October 2, 2008.

15. Dan Breznitz and Michael Murphree, *Run of the Red Queen: Government, Innovation, Globalization, and Economic Growth in China* (New Haven: Yale University Press, forthcoming); John Seely Brown and John Hagel III, "Innovation Blowback: Disruptive Management Practices from Asia," *McKinsey Quarterly*, no. 1 (2005).

16. "Makeshift Miracles: The Indian Genius for Jugaad," *Times of India*, January 1, 2004, available at http://timesofindia.indiatimes.com/articleshow/398740.cms.

17. Analyst quoted in Michael Keane, "Why China Wants Creativity," *Australian Policy Online*, March 12, 2009, available at http://apo.org.au/commentary/why-china-wants-creativity/.

18. Jan Fagerberg, "Innovation: Guide to the Literature," in Jan Fagerberg, David C. Mowery, and Richard R. Nelson (eds.), *The Oxford Handbook of Innovation* (Oxford: Oxford University Press, 2004), p. 8.

19. Bhidé quoted in Steve Lohr, "Do We Overrate Basic Research?" *New York Times*, November 29, 2008.

20. Charles Krauthammer, "The Unipolar World," *Foreign Affairs* 70, no. 1 (1990/1991): 23–33.

21. Brahma Chellaney, "The Orient Express," *India Today*, June 20, 2008.

22. John Ikenberry, *Liberal Order and Imperial Ambition* (Malden, MA: Polity Press, 2006), p. 2.

23. Alexander J. Field, "The Most Technologically Progressive Decade of the Century," *American Economic Review* 93 (September 2003): 1399–1414.

24. Immelt quoted in "A Gathering Storm?" *The Economist*, November 20, 2008.

25. "Remarks by the President at the National Academy of Sciences Annual

Meeting," White House Office of the Press Secretary, April 27, 2009, available at http://www.whitehouse.gov/the_press_office/Remarks-by-the-President-at-the-National-Academy-of-Sciences-Annual-Meeting/.

26. Paras D. Bhayani, "Surveying the Class," *Harvard Crimson*, June 1, 2009.

CHAPTER 2: STAKES AND FORCES

1. "Global Trends in Venture Capital 2006 Survey," Deloitte & Touche USA, July 12, 2006, available at http://www.nvca.org/index.php?option=com_docman&task=doc_download&gid=339&Itemid=93.

2. Richard Freeman, "Does Globalization of the Scientific/Engineering Workforce Threaten U.S. Economic Leadership?" *Innovation Policy and the Economy* 6 (2006): 123–158.

3. "Science and Engineering Indicators 2010," National Science Foundation, available at http://www.nsf.gov/statistics/seind10/pdf/at.pdf.

4. "The InfoTech 100," *BusinessWeek*, n.d., available at http://bwnt.businessweek.com/interactive_reports/it100_2009.

5. Craig Barrett, "The Next Economy," *Foreign Policy* 144 (September/October 2004):76–77.

6. Singh quoted in Jo Johnson and Mure Dickie, "India, China Heading to Moon," *Financial Times*, June 11, 2007.

7. Hu quote in "Full Text of Hu Jintao's Report at 17th Party Congress," *People's Daily*, October 24, 2007, available at http://english.peopledaily.com.cn/90001/90776/90785/6290142.html.

8. Fang quoted in Robert Marquand, "Research Fraud Rampant in China," *Christian Science Monitor*, May 16, 2006.

9. Cheng quoted in David Stipp, "Can China Overtake the U.S. in Science?" *Fortune*, October 4, 2004.

10. Max Weber, *From Max Weber: Essays in Socioiogy* (New York: Oxford University Press, 1946), pp. 129–156.

11. Nicholas Wade and Choe Sang-Hun, "Human Cloning Was All Faked, Koreans Report," *New York Times*, January 10, 2006.

12. Xu quoted in "China Aims to Be One of Science Powers in World," *Xinhua*, February 10, 2006.

13. Quotes from Barbara Demick, "South Korean Cloning Scandal Takes Toll on Whistle-Blowers," *Los Angeles Times*, February 14, 2006.

14. Richard Samuels, *"Rich Nation, Strong Army": National Security and the Technological Transformation of Japan* (Ithaca: Cornell University Press, 1996).

15. Alexander Hamilton, *Report on the Subject of Manufactures* [1791] , in Har-

old C. Syrett (ed.), *The Papers of Alexander Hamilton* (New York: Columbia University Press, 1979), p. 633.

16. Edward Teller, "Secret-Stealing, Then and Now," *New York Times*, May 14, 1999.

17. Karen G. Mills, "Growing Maine's Own Is Economic Development Key," *Kennebec Journal*, March 25, 2007.

18. Richard K. Lester, "The Future of Manufacturing & the Role of Innovation," Presentation at the Conference on the Future of Manufacturing in Ireland: The Role of Partnership, Dublin, Ireland, June 28, 2007.

19. Michael E. Porter, *Competitive Advantage of Nations* (New York: Free Press, 1990).

20. Arie de Geus, "The Living Company," *Harvard Business Review* (March/April 1997): 51–59.

CHAPTER 3: KNOW THY COUPLETS

1. "China Cell Phone Subscriber Gets 10 Junk Messages Every Week," *Xinhua*, January 7, 2009.

2. "A New World Economy: The Balance of Power Will Shift to the East as China and India Evolve," *BusinessWeek*, August 22, 2005.

3. "The Mobile Phone Man (Shoujiren)," *New Weekly (Xinzhoukan)*, January 15, 2007.

4. George Scalise, "China's High-Technology Development," Testimony before the U.S.-China Economic and Security Review Commission, Palo Alto, California, April 21, 2005, available at http://www.uscc.gov/hearings/2005hearings/written_testimonies/05_21_22wrts/scalise_george_wrts.pdf.

5. Barrett quoted in K. Heim, "U.S. High-Tech Giants Invest in Future Competitor," *San Jose Mercury News*, March 15, 2004; "Microsoft Aims to Trounce Google," *BBC*, October 27, 2005, available at http://news.bbc.co.uk/2/hi/technology/4382112.stm.

6. C. N. R. Rao quoted in Indrajit Basu, "Indian Science: Alive but Not Kicking," *Asia Times*, August 15, 2006.

7. "Evalueserve Study: India to Emerge as Global Innovation Hub," *Marketwire*, December 15, 2008.

8. Ashok Parthasarathi, "Making India a Scientific Power," *Business Standard*, August 30, 2006.

9. Anita Mehta, "Science in the Sick Bay," *Times of India*, April 23, 2008.

10. Yi quoted in Hao Xin and Gong Yidong, "China Bets on Big Science," *Science* 311, no. 5767 (March 17, 2006): 1548–1549.

11. Diana Farrell, Noshir Kaka, and Sascha Stürze, "Ensuring India's Offshoring Future," *McKinsey Quarterly*, September 2005; Diana Farrell and Andrew Grant, "Addressing China's Looming Talent Shortage," McKinsey Global Institute, October 2005; Cong Cao and Denis Fred Simon, *China's Emerging Technological Edge: Assessing the Role of High-End Talent* (New York: Cambridge University Press, 2009).

12. Paul Mooney, "The Long Road Ahead for China's Universities," *Chronicle of Higher Education*, May 19, 2006.

13. Liu quoted in Gong Yidong, "Cry for Freedom," *China Daily*, May 7, 2009.

14. Mu-Ming Poo, "Cultural Reflections," *Nature*, March 11, 2004.

15. James Wilsdon and James Keeley, "China: The Next Science Superpower?" DEMOS, January 2007, available at http://www.demos.co.uk/files/China_Final.pdf.

16. Zhu Zhe, "Plagiarism, Fake Research Plague Academia," *China Daily*, March 15, 2006; for the prominent cases, see "Chinese Academia Ghost-Writing 'Widespread'," BBC, January 5, 2010, and Rui Yang, "Corruption in China's Higher Education: A Malignant Tumor," *International Higher Education*, Spring 2005.

17. Paul Mooney, "Plagued by Plagiarism," *Chronicle of Higher Education*, May 19, 2006.

18. Mark A. Dutz (ed.), *Unleashing India's Innovation: Toward Sustainable and Inclusive Growth*, World Bank, 2007, available at http://siteresources.world bank.org/SOUTHASIAEXT/Resources/223546-1181699473021/3876782-1 191373775504/indiainnovationfull.pdf; R. Venkatesan and Wlima Wadwha, National Council of Applied Economic Research, *The Evolving Global Talent Pool*, Levin Institute, October 2009.

19. Anand Giridharadas, "A College Education without Job Prospects," *New York Times*, November 30, 2006.

20. Kalam quoted in "Presidential Plain-Speaking," *Mumbai DNA*, December 24, 2006.

21. Joe Leahy, "India Puts Research under Microscope," *Financial Times*, October 11, 2007.

22. Shailaja Neelakantan, "In India, Economic Success Leaves Universities Desperate for Professors," *Chronicle of Higher Education*, October 12, 2007.

23. "The Delusion of University Oriented Ventures," *Nikkei Business*, November 14, 2005.

24. Robert Kneller, *Bridging Islands: Venture Companies and the Future of Japanese and American Industry* (Oxford: Oxford University Press, 2007).

25. George J. Gilboy, "The Myth Behind China's Miracle," *Foreign Affairs* 83, no. 4 (July/August 2004): 33–48.

26. Jin quoted in Wei Gu, "Why China's 'Start-up' Bourse Won't Produce a Microsoft," *Reuters*, April 1, 2008.

27. William N. Goetzmann and Philippe Jorion, "A Century of Global Stock Markets," NBER Working Paper 5901, National Bureau of Economic Research, 1997, available at http://ideas.repec.org/p/nbr/nberwo/5901.html.

28. Sungchul Chung, "Excelsior: The Korean Innovation Story," *Issues in Science and Technology* 24 (Fall 2007): 62–69.

29. Quoted in Molly Webb, *South Korea: Mass Innovation Comes of Age* (London: DEMOS, 2007), p. 20.

30. Yasheng Huang, "China is No Haven for Entrepreneurs," *Financial Times*, February 1, 2007.

31. Liu Zhaoqiong, Xi Si, Wei Liming, and Li Ping, "Private Business Sidelined by China's Stimulus," *Economic Observer*, March 16, 2009, available at http://www.eeo.com.cn/ens/Industry/2009/03/16/132582.shtml.

32. *Study on the Future Opportunities and Challenges in EU-China Trade and Investment Relations 2006–2010*, European Commission, February 15, 2007, available at http://ec.europa.eu/trade/issues/bilateral/countries/china/legis/index_en.htm.

33. Frederic Golden, "Closing the Gap with the West," *Time*, August 1, 1983.

34. Christian Caryl, "Why Bow to China?" *Newsweek*, May 16, 2009.

35. "Opening the Doors," *The Economist*, October 7, 2006; Kalluri quoted in S. Mitra Kalita, "A Reversal of the Tide in India," *Washington Post*, February 28, 2006.

36. AnnaLee Saxenian, *The New Argonauts: Regional Advantage in a Global Economy* (Cambridge: Harvard University Press, 2006), p. 18.

37. Wadhwani quoted in "Serial Entrepreneur Offers Success Lessons," *Financial Express*, April 2, 2003.

38. Nannan Lundin and Sylvia Schwaag Serger, "Globalization of R&D and China—Empirical Observations and Policy Implications," No. 710, Working Paper Series, Research Institute of Industrial Economics, Stockholm, Sweden, 2007, available at: http://econpapers.repec.org/RePEc:hhs:iuiwop:0710.

39. Lee quoted in Sarah Lacy, "Will China's Best Coders Flock to Kai-Fu Lee's New Incubator?" *Techcrunch*, September 6, 2009.

40. "American Professor Mu-ming Poo Forces CAS Researcher Li Chaoyi to Resign," National Chekiang University Forum, January 16, 2007, available at http://ncku1897.net./post/topic.aspx?tid=2759497.

41. Gong Yidong, "China Science Foundation Takes Action against 60 Grantees," *Science* 309, no. 5742 (September 2005): 1798–1799.

42. Zi Xun, "China to Tackle Misuse of Science Funding," *SciDev.Net*, July 12, 2006, available at http://www.scidev.net/en/news/china-to-tackle-misuse-of-

science-funding.html; "China to Set Up Credibility Evaluation System for Scientists," *Xinhua*, July 5, 2006.

43. "China Urges U.S. to Stop Accusations on So-Called Internet Freedom," *Xinhua*, January 22, 2010.

44. Jane Qiu, "A Land without Google?" *Nature*, February 24, 2010.

45. Rishikesha T. Krishnan, "India in Transition: In Search of an Innovation Paradigm," Center for the Advanced Study of India, University of Pennsylvania, November 25, 2008, available at http://casi.ssc.upenn.edu/iit/krishnan.

46. "How Technology Sectors Grow," *Economist Intelligence Unit*, September 2008, available at http://graphics.eiu.com/upload/BSA_2008.pdf.

47. Pew Research Center for the People & the Press, "Views of a Changing World," June 2003, available at http://people-press.org/reports/pdf/185.pdf; Pew Global Research Center, "47-Nation Pew Global Attitudes Survey," October 7, 2007, available at http://pewglobal.org/reports/pdf/258.pdf.

48. Kenji E. Kushida, "Leading without Followers: The Political Economy of Japan's ICT Sector," *Berkeley Roundtable on the International Economy*, Working Paper 184, December 2008, pp. 1–54; Hiroko Tabuchi, "Why Japan's Cellphones Haven't Gone Global," *New York Times*, July 19, 2009.

CHAPTER 4: THE OPEN DOOR

1. Editorial, "Such a Long Journey, but India Is Getting There," *Hindustan Times*, January 25, 2008.

2. Xianfeng Zhang, "When Will Cell Phones No Longer Use 'Imported Chinese Characters,'" *People's Daily*, November 2, 2006, available at http://news.people.com.cn/GB/37454/37459/4988909.html.

3. "Guidelines on National Medium- and Long-Term Program for Science and Technology Development" (2006–2020), People's Republic of China State Council, February 6, 2009, available at www.gov.cn/jrzg/2006-02/09/content_183787.htm.

4. Barrett quoted in Sumner Lemon, "No Compromise on WAPI as Intel's Barrett Heads to China," IDG News Service, April 5, 2004, available at http://www.infoworld.com/article/04/04/05/HNbarrettochina_1.html.

5. Quoted in Michael Kanellos, "Intel, Others to Stop Shipping Wi-Fi to China," *CNET News*, March 10, 2004, available at http://news.cnet.com/Intel,-others-to-stop-shipping-Wi-Fi-to-China/2100-7351_3-5172127.html.

6. See Mike Clendenin, "WAPI Battle Exposes Technology Rifts with China," *EE Times*, March 17, 2006, available at http://www.eetimes.com/news/semi/showArticle.jhtml?articleID=183700631; quoted in Liang Chen, "How Long Will the Tug of War on WAPI with International Forces Persist?" *eNet*,

March 23, 2005, available at http://www.enet.com.cn/article/2005/0323/A20050323401099.shtml.

7. Scott Kennedy, "The Political Economy of Standards Coalitions: Explaining China's Involvement in High-Tech Standards Wars," *Asia Policy*, no. 2 (July 2006): 41–62.

8. Barry Naughton, "The Emergence of the China Circle," in Barry Naughton (ed.), *The China Circle: Economics and Electronics in the PRC, Taiwan, and Hong Kong* (Washington, DC: Brookings Institution Press, 1997).

9. *Export Controls: Rapid Advances in China's Semiconductor Industry Underscore Need for Fundamental U.S. Policy Review*, U.S. General Accounting Office, April 2002, available at http://www.gao.gov/new.items/d02620.pdf.

10. Liu quoted in "Legend in the Making," *The Economist*, September 15, 2001.

11. Gurcharan Das, *India Unbound: The Social and Economic Revolution from Independence to the Global Information Age* (New Delhi: Penguin Books, 2002), pp. 94–95.

12. Quoted in Sumantra Sen and Francine Frankel, *India's Strategy of IT-Led Growth: Challenges of Asymmetric Dependence*, Center for the Advanced Study of India, University of Pennsylvania, 2005, http://casi.ssc.upenn.edu/research/DBI/IIT_Summer_2005.pdf, accessed Aug. 2, 2005.

13. Montek S. Ahluwalia, "Economic Reforms in India since 1991: Has Gradualism Worked?" *Journal of Economic Perspectives* 16, no. 3 (Summer 2002): 67–88.

14. "India's IT-BPO Market to Touch $285 Billion by 2020," KPMG Press Release, February 9, 2010, available at http://www.kpmg.com/IN/en/Press%20Release/India%E2%80%99s%20IT-BPO%20market%20to%20touch%20$285%20billion%20by%202020.pdf.

15. "Cisco: Sold on India," *BusinessWeek*, November 28, 2005.

16. "Publics of Asian Powers Hold Negative Views of One Another," Pew Research Center Pew Global Attitudes Project, September 21, 2006, available at http://pewglobal.org/reports/display.php?ReportID=255.

17. Richard J. Samuels, *Securing Japan: Tokyo's Grand Strategy and the Future of East Asia* (Ithaca: Cornell University Press, 2007).

18. "Task Force on Industrial Competitiveness and Intellectual Property Policy," Japan Ministry of Economy, Trade, and Industry, June 5, 2002, available at http://www.meti.go.jp/english/information/downloadfiles/cICIPPoutlinee.pdf.

19. Japan Business Federation, "Japan 2025," 2003, available at http://www.keidanren.or.jp/english/policy/vision2025.pdf.

20. Samuels, *Securing Japan*.

21. Patnaik quoted in "Call for Technological Innovation," *Hindu*, December 19, 2006.

22. "Amartya Sen: Completion of Land Reforms a Must," *Hindu*, January 4, 2006.

23. Matthew Rudolph, "Indo-American Relations in the Digital Age: Part I," *ICWA Letters*, November 4, 2004.

24. The Rediff Election Andhra Pradesh Homepage, September 30, 1999, available at http://www.rediff.com/election/1999/sep/30naidu.htm.

25. "The Rediff Interview: Nara Chandrababu Naidu," February 8, 2000, available at http://www.rediff.com/news/2000/feb/08naidu.htm.

26. "Prime Minister Vajpayee's Speech at the Delhi Sustainable Development Summit," February 7, 2001, available at http://www.indianembassy.org/spe cial/cabinet/Primeminister/pm_february_07_2001.htm.

27. Pranab Bardhan, "Resistance to Economic Reform in India," *Yale Global Online*, October 2006.

28. Ashutosh Varshney,"India's Democratic Challenge," *Foreign Affairs* 86, no. 2 (March/April 2007): 93–106.

29. Ibid.

30. Nath quoted in "Tata's Nano Is an Example of India's Technical Abilities: Nath," *United News of India*, January 10, 2008; Avijit Ghosh, "Tata Reinvents the Wheel," *Times of India*, January 11, 2008.

31. Peter Wonacott, "Lawless Legislators Thwart Social Progress in India," *Wall Street Journal*, May 4, 2007; "News: Asset Comparison for Recontesting MPs, Phase 4 Report and Phase 1234 Report," National Election Watch, available at http://nationalelectionwatch.org/pages/34.

32. Jo Johnson, "Report Says India to Grow 8% until 2020," *Financial Times*, January 24, 2007; Jim O'Neill and Tushar Poddar, "Ten Things for India to Achieve Its 2050 Potential," Goldman Sachs Global Economics Paper No. 169, June 16, 2008, available at http://www2.goldmansachs.com/ideas/brics/ ten-things-doc.pdf.

CHAPTER 5: TRADING WITH THE (POTENTIAL) ENEMY

1. Hu quoted in Allison Linn, "Chinese President Extols Trade Tie Benefits at Airplane Plant," Associated Press, April 19, 2006.

2. Craig S. Smith, "China Moves to Cut Power of Microsoft," *New York Times*, July 8, 2000.

3. Andrew Orlowski, " 'China has f*cked us'—Bill Gates," *Register*, September 7, 2005, available at http://www.theregister.co.uk/2005/09/07/ microsoft_google/.

4. Kai-Fu Lee, "Making It in China," September 2003, available at http:// www.360doc.com/content/05/0917/11/494_12942.shtml; see also discussion

of Lee in Robert Buderi and Gregory T. Huang, *Guanxi (The Art of Relationships): Microsoft, China, and Bill Gates' Plan to Win the Road Ahead* (New York: Simon & Schuster, 2006), pp. 264–265.

5. Chen quoted in David Kirkpatrick, "How Microsoft Conquered China," *Fortune*, July 9, 2007.

6. Loretta Chao, "In Piracy Case, China Fights Hero," *Wall Street Journal*, September 1, 2009.

7. Kimball quoted in Lyle J. Goldstein and Andrew S. Erickson, "China's Nuclear Force Modernization," *Naval War College Newport Papers*, no. 22 (2005): 51.

8. This paragraph draws from Iris Chang, *Thread of the Silkworm* (New York: Basic Books, 1996), p. 192.

9. Ibid., p. 229.

10. K. Oanh Ha, "Stealing a Head Start," *San Jose Mercury News*, September 28, 2006.

11. Szady quoted in Jay Solomon, "FBI Sees Big Threat from Chinese Spies," *Wall Street Journal*, August 20, 2005.

12. Deemed Export Advisory Committee, *The Deemed Export Rule in the Era of Globalization*, December 20, 2007, available at http://tac.bis.doc.gov/2007/deacreport.pdf.

13. Jim Richberg, "The Counterintelligence Implications of Deemed Export Control," Workshop on the Globalization of the University and Deemed Export Policy, Oak Ridge Center for Advanced Studies, March 6–7, 2006.

14. Donald Rumsfeld, Secretary of Defense, Remarks to the International Institute for Strategic Studies, Singapore, June 4, 2005, available at http://www.defense.gov/speeches/speech.aspx?speechid=77.

15. Negroponte quoted in Foster Klug, "U.S. Spy Chief Says North Korea Remains Grave Threat, China Military Growing," Associated Press, January 11, 2007.

16. Zhang quoted in Stephen Fidler, "China Tries to Allay Fears about 17.8% Defense Budget Rise," *Financial Times*, June 4, 2007.

17. Liang quoted in "China Confirms It Will Build Aircraft Carrier," AFP, March 24, 2009.

18. Department of Defense, *Annual Report to Congress: Military Power of the People's Republic of China*, 2009, available at http://www.defense.gov/pubs/pdfs/China_Military_Power_Report_2009.

19. *Some Key Uncertainties: Transformations in Defense Markets and Industries*, National Intelligence Council, January 8, 2002, available at http://www.fas.org/irp/nic/battilega/transformations_summary.htm.

20. Evan S. Medeiros, Roger Cliff, Keith Crane and James C. Mulvenon, *A New*

Direction for China's Defense Industry (Santa Monica, CA: RAND Corporation, 2005).

21. James Mulvenon, "Digital Triangle: A New Defense-Industrial Paradigm," in *Economics and National Security: The Case of China* (Washington, DC: U.S. Army War College, August 2002).

22. Medeiros, Cliff, Crane, and Mulvenon, *New Direction for China's Defense Industry*.

23. Bill Gertz, "China Sub Secretly Stalked U.S. Fleet," *Washington Times*, November 13, 2006.

24. Analyst quoted in Lyle Goldstein and William Murray, "Undersea Dragons: China's Maturing Submarine Force," *International Security* 28, no. 4 (Spring 2004): 162.

25. Wortzel quote from "Reframing China Policy Debate 3: Is China's Military Modernization Program a Growing Threat to the United States and Asia?" Debate Transcript. Debate was held at Dirksen Senate Office Building, organized by Carnegie Endowment for International Peace, February 6, 2007, available at www.carnegieendowment.org/files/debate_3%20final%20 transcript.pdf.

26. "Report of the Defense Science Board Task Force on High Performance Microchip Supply," Defense Science Board, February 2005, quoted in John Tkacik, "Trojan Dragon: China's Cyber Threat," Heritage Foundation Backgrounder on Asia, February 8, 2008, available at http://www.heritage.org/ Research/Reports/2008/02/Trojan-Dragon-Chinas-Cyber-Threat#_ftn51.

27. Official quoted in Daniel Twining, "America's Grand Design in Asia," *Washington Quarterly* 30, no. 3 (Summer 2007): 82.

28. Stephen P. Cohen, *India: Emerging Power* (Washington, DC: Brookings Institution Press, 2001), p. 283.

29. Virginia Foran, "Indo-Relations after the 1998 Tests: Sanctions versus Incentives," in Seema Gahlaut, Gary K. Bertsch, and Anupam Srivastava (eds.), *Engaging India: US Strategic Relations with the World's Largest Democracy* (London: Routledge, 2007).

30. Pallava Bagla, "Indian Scientists Shaken by Bomb Test Aftershocks," *Science* 281, no. 5376 (July 24, 1998): 494–495; James Glanz, "DOE Blocks Physicists from Indian Meeting," *Science* 283, no. 5400 (January 15, 1999): 307.

31. Robert D. Blackwill, "A Friend Indeed," *National Interest* 89, no. 3 (May/ June 2007): 16–19.

32. James B. Steinberg, "Engaging Asia 2009: Strategies for Success," Remarks at National Bureau of Asian Research Conference, Washington, DC, April 1, 2009.

33. David McCormick, "Win-Win High Technology Trade With China," Speech

to the Center for Strategic and International Studies, Washington, DC, June 9, 2006.

34. Judy Franz, Letter to Chairs of PhD-Granting Physics Department, re: Proposed Dept. of Commerce Rules Pose Threat to Research, April 22, 2005, available at http://preposterousuniverse.blogspot.com/2005_04_01_prepos terousuniverse_archive.html#111418166734004943.

35. Quoted in "William Reinsch Addresses ACI," National Foreign Trade Council Press Release, April 27, 2005, available at http://www.nftc.org/newsflash/newsflash.asp?id=236&mode=View&articleid=2492.

36. "Cross Sector Report," American Chamber of Commerce, December 4, 2006, available at http://web.resource.amchamchina.org/news/ECWGCrossSec torReportFinal.pdf.

37. Jonathan Fink, Presentation on Competitiveness of Chinese R&D, Air Force Asian S&T Forum, Washington, DC, June 27, 2007.

38. Locke quoted in Mark Drajem, "U.S. May Lift Export Controls for Some Warfare Items," *Bloomberg.com*, January 28, 2010.

CHAPTER 6: AN OPEN WORLD

1. Bruce Schneier, "The Difference between Feeling and Reality in Security," *Wired News*, April 3, 2008, available at http://www.wired.com/politics/security/commentary/securitymatters/2008/04/securitymatters_0403.

2. Accenture, "China Spreads Its Wings," 2005, available at http://www.accen ture.com/NR/rdonlyres/6A4C9C07-8C84-4287-9417-203DF3E6A3D1/0/Chinaspreadsitswings.pdf; Lawrence Brainard and Jonathan Fenby, "Chinese Takeout," *Wall Street Journal*, February 20, 2007; Andreas Lunding, "Global Champions in Waiting," *Deutsche Bank Research*, August 4, 2006, available at http://www.dbresearch.com/PROD/DBR_INTER NET_EN-PROD/PROD0000000000201318.PDF; "2007 Statistical Bulletin of China's Outward Foreign Direct Investment," People's Republic of China Ministry of Commerce, 2008, quoted in Françoise Nicolas, "Chinese Direct Investment in Europe," Chatham House Briefing Paper, June 2009, available at http://www.chathamhouse.org.uk/files/14121_0609ch_odi .pdf.

3. Ma quoted in "Chinese Companies Abroad," *The Economist*, June 30, 2005.

4. Tata quoted in Joe Leahy, "Indian Pride Fueled Tata's Push for Corus," *Financial Times*, February 2, 2007.

5. Quoted in Jo Johnson, "India's Steely Drive is Overcoming Colonial Attitudes," *Financial Times*, February 2, 2007.

6. "Country Fact Sheet: India," United Nations Conference on Trade and

Development, World Investment Report 2009, available at http://www
.unctad.org/sections/dite_dir/docs/wir09_fs_in_en.pdf.

7. David Marchick and Matthew Slaughter, "Global FDI Policy," Council on
Foreign Relations, Council Special Report no. 34, June 2008, available at
www.cfr.org/content/publications/attachments/FDl_CSR34.pdf.

8. Thomas Anderson, "U.S. Affiliates of Foreign Companies Operations in
2005," Bureau of Economic Analysis, Washington, DC, August 2007, available at http://www.bea.gov/scb/pdf/2007/08%20August/0807_foreign.pdf.

9. Official quoted in "Government Stops Huawei March," *SiliconIndia*, August
16, 2005; Khozem Merchant, "Indian Security Fears Voiced on Huawei,"
Financial Times, August 28, 2005.

10. Estimates of growth come from Gerard Lyons, "State Capitalism: The Rise
of Sovereign Wealth Funds," *Standard Chartered Global Research*, November 13, 2007.

11. Quoted in Brad Setser, "Maybe the CIC Isn't Motivated Entirely by Commercial Gain . . . ," Roubini Global Economics Asia Economonitor blog, June
20, 2008, available at http://www.roubini.com/asia-monitor/archive/200806/.

12. Call for "strategic resources" quoted in Brad Setser, "Maybe the CIC Isn't
Motivated Entirely by Commercial Gain . . . ," *RGE Monitor*, June 20, 2008.

13. See, for example, Ian Bremmer, "State Capitalism Comes of Age," *Foreign
Affairs* 88, no. 3 (May/June 2009): 40–55; Joshua Kurlantzick, "State Inc.,"
Boston Globe, March 16, 2008; Azar Gat, "The Return of Authoritarian
Great Powers," *Foreign Affairs* 86, no. 4 (July/August 2007): 59–69; Martin
Wolf, "The Brave New World of State Capitalism," *Financial Times*, Octo-
ber 16, 2007.

14. Gao quoted in Jamil Anderlini, "China Fund Shuns Guns and Gambling,"
Financial Times, June 13, 2008.

15. President Bush's Statement on Open Economies, White House Office of the
Press Secretary, May 10, 2007.

16. Barack Obama, "A Time for Global Action," *Chicago Tribune*, March 24,
2009.

17. Alan P. Larson and David M. Marchick, "Foreign Investment and National
Security: Getting the Balance Right," Council on Foreign Relations; Council
Special Report no. 18, July 2006, available at http://www.cfr.org/publication
/11146/foreign_investment_and_national_security.html?breadcrumb=%2F
publication%2Fpublication_list%3Ftype%3Dspecial_report%26page%3D2.

18. Innman quoted in National Academy of Sciences, *Scientific Communication
and National Security* (Washington, DC: National Academies Press, 1982),
p. 10, available at http://www.nap.edu/catalog.php?record_id=253.

19. Casey quoted in Daniel Southerland, "America's Spies," *Christian Science
Monitor*, October 28, 1982.

20. David Buchan, "Western Security and Economic Strategy towards the East," *Adelphi* series 24 no. 192 (1984): 11–19.

21. Keyworth quoted in Alice P. Gast, "The Impact of Restricting Information Access on Science and Technology," in Peter M. Shane, John Podesta, and Richard C. Leone (eds.), *A Little Knowledge: Privacy, Security, and Public Information after September 11* (New York: Century Foundation, 2004).

22. Pierre Chao, "Health of the U.S. Space Industrial Base and the Impact of Export Control," Presentation at Center for Strategic and International Studies, Washington, DC, February 19, 2008.

23. Paul N. Edwards, *The Closed World: Computers and the Politics of Discourse in Cold War America* (Cambridge: MIT Press, 1996); Donald Hicks, *Final Report of the Defense Science Board Task Force on Globalization and Security* (Washington, DC: Defense Science Board, December 1999), p. ii.

24. Lily E. Johnston, "Meeting a Critical Challenge," *Studies in Intelligence* 52, no. 2 (June 2008): 1–10.

25. Charles Vest, "Openness and Globalization in Higher Education," Lecture at University of California, Berkeley, June 2006.

26. Kishore Mahbubani, "Wake Up Washington," *Global Asia* 2, no. 2 (Fall 2007): 16–23.

27. Richard Freeman, Paula Stephan, and John Trumpbour, "Career Patterns of Foreign Born Scientists and Engineers Trained and or Working in the U.S.," National Bureau of Economic Research (NBER) Workshop Report, January 2008.

28. National Academies, Committee on a New Government-University Partnership for Science and Security, Southeast Regional Meeting, hosted by Georgia Tech, June 5–6, 2006, http://www7.nationalacademies.org/stl/SS_Regional%20meetings.html, accessed June 2008.

29. Sara Rimer, "At 71, Physics Professor Is a Web Star," *New York Times*, December 19, 2007.

30. Vivek Wadhwa, AnnaLee Saxenian, Ben Rissing, and Gary Gereffi, "America's New Immigrant Entrepreneurs," University of California, Berkeley, School of Information, January 4, 2007, available at http://people.ischool.berkeley.edu/~anno/Papers/Americas_new_immigrant_entrepreneurs_I.pdf.

31. Gates quoted in "High-Tech Titans Unite on Lifting Visa Caps," *Wall Street Journal*, June 14, 2006.

32. Ron Hira, "Outsourcing America's Technology and Knowledge Jobs," Economic Policy Institute, March 28, 2007, available at http://www.sharedprosperity.org/bp187.html.

33. John Miano, "The Bottom of the Pay Scale: Wages for H-1B Computer Programmers," Center for Immigration Studies, December 2005, available at http://www.cis.org/node/261.

34. Marianne Kolbasuk McGee, "Who Gets H-1B Visas? Check Out This List," *Information Week*, May 16, 2007.

35. "H-1B Visas and Job Creation," National Foundation for American Policy, March 2008, available at http://www.nfap.com/pdf/080311h1b.pdf.; Microsoft quoted in "More Visas, More Jobs," *Wall Street Journal*, March 19, 2008.

36. Gary S. Becker, "Give Us Your Skilled Masses," *Wall Street Journal*, December 1, 2005.

37. "Recommendations for Enhancing the U.S. Visa System to Advance America's Scientific and Economic Competitiveness and National Security Interests," National Academies, Office of News and Public Information, May 18, 2005, available at http://www8.nationalacademies.org/onpinews/newsitem .aspx?RecordID=s05182005.

38. Vivek Wadhwa, Guillermina Jasso, Ben Rassing, Gary Gereffi, and Richard Freeman, "Intellectual Property, the Immigration Backlog, and a Reverse Brain-Drain," Kauffman Foundation, August 2007.

39. Paul Graham, "The Founder Visa," April 2009, available at http://www.paul graham.com/foundervisa.html.

CHAPTER 7: ATOMS AND SMART GRIDS

1. Steven Weisman, "U.S. and China Set Up Teams for Economic Talks," *New York Times*, September 21, 2006.

2. Morris Goldstein and Nicholas R. Lardy, "China's Revaluation Shows Size Really Matters," *Financial Times*, July 22, 2005; Morris Goldstein, "A (Lack of) Progress Report on China's Exchange Rate Policies," Peterson Institute for International Economics Working Paper, May 2007, available at http:// www.iie.com/publications/papers/goldstein0507.pdf.

3. Grassley quoted in Peter S. Goodman, "This Time, Bill to Raise Yuan Might Pass," *Washington Post*, August 1, 2007.

4. Quoted in Steve Lohr, "The Big Tug of War over Unocal," *New York Times*, July 6, 2005.

5. "Remarks by Secretary Clinton En Route to Tokyo, Japan," Department of State, February 15, 2009, available at http://www.state.gov/secretary/ rm/2009a/02/117345.htm.

6. Chu and Fludder quoted in Andrew C. Revkin and Kate Galbraith, "Energy Chief Seeks Global Flow of Ideas," Dot Earth, *New York Times*, March 26, 2009.

7. "U.S. House Votes to Protect American Green Collar Jobs in New Climate Change Treaty," Press Release by Representative Rick Larsen, June

10, 2009, available at www.house.gov/list/press/.../pr_090610_greencollar .shtml.

8. "Commerce Secretary Gary Locke to Lead Administration's First Cabinet-Level Trade Mission," U.S. Department of Commerce Press Release, January 28, 2010, available at http://www.commerce.gov/NewsRoom/ PressReleases_FactSheets/PROD01_008856.

9. *2008 National Trade Estimate Report on Foreign Trade Barriers*, Office of the United States Trade Representative, Executive Office of the President, March 28, 2008.

10. Andrew Mertha, "Putting Your Mouth Where Your Money Is: How US Companies' Fear of Chinese Retaliation Influences US Trade Policy," in Ka Zeng (ed.), *China's Foreign Trade Policy* (New York: Routledge, 2007), pp. 59–72.

11. Wang Qishan, "No More Chinese Knock-Offs," *Wall Street Journal*, June 17, 2008.

12. James Baker III, "The Future of Sino-American Relations," Speech (as prepared for delivery) to U.S.-China Business Council, Washington, DC, June 5, 2007.

13. Doron Ben-Atar, "A U.S. Technology Double Standard?" *Globalist*, October 20, 2004, available at http://www.theglobalist.com/StoryId.aspx?StoryId=4222.

14. Alexander Hamilton, *Report on the Subject of Manufactures* [1791], in Susan Dunn (ed.), *Something That Will Surprise the World* (New York: Basic Books, 2006), p. 159.

15. Anne Stevenson-Yang and Ken DeWoskin, "China Destroys the IPR Paradigm," *Far Eastern Economic Review* 168, no. 3 (March 2005): 9–18.

16. Yasheng Huang, *Capitalism with Chinese Characteristics: Entrepreneurship and the State* (Cambridge, UK: Cambridge University Press, 2008).

17. Daniel Chow, Testimony before the U.S.-China Economic and Security Review Commission, Washington, DC, June 7–8, 2006.

18. Zoellick quoted in "U.S. Files WTO Case against China over Discriminatory Taxes That Hurt U.S. Exports," Office of the United States Trade Representative, Executive Office of the President, March 18, 2004.

19. Keith E. Maskus, "Reforming U.S. Patent Policy," Council on Foreign Relations, Council Special Report no. 19, November 2006, available at http://www .cfr.org/publication/12087/reforming_us_patent_policy.html?breadcrumb=% 2Fpublication%2Fpublication_list%3Ftype%3Dspecial_report%26page%3D2.

20. Ibid.

21. Daniel K. Correa, "Assessing Broadband in America," Information Technology and Innovation Foundation, April 2007, available at http://www.itif.org/ files/BroadbandRankings.pdf.

22. John Peha, *Bringing Broadband to Unserved Communities* (Washington, DC: Brookings Institution Press, July 2009), p. 2.
23. "Broadband Blockage," *Wall Street Journal*, December 30, 2009.
24. Tim Wu, "OPEC 2.0," *New York Times*, July 30, 2008.
25. Alan Parkinson, "Engineering Study Abroad Programs: Formats, Challenges, Best Practices," *Online Journal for Global Engineering Education* 2, no. 2 (2007): 1–15.
26. Kelly quoted in Steve Hamm, "Big Blue's Global Lab," *BusinessWeek*, August 17, 2009; Peter R. Orszag and John P. Holdren, Memorandum for the Heads of Executive Departments and Agencies, re: Science and Technology Budget Priorities for the FY 2011 Budget, White House, August 4, 2009.

CHAPTER 8: PROMOTING INNOVATION AT HOME

1. Samuel J. Palmisano, "Globally Integrated Enterprises," *Foreign Affairs* 85, no. 3 (May/June 2006): 127–36.
2. "World Investment Report 2005," United Nations Conference on Trade and Development, available at http://www.unctad.org/en/docs/wir2005ch4_en.pdf.
3. Richard C. Levin and Linda Koch Lorimer, "The Internationalization of Yale: 2005–2008: The Emerging Framework," Yale University, December 2005.
4. "University Top 200 in Full," *Times Online*, October 9, 2008, available at http://www.timesonline.co.uk/tol/news/uk/education/article4910798 .ece; *Global Student Mobility 2025*, Media Briefing IDP Education Australia, September 2002, available at http://www.aiec.idp.com/PDF/ Bohm_2025Media_p.pdf.
5. Jeffrey T. Macher and David C. Mowery (eds.), *Innovation in Global Industries* (Washington, DC: National Academies Press, 2008), p. xi.
6. Chambers quoted in "Tech Companies Building Bridges with China," IDG News Service, September 27, 2004, available at http://www.itworld .com/040927techchina.
7. Rohrabacher quoted in "The Globalization of R&D and Innovation, Pt. II: The University Response," U.S. House of Representatives Committee on Science and Technology Hearing Charter, July 26, 2007, available at http:// democrats.science.house.gov/Media/File/Commdocs/hearings/2007/ full/26jul/hearing_charter.pdf.
8. Jere N. Glover, "The Role of the SBIR and STTR Programs in Stimulating Innovation at Small High-Tech Businesses," Testimony before the Subcommittee on Technology and Innovation, United States House of

Representatives, April 23, 2009, available at http://www.sbtc.org/docs/09-04Testimony_Glover.pdf; Carl Schramm, Robert Litan, and Dane Stangler, "New Business, Not Small Business, Is What Creates Jobs," *Wall Street Journal*, November 6, 2009; Dane Stangler and Robert E. Litan, "Where Will the Jobs Come From?" Kauffman Foundation Research Series, November 2009, available at http://www.kauffman.org/uploadedFiles/where_will_the_jobs_come_from.pdf.

9. Fred Block and Matthew R. Keller, "Where Do Innovations Come From? Transformations in the U.S. National Innovation System, 1970–2006," Information Technology and Innovation Foundation, Washington, DC, July 2008.

10. Daniel Lyons, "Holy Chip," *Forbes*, January 30, 2006.

11. Walshok quoted in Bradley Fikes, "What's Next for UCSD Connect?" *San Diego Metropolitan*, March 2004.

12. Chad Graham, "Ariz.'s Choice: Lead or Follow," *Arizona Republic*, October 28, 2007.

13. Gammage quote from "Phoenix Grows and Grows," *NPR Morning Edition*, March 13, 2006.

14. Miller quoted in Collaborative Economics, "The Innovation Driven Economic Development Model: A Practical Guide for the Regional Innovation Broker," Bay Area Council Economic Institute, September 2008, available at http://www.bayeconfor.org/media/files/pdf/InnovationDrivenEconomic DevelopmentModel-final.pdf.

15. Anjanette Riley, "Not Enough to Compete: Arizona's Emphasis on Gene-Based Therapy Could Be the State's Best Bet," *Arizona Capitol Times*, April 3, 2009.

16. Jessica Tan, "Building a Pillar," *Forbes*, April 13, 2009.

17. Luci Scott, " 'Stars Aligning' Landed Chinese Solar Firm," *Arizona Republic*, November 18, 2009.

18. Paul A. Gompers and Josh Lerner, *The Money of Invention: How Venture Capital Creates New Wealth* (Boston: Harvard Business School Press, 2001).

19. Statistics from "Latest Industry Statistics," National Venture Capital Association, available at http://www.nvca.org/index.php?option=com_content& view=article&id=78&Itemid=102; Robert N. Schmidt, "Reauthorization of the Small Business Innovation Research Programs and 'Unleashing American Innovation,'" Testimony before the Subcommittee on Technology and Innovation, Committee on Science and Technology, House of Representatives, April 26, 2007, available at http://democrats.science.house.gov/Media/ File/Commdocs/hearings/2007/tech/26apr/schmidt_testimony.pdf.

20. Committee on Capitalizing on Science, Technology, and Innovation, "An Assessment of the SBIR Program," National Research Council, 2008.

21. Sramana Mitra, "Stimulus Package for Entrepreneurs," *Forbes*, September 12, 2008.
22. Jerry Thursby and Marie Thursby, "Here or There? A Survey of Factors in Multinational R&D Location," National Academy of Sciences, February 2006, available at http://www.kauffman.org/uploadedFiles/thursby_final_1206.pdf.
23. Jane E. Fountain and Robert D. Atkinson, *Innovation, Social Capital, and the New Economy* (Washington, DC: Progressive Policy Institute, July 1, 1998).
24. "Innovation's Golden Goose," *The Economist*, December 14, 2002.
25. Reference to 2003 study is in Joseph Cortright, "Time for a More Open Approach?" *Science Progress*, April 28, 2009, available at http://www.scienceprogress.org/2009/04/university-patents/; Donald Kennedy, "Bayh-Dole: Almost 25," *Science* 307, no. 5714 (March 2005): 1375.
26. R. Stanley Williams, HP Fellow, Hewlett-Packard Laboratories, Testimony on behalf of the Hewlett-Packard Company before the Subcommittee on Science, Technology and Space of the Senate Committee on Commerce, Science and Transportation of the United States Senate, September 17, 2002, available at http://www.hp.com/hpinfo/abouthp/government/testimony-nanotechnology.pdf.
27. Robert E. Litan, Lesa Mitchell, and E. J. Reedy, "The University as Innovator: Bumps in the Road," *Issues in Science and Technology* (Summer 2007), and *Moving Innovations to Market*, available at http://www.bsues.org/23.4/litan.html.

CHAPTER 9: COMMUNITIES OF INNOVATION

1. National Academy of Sciences, *Rising above the Gathering Storm*.
2. Norman R. Augustine, "Learning to Lose?" *Washington Post*, December 6, 2005; David S. Broder, "Math and Science Test for Bush," *Washington Post*, December 18, 2005; Thomas L. Friedman, "Keeping Us in the Race," *New York Times*, October 14, 2005; Bill Gates, "Strengthening American Competitiveness for the 21st Century," Testimony before United States Senate Committee on Health, Education, Labor, and Pensions, March 7, 2007.
3. "Framing the Engineering Outsourcing Debate," Duke University Master of Engineering Management Program, December 2005, available at http://www.soc.duke.edu/resources/public_sociology/duke_outsourcing.pdf; Denis Fred Simon and Cong Cao, *China's Emerging Technological Edge* (Cambridge, UK: Cambridge University Press, 2009).
4. Michael Teitelbaum, "Do We Need More Scientists?" *Public Interest*, no. 153 (Fall 2003): 40–53.

5. Beryl Lieff Benderly, "Rising above 'The Gathering Storm,'" *Science*, December 14, 2007.

6. B. Lindsay Lowell and Hal Salzman, "Into the Eye of the Storm: Assessing the Evidence on Science and Engineering Education, Quality, and Workforce Demand," Urban Institute, October 2007, available at http://www.urban.org/UploadedPDF/411562_Salzman_Science.pdf.

7. Paula Stephan, "Early Careers for Biomedical Scientists," Talk at Harvard University as part of National Bureau of Economic Research project, February 26, 2007, available at http://www.nber.org/~sewp/Early%20Careers%20for%20Biomedical%20Scientists.pdf.

8. Mellman quoted in John Carey, "Why the Biomedical 'Crisis' Really Isn't," *BusinessWeek*, March 20, 2007.

9. Richard Freeman, "The Human Resource Leapfrog Model and US Economic Leadership," Presentation at Council on Foreign Relations Roundtable, New York, October 31, 2005; Jonah Lehrer, "Fleeting Youth, Fading Creativity in Sceince," *Wall Street Journal*, February 19, 2010.

10. "Indentured Labour," *Nature*, August 23, 2007.

11. Richard B. Freeman, "Does Globalization of the Scientific/Engineering Workforce Threaten U.S. Economic Leadership?" National Bureau of Economic Research Working Paper 11457, June 2005, available at http://www.nber.org/papers/w11457.

12. William J. Broad, "Congressional Budget Delay Stymies Research," *New York Times*, January 7, 2007.

13. Michael Teitelbaum, "A New Science Degree to Meet Industry Needs," *Issues in Science and Technology* 23, no.1 (Fall 2006): 27–30.

14. Bruce Alberts, "Science for Science," *Science* 324 (April 3, 2009): 13.

15. Chris Woolston, "Reviving a 'Lesser' Degree in the Sciences," *Chronicle of Higher Education*, June 17, 2003, available at http://chronicle.com/jobs/news/2003/06/2003061701c.htm.

16. Freeman, "Does Globalization of the Scientific/Engineering Workforce Threaten U.S. Economic Leadership?"

17. Daniel L. Goroff, "Undergraduate Science, Math, and Engineering Education: What's Working?" Testimony before the Subcommittee on Research, Committee on Science, House of Representatives, March 15, 2006, available at http://commdocs.house.gov/committees/science/hsy26481.000/hsy26481_0.htm.

18. Kevin Eagan, "Freshmen Show Gains in Aspirations for Science Degrees, but Not All Arrive at Finish Line," UCLA News Release, February 16, 2010, available at http://newsroom.ucla.edu/portal/ucla/freshmen-show-gains-in-aspirations-153723.aspx.

19. Elaine Seymour and Nancy Hewett, *Talking about Leaving: Why Undergraduates Leave the Sciences* (Boulder, CO: Westview Press, 1997).

20. Carl Wieman, "Undergraduate Science, Math and Engineering Education: What's Working?" Testimony before the Subcommittee on Research, Committee on Science, House of Representatives, March 15, 2006, available at http://commdocs.house.gov/committees/science/hsy26481.000/hsy26481_0.htm.

21. Paul Romer, "Growth Hinges on Science Education," *Stanford Business* 70, no. 3 (May 2002).

22. Building Engineering and Science Talent, *A Bridge for All: Higher Education Design Principles to Broaden Participation in Science, Technology, Engineering and Mathematics*, February 2004, available at http://www.bestworkforce.org/PDFdocs/BEST_BridgeforAll_HighEdFINAL.pdf; Mary K. Boyd and Jodi L. Wesemann (eds.), *Broadening Participation in Undergraduate Research: Fostering Excellence and Enhancing the Impact* (Washington, DC: Council on Undergraduate Research, 2009).

23. BEST, *A Bridge for All: Higher Education Design Principles to Broaden Participation in Science, Technology, Engineering, and Mathematics*.

24. Susan Kinzie, "A Magnetic Force," *Washington Post*, May 30, 2007.

25. Baker quoted in "Hold Fast to Dreams," UMBC Meyerhoff Scholars Program, April 1, 2008, available at http://www.umbc.edu/window/meyerhoff20.html.

26. "Scholar Research," UMBC Meyerhoff Scholars Program, available at http://www.umbc.edu/meyerhoff/scholar_research.html.

27. See, for example, Shirley Ann Jackson, "The Graying of NASA," *Research USA*, April 28, 2003.

28. Scott E. Page, *The Difference* (Princeton, NJ: Princeton University Press, 2007).

29. Vannevar Bush, *Science—The Endless Frontier*, Report to the President, July 1945, available at http://www.nsf.gov/od/lpa/nsf50/vbush1945.htm.

30. "President Barack Obama's Inaugural Address," White House, January 21, 2009, available at http://www.whitehouse.gov/blog/inaugural-address/.

31. "Science: The Endless Frontier: Learning from the Past, Designing for the Future," Conference series held at Columbia University, New York, December 9, 1994, June 9, 1995, and September 21–22, 1996, available at http://www.cspo.org/products/conferences/.

CHAPTER 10: THE FUTURE OF INNOVATION

1. C. N. R. Rao quoted from Proceedings of the China-India-US Workshop on Science, Technology and Innovation Policy, National Institute of Advanced Studies, Bangalore, India, July 7–9, 2008.

2. Daniel McGinn, "The Decline of Western Innovation," *Newsweek*, November 23, 2009.

3. Thomas Friedman, "Our One-Party Democracy," *New York Times*, September 8, 2009.

4. China Greentech Initiative, *China Greentech Report 2009*, available at http://www.china-greentech.com/report.

5. Michael Nielsen, "Doing Science in the Open," *Physics World*, May 1, 2009, available at http://physicsworld.com/cws/article/print/38904.

6. Hendershott quoted in Claire Cain Miller, "Do Web Entrepreneurs Still Need Venture Capitalists?" *New York Times* Blog, May 14, 2009, available at http://bits.blogs.nytimes.com/2009/05/14/do-web-entrepreneurs-still-need-venture-capitalists/.

7. Thomas Cech, "Strategies for Nurturing Science's Next Generation," *Science News*, June 20, 2008, available at http://www.sciencenews.org/view/generic/id/33368/title/Comment__Strategies_for_nurturing_science%E2%80%99s_next_generation.

8. Smolin quoted in "In Search of the Black Swans," *Physics World*, April 1, 2009, available at http://physicsworld.com/cws/article/print/38468.

9. Lawrence H. Summers, "The Global Middle Cries out for Reassurance," *Financial Times*, October 29, 2006.

10. Uri Berliner, "Haves and Have-Nots: Income Inequality in America," *NPR*, February 5, 2007; "Top One Percent of Tax Filers Pay Highest Share in Decades," Press Release, Congress of the United States Joint Economic Committee, October 29, 2008.

11. The Innovation Economy Conference, Washington, DC, December 1, 2009, transcript available at http://www.theinnovationeconomy.org/_layouts/IEC/PDF/Transcripts/Leadership_And_The_Innovation_Economy.pdf.

12. Japan Science and Technology Agency, China Research Center, *Scientific and Technological Capabilities of China*, September 2008, pp. 65–66.

13. Remarks by President Barack Obama at the National Academy of Sciences Annual Meeting, National Academy of Sciences, Washington, DC, April 27, 2009, available at http://www.whitehouse.gov/the_press_office/Remarks-by-the-President-at-the-National-Academy-of-Sciences-Annual-Meeting/.

14. Alexis de Tocqueville, *Democracy in America* (New York: Colonial Press, 1900), p. 234.

Index

About the Author

Adam Segal is the Ira A. Lipman Senior Fellow for Counterterrorism and National Security Studies at the Council on Foreign Relations. He is the author of *Digital Dragon: High Technology Enterprises in China*, and his writing has appeared in publications such as the *Financial Times*, *Foreign Affairs*, *Asian Wall Street Journal*, and *International Herald Tribune*. He has appeared as a commentator on several networks including Bloomberg, CNN, NBC, NPR, and the BBC. He lives in New York City with his wife and two children.